Every Day is a GOOD Day

Robert Shea on
Illuminatus!, Writing and Anarchism

Edited by Tom Jackson

G

Every Day is a GOOD Day

Print ISBN: 978-1-952746-43-7

eBook ISBN: 978-1-952746-44-4

Cover Design by Richard Rasa
eBook design by Pelorian Digital

Hilaritas Press, LLC.
P.O. Box 1153
Grand Junction, Colorado 81502

www.hilaritaspress.com

Ǥ

The small graphic of a G with a line through it used throughout this book was borrowed from Robert Shea's zine, *No Governor*, where it served there as a section-dividing glyph.

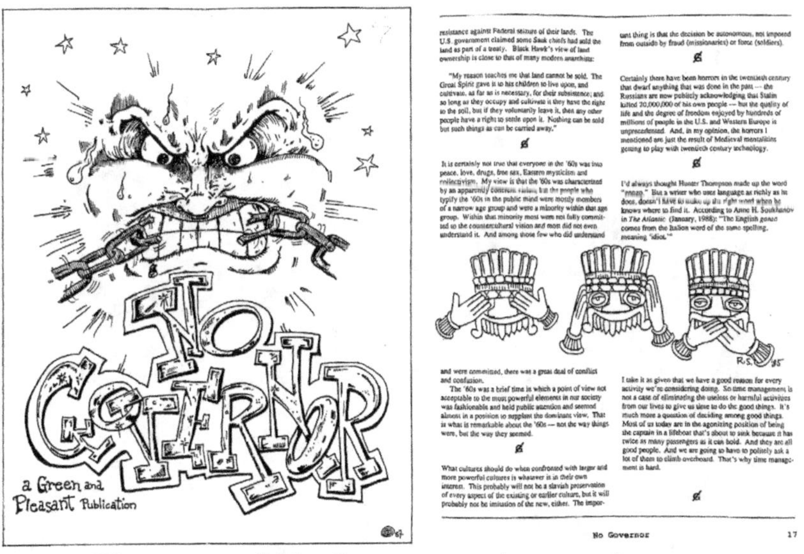

resistance against Federal seizure of their lands. The U.S. government claimed some Sauk chiefs had sold the land as part of a treaty. Black Hawk's view of land ownership is close to that of many modern anarchists:

"My reason teaches me that land cannot be sold. The Great Spirit gave it to his children to live upon, and cultivate, as far as is necessary, for their subsistence; and so long as they occupy and cultivate it they have the right to the soil, but if they voluntarily leave it, then any other people have a right to settle upon it. Nothing can be sold but such things as can be carried away."

Ǥ

It is certainly not true that everyone in the '60s was into peace, love, drugs, free sex, Eastern mysticism and collectivism. My view is that the '60s was characterized by an apparently coherent [illegible] but the people who typify the '60s in the public mind were mostly members of a narrow age group and were a minority within that age group. Within that minority most were not fully committed to the countercultural vision and most did not even understand it. And among those few who did understand and were committed, there was a great deal of conflict and confusion.

The '60s was a brief time in which a point of view not acceptable to the most powerful elements in our society was fashionable and held public attention and seemed almost in a position to supplant the dominant view. That is what is remarkable about the '60s — not the way things were, but the way they seemed.

Ǥ

What cultures should do when confronted with larger and more powerful cultures is whatever is in their own interest. This probably will not be a slavish preservation of every aspect of the existing or earlier culture, but it will probably not be imitation of the new, either. The important thing is that the decision be autonomous, not imposed from outside by fraud (missionaries) or force (soldiers).

Ǥ

Certainly there have been horrors in the twentieth century that dwarf anything that was done in the past — the Russians are now publicly acknowledging that Stalin killed 20,000,000 of his own people — but the quality of life and the degree of freedom enjoyed by hundreds of millions of people in the U.S. and Western Europe is unprecedented. And, in my opinion, the horrors I mentioned are just the result of Medieval mentalities getting to play with twentieth century technology.

Ǥ

I'd always thought Hunter Thompson made up the word "gonzo." But a writer who uses language as richly as he does, doesn't have to make up the right word when he knows where to find it. According to Anne H. Soukhanov in *The Atlantic* (January, 1988): "The English *gonzo* comes from the Italian word of the same spelling, meaning 'idiot.'"

I take it as given that we have a good reason for every activity we're considering doing. So time management is not a case of eliminating the useless or harmful activities from our lives to give us time to do the good things. It's much more a question of deciding among good things. Most of us today are in the agonizing position of being the captain in a lifeboat that's about to sink because it has twice as many passengers as it can hold. And they are all good people. And we are going to have to politely ask a lot of them to climb overboard. That's why time management is hard.

Ǥ

No Governor 17

The cover of *No Governor* and a sample page.

Ǥ

Books by Robert Shea

The Illuminatus Trilogy (with Robert Anton Wilson):

- *The Eye in the Pyramid*
- *The Golden Apple*
- *Leviathan*

Shike: Time of the Dragons

Shike: Last of the Zinja

All Things Are Lights

From No Man's Land to Plaza del Lago

The Saracen: Land of the Infidel

The Saracen: The Holy War

Shaman

Table of Contents

Robert Shea with the manuscript of Shike, his first published “solo” novel.

Ǥ

Introduction

When American author Robert Shea died in 1994, an obituary published in the summer 1994 issue of *Green Egg*, a pagan magazine, said Shea's fans can expect more of his books to be published. The obit stated, "In the next few years, several more of Bob Shea's works will be published, including a collection of essays. Patricia requests that anyone having copies of Bob's work from magazines or other publications, or having letters from him which might be publishable, to please send copies to her at [address omitted as it is no longer relevant]."

The "Patricia" referred to in the obituary is Patricia Monaghan, a writer and scholar and Shea's widow. She died in 2012. And in fact, no additional books were published after Shea's death.

This book, coming out about 30 years after Shea's death, is an attempt to make that planned collection of Shea's short pieces a reality.

Shea's collaborator in writing the *Illuminatus!* trilogy, Robert Anton Wilson, published many books that are similar in format to what I am publishing here: collections of short pieces and interviews. So although this is the first such collection of Shea's short work, the format should be familiar to RAW fans who have read books such as *Email to the Universe* and *Right Where You Are Sitting Now.*

Robert Anton Wilson died in 2007, yet he remains a cult author with many books still in print. In fact, many of his books have been republished by Hilaritas Press, the publishing imprint of the Robert Anton Wilson Trust.

I have worked as hard as almost anyone to try to promote Wilson's literary reputation. Since 2010, I have published a blog at RAWIllumination.net largely devoted to news and commentary about Wilson, Wilson's community of fans, and topics that Wilson clearly was interested in.

Yet, I have come to think that Shea also should not be neglected. This opinion has grown in recent years, as I've gone through his historical novels, fine books such as the *Shike* novels, *All Things Are Lights* and *Shaman.*

Wilson and Shea both remain best known for the *Illuminatus!* trilogy, written when the two became close friends when they both worked at *Playboy* magazine in Chicago as editors of the *Playboy* Forum, where the two interacted with readers who wrote in to discuss the issues of the day.

While Wilson is the better known of the two, I would note that without Shea, there would have been no *Illuminatus!* The original idea for the book came from Shea. It was Shea who obtained a contract from Dell to get the work published after contacting his old friend, Bob Abel. (See my piece in the Appendix, "Three Bobs and the Origin of the *Illuminatus!* trilogy.")

After Abel bought *Illuminatus!*, subsequent Dell editors brought it to publication, and during that process, Shea played the role of diplomat in helping to bring the work to actual publication. For example, it was not considered commercially possible for Dell to publish the work as one large volume, particularly a work by two unknown editors, but Wilson fought the decision to publish the work as a trilogy, while Shea accepted it. When I interviewed him for my blog, former Dell editor David M. Harris remembered, "I do clearly remember Bob Wilson as one of the most difficult authors I ever worked with. He seemed to think of me as his enemy, rather than his ally in getting the book into print. Fortunately for me and the book, Shea was more easygoing – in those days I would have said rational. We had lunch once when he was in New York, and had a nice time as I recall."

Many of the ideas explored in *Illuminatus!* are discussed in this anthology. Shea retained a lifelong interest in the concepts of anarchism and libertarianism discussed in *Illuminatus!* He also was interested in freedom of speech, Zen Buddhism, literature and the writing process itself.

But while *Illuminatus!* helped launch the literary careers of Wilson and Shea, Wilson was the first of the two to take advantage of the work's success. If you have followed Wilson's career, you have probably noticed that *Illuminatus!* served as a template for his career. His novels all resemble the text of *Illuminatus!*, sometimes even sharing some of the same characters, while all of Wilson's nonfiction books resemble the appendices of *Illuminatus!* And Wilson immediately published many books in the wake of *Illuminatus!* After the trilogy was published, Wilson soon left *Playboy* to pursue his dream of being a freelance writer and pundit.

Although Shea had always wanted to work as a novelist, he stayed at *Playboy* magazine and only became serious about writing novels when he was laid off from *Playboy* in 1977.

Robert Anton Wilson writes in *Cosmic Trigger 3* about what happened: "When *Playboy* fired him, Shea endured terrible anxiety about keeping his house, and dashed out a few novel outlines while looking for another job. He sold his first novel before finding a job and never stopped writing again."

That first novel was *Shike*, which was published originally in two volumes, with the first one coming out in June 1981. Set in medieval Japan, China and Mongolia, it was the first of a series of historical novels, many of them featuring *Illuminatus!* style secret societies as a plot element. The other novels were *All Things Are Lights, The Saracen* published as two novels (like *Shike)*, and *Shaman.* Shea was working on additional fiction at the time of his death from cancer in 1994, at age 61.

Shea's novels, which I strongly recommend, have been released as eBooks under a Creative Commons license by his son and literary executor, Michael Shea; they also can be tracked down as modestly priced used books.

While Wilson remains a writer with a strong cult following, I believe Shea's solo work also deserves to be read and remembered; this book is part of my contribution to that ongoing effort.

– Tom Jackson,
Berea, Ohio, December 2024.

Ǥ

Introduction to Illuminati game

When Lewis Shiner interviewed Robert Anton Wilson in 1988, Wilson was asked about Steve Jackson Games' Illuminati game. Wilson answered, "Everybody I meet thinks it's based on my Illuminatus! novels and I'm getting royalties on it. He claims it's not based on the novels, so I'm not getting royalties on it. Different lawyers give me different opinions. Decide for yourself."

Shea apparently was fine with the game, and even wrote the following piece for an edition of the game, which I reprint below with the permission of Mr. Jackson. – The Editor

Indeed, do many strange things come to pass. When Robert Anton Wilson and I first became aware of the Ancient Illuminated Seers of Bavaria, and the extent of their conspiratorial power over historical events, we soon realized there was nothing to stop them from taking over the world completely. Why, then, did they choose to lurk behind the scenes, manipulating people and happenings through their many guises and front groups, when they could, at any time, have stepped forward to center stage and taken command?

After pondering this for a long time, we told each other, "They don't want to rule the world, they just want to play with it." (We often talk to each other in chorus.) This struck us as pretty sick – even sicker than wanting to control the world openly. Little did we reckon then that some twisted mind would come forward with something even sicker – a game in which people could play at being Illuminati playing at ruling the world.

Wilson and I have been accused of writing *Illuminatus!* to satirize conspiracy paranoia, when of course, as anybody who knows us will testify, we have always been dreadfully serious. Indeed, we have suffered greatly since going public about the Illuminati. Many of our best friends disappeared. Some because they didn't want to associate with the authors of a crazy, dirty, anarchist book. Others because we bored them silly by incessantly talking about the Illuminati. Still others to start cults of their own. So it goes.

But while we may have been called satirists, even satyrists, we have never been accused of making a game out of the whole thing. That remained for other and worser minds than ours to conceive. And if the person or persons who made up this game can be accused of whistling Dixie in the face of universal awfulness, what are we to say about the kind of people who would sit around and play such a game while outside, and maybe inside their doors, the world is going to pot? An even more chilling thought: maybe the Illuminati are behind this game. They must be – they are by definition behind everything, after all. So, play on, laugh if you will. But while you do, could mysterious fingers be moving you hither and yon on the gameboard of the world? Best not to think about it . . .

Ǥ

Illuminatus! and the Prometheus Award

Robert Shea and Robert Anton Wilson both largely launched their literary careers with the Illuminatus! *trilogy, published in the 1970s by Dell books. The book was written while the two were serving as editors for the Playboy Forum feature at* Playboy *magazine. The trilogy soon gained a large cult following and has remained in print ever since.*

It was very much a joint effort of the two writers. While the book's style sounds more like Wilson – in one interview, Wilson states that he rewrote the final draft so it would have a consistent tone – it was Shea who came up with the idea of writing a book based on the crazy conspiracy theories espoused by Playboy *readers who wrote in to the Playboy Forum. And it was Shea who convinced his editor friend, Bob Abel, to buy the proposed book for Dell.* *See "Appendix 1: Three Bobs and the Origin of the* Illuminatus! *Trilogy," my article at the back of this book.*

The trilogy won only one literary award. In 1986, it received a science fiction award, the Prometheus Hall of Fame Award, in a tie with The Syndic, a novel by Cyril Kornbluth.

The oldest awards in American science fiction are

the Hugo, awarded by fans at the annual world science fiction convention (or "worldcon"), and the Nebula, given by the Science Fiction Writers of America. But among the proliferation of other science fiction awards, the Prometheus, given for science fiction that emphasizes individual liberty, is one of the oldest. It began as a onetime award, created and given in 1979 by the libertarian science fiction writer L. Neil Smith. That first award was presented to F. Paul Wilson for his novel, Wheels Within Wheels, *and the master of ceremonies for that first award was Robert Anton Wilson. Smith was heavily influenced by* Illuminatus! *and often referenced the trilogy in his own fiction.*

Smith, wanting to turn the Prometheus into an annual award and sensing that he lacked the organizational abilities to turn it into an institution, asked a newspaper journalist and science fiction fan named Michael Grossberg to help him. Grossberg in turn founded a group called the Libertarian Futurist Society, which since 1982 has presented annual Prometheus Awards and Prometheus Hall of Fame Awards. A list of the awards is available at lfs.org.

Robert Shea was a member of the Libertarian Futurist Society. Members of the group are allowed to nominate works for the two awards, and in fact, it was Shea who nominated Illuminatus! *Here is a letter he published in the organization's newsletter, explaining why he nominated a work he also had written.*

Letter

I feel somewhat sheepish about having nominated my own novel. I am not claiming that *Illuminatus!* is as good as the novels that have already been chosen for the Hall of Fame. There are at least two books on this year's list of nominees that I would vote for before voting for *Illuminatus!* But I do believe it deserves to be nominated and considered. Eventually, I feel, there will come a year when all the more deserving books will have already been inducted into the Hall of Fame and *Illuminatus!* will have its turn.

That it has not been nominated by anybody else must be due, it seems to me, to one or more of these five reasons: 1) it was just an oversight; 2) everybody was expecting someone else to do it; 3) the Advisory membership of the Libertarian Futurists is not a representative cross-section of libertarian/anarchist science fiction fans; 4) the Goddess Eris wants me to know how she felt when she wasn't invited to the party on Mount Olympus; 5) it is the work of a Conspiracy.

While liberal Gimps might consider it bad form for an author to toot his own horn like this (one can imagine what Ellsworth Toohey would say). I am sure the individualists, egoists, objectivists, libertarians and anarchists who make up the L.F.S. will applaud it as an act of rational self-interest and healthy self-esteem.

Besides, if I need a more altruistic motive I can always say I'm doing it for Bob Wilson's sake.

Robert Shea,
Glencoe, Illinois

After Illuminatus! won the Prometheus Hall of Fame Award, the award was presented in a ceremony held in 1986 at a world science fiction convention held in Atlanta. Here is Shea's acceptance speech, which was printed in the LFS newsletter:

Acceptance speech

I would not be doing this today were it not for the other half of the team, one of the wittiest, most erudite and lovable people I've ever met, a man capable of sawing the most difficult ideas in two without hurting them, making them jump through hoops, walk into cabinets and disappear and pop out of trick top hats, a man with a universe up each sleeve. He is my very good friend and I miss his presence here today more than I can say – Robert Anton Wilson. So I very gratefully accept this award on behalf of Bob Wilson and myself.

I asked Bob if there was anything he wanted me to say in his place since he could not be here, and he wrote back, "Well, it sure was good news to hear we finally got an award of some sort for *Illuminatus!* . . . The only thing you can do for me in Atlanta is tell as many people as possible that my next American lecture tour begins in January, and anyone who is interested in lectures by me or seminars by Arlen and me should contact us at 3 the Haggard, Howth, Dublin, Ireland." So I have just passed that on to as many people as possible.

I also want to thank the members of the Libertarian Futurist Society who thought enough of *Illuminatus!* to vote it into their Hall of Fame. The greatest honor of all, I think, is to have our work mentioned in the same breath with the seven great novels that make up the Libertarian Futurist Society's Hall of Fame.* Heady company. And I am very, very grateful to the thousands of readers who have kept *Illuminatus!* alive from the day it was first published to this moment. It is claimed that *Illuminatus!* started a cult. I am happy to be a member of the *Illuminatus!* nut cult, which is responsible for my meeting some of the most delightful people it has ever been my pleasure and privilege to know.

I sometimes think it's remarkable that anybody at all read *Illuminatus!* When it first came out in 1975 the publisher decided to label it "Science Fiction," which meant that it would be put in an obscure corner of the bookstore where, as we all know, only a handful of weird people ever venture. On the other hand, the editors of all the science fiction magazines then extant refused to review *Illuminatus!* on the grounds that it was not science fiction – by whatever definition they were using that year. So we were banished from the mainstream but also rejected by the ghetto. A novel without a home. The fact that *Illuminatus!* survived this inauspicious start is proof that the weird people are even weirder than anybody gave them credit for.

Wilson and I initially had it in mind to write a fairly short international espionage paperback thriller based upon the conspiracy theories in the air at that moment, particularly those about the Bavarian Illuminati and the assassination of John F. Kennedy. Well, things got rather out of hand. Bob sometimes puts forward the notion that our minds were taken over by a bunch of super-intelligent dogs living on a planet circling Sirius. It's not hard to believe that, because in my home we have two ordinary Earth-type dogs who pretty much run our lives. But my own more prosaic idea is that the madness of *Illuminatus!* was implicit in our decision to satirize the theories we were using as premises. To satirize you have to exaggerate, and since the theories themselves were already so wild in their natural state, we had to go to incredible lengths to make them look even more ridiculous. But for satire to work it also has to have a grounding in reality. So we carefully mixed strange things that were true with strange things that were not true.

We put into the book things we believed and things we did not believe, things one of us believed and the other did not and things we sometimes believed and sometimes did not. And while writing the book, and afterwards as well, we often forgot which was which. Eventually it dawned on us that we were trying to make a statement about the nature of reality. We didn't start out trying to do anything so grandiose. It just grew on us.

I've been thinking about *Illuminatus!* in comparison to the other novels that have been chosen for the Hall of Fame, and one major difference has occurred to me. In the other Hall of Fame novels the distinction between fact and fiction is quite clear. In *Illuminatus!* we made a deliberate attempt to blur that distinction, to suggest that fact may be fiction and fiction may be fact. This blurring is consistent with that statement about reality we were trying to make. But even though our attitude toward reality may be somewhat confusing, I think our values are quite clear. I hope and think it is plain that the message of *Illuminatus!* is an anarchist message. The novel stands as a record of the anarchists we were in the 1960s and 70s. I still consider myself an anarchist. Bob Wilson does not, more, as I understand it, because he rejects labeling than because he is out of sympathy with anarchism.

We say in the novel that the original Illuminati were dedicated to religious and political freedom and that this secret organization somehow became perverted so that in recent centuries the Illuminati had become a vehicle for a monstrous authoritarianism. Thus the myth of the Illuminati is an archetype for every political movement, from Lenin's Bolshevism to Reagan's Republicanism, that has promised people greater freedom while loading them down with more government. People can be fooled in this way because they are not sure what freedom is. Freedom is a word whose meaning has been worn away by overuse, like a coin that has passed through too many hands. We need to be clear about what it means to us when we use it and maybe not use it quite so much, but use other, more precise words instead.

In *Illuminatus!* we suggest that freedom begins in your right to define yourself and to insist on the validity of your own perceptions and your own thoughts. To change to a new point of view because you find it convincing is, of course, merely an exercise of that freedom. But freedom is lost when you are coerced or frightened into denying your own way of seeing reality and into accepting a point of view you cannot really believe in, be it that of a family, a teacher, a boss, a party, a church, a state. And an amazing thing is that when each of us insists on his or her own vision, it does not divide us. It unites us as no externally imposed unity ever could. It unites us in reverence for that inner light which we can only find by knowing ourselves, never by denying ourselves, that light by which each one of us can truly be said to be illuminated – the true Illuminati.

* *[Those first seven honorees are The Moon is a Harsh Mistress, Robert Heinlein; Atlas Shrugged, Ayn Rand; Nineteen Eighty-Four, George Orwell; Fahrenheit 451, Ray Bradbury; Trader to the Stars, Poul Anderson; The Great Explosion, Eric Frank Russell, and The Syndic, Cyril Kornbluth.]*

Ᵹ

Questions About *Illuminatus!*

These answers from Robert Shea from a March 1977 interview of Shea and Robert Anton Wilson originally were published in a document given to people attending Ken Campbell's British theater adaptation of the Illuminatus! trilogy.

Fanatic: How far is *Illuminatus!* a work of fiction and how far is it a work of fact?

Bob Shea: An intelligent person who looks at it will immediately recognise that it's a put-on. But then there's another level beyond that, where the fantasy blends in with the reality to the point where it's not that easy to determine whether you're being put on or whether it's real. I myself keep changing my judgment about which parts of the book are real and which parts are fantasy.

Fanatic: Has anything happened since you finished the book to confirm you in your uncertainty?

Bob Shea: Yes, there have been a number of things that seem to bear out the direction we were going in: the discovery of the link between the Mafia and the CIA and their attempt to assassinate Castro. The existence of the informal international organisation of financiers called he Bilderbergers, who meet once a year and seem to determine the financial fate of the

Earth. The Trilateral Commission, similar to the Bilderbergers, headed by David Rockerfeller. This Commission seems to have numbered at least two recent presidents of the US. The symbol of the Trilateral Commission is a triangle and the symbol of the Illuminati is an eye in a triangle. So as soon as I heard of the Trilateral Commission I couldn't help but wonder if it wasn't the Illuminati at work again! Then there's the groups in *Illuminatus!* that seemed to foreshadow little suicidal terrorist groups like the Symbionese Liberation Army.

Fanatic: What the powerful call Utopia is now the condition for human survival.

Bob Shea: The point is to appropriate the technology and use it. It's not something that's just going to happen because the technology is there. Solar power from space colonies could be the private preserve of monopolies like General Electric . . . It's going to come – something that's absolutely necessary, so people have to prepare themselves for this development and begin to work to ensure that when solar power comes it isn't like oil or gas – just another thing that enslaves people.

Fanatic: What do you think of the stage version of *Illuminatus!*?

Bob Shea: I think it's superb. I was thunderstruck at what a magnificent job they did in capturing the exact tone, the exact mixture of fantasy and reality in the book. It really does keep you guessing, which is what we intended. I've come round to the conclusion that this isn't literature. It's too late in the day for literature. This is magick!

Ǥ

Robert Shea on *The Dispossessed*

As previously mentioned, Robert Shea was a member of the Libertarian Futurist Society, the group that gives the Prometheus Award. A debate raged for years within the group whether Ursula K. LeGuin should receive the group's Hall of Fame Award. LeGuin had predicted the book would never get the award, but she was wrong. Shea's side eventually won, when the novel finally received the award in 1993. Here is a piece by Shea, in the LFS newsletter, arguing for LeGuin's novel to be honored.

After reading the two commentaries on Ursula Le Guin's *The Dispossessed* in the Summer 1987 *Prometheus*, I had to offer my opinion. I was happy to vote for *The Dispossessed* for the Hall of Fame award this year. I think Le Guin does a remarkably good job of portraying a real live anarchist society.

The objections I've seen to this novel as libertarian science fiction seem to come from people I would call right-wing anarchists – I can think of no more efficient way to describe them – who believe that freedom is impossible without private property. If Le Guin had portrayed everything as hunky-dory in her anarcho-collectivist society their criticisms would be easier to understand, although *The Dispossessed* would in that case be a small, flat, banal, propagandistic book. But Le Guin's novel is primarily about the things that have gone wrong in this society.

The Odonians, banished to a world where everything is scarce, have managed to create a society that is, in many ways, quite attractive. It is non-violent, nonhierarchical, ascetic, sexually free. But in the generations since it was established, it has ossified. Shevek begins a rebellion against this ossification.

Annares has oppressive institutions, but not because Le Guin fails to understand the nature of freedom. She understands freedom quite well. The Annaresti, in their struggle to survive on an inhospitable planet, came up with solutions that later led to more problems. Le Guin knows that the business of any revolution – perhaps especially an anarchist revolution – is never finished.

Other SF novels advocating anarchism often show the society's problems as stemming from internal subversives. Everything would be just peachy were it not for the small group of evil people who want to bring back the state. Odonian problems stem from their society itself, which makes for a far more subtle and profound thought experiment.

Robert Heinlein's *The Moon is a Harsh Mistress*, which deservedly won LFS's Hall of Fame award, describes an anarchist society on the Moon which many libertarians find attractive. But his more recent *The Cat Who Walked Through Walls* returns a few generations later to find it, like Le Guin's Odonian society, plagued by creeping archism. This does not mean Heinlein's view of freedom is flawed. Like Le Guin, he knows that freedom is never won once and for all and there is no perfect blueprint for a free society.

George Orwell pointed out in an essay on Gandhi that in an anarcho-pacifist society people would be subjected to the most pervasive tyranny of all, the unlimited power of collective opinion. Orwell, who created the archetype of tyrannies that rule by force and fraud, might have given us a novel about tyranny by guilt and shame had he developed his insight. What Orwell did not do, Le Guin has done.

The Dispossessed is a cautionary tale for anarchists. The people who hate it remind me of those who want *Huckleberry Finn* taken off bookshelves because they see it as a sympathetic portrait of a slaveholding society. Because Le Guin shows that life on Annares has its positive side, people who want their fiction to have a simple good vs. evil message are offended.

Le Guin is too fine a writer to appeal to people who insist on taking their propaganda straight. But that's why *The Dispossessed* deserves a place in LFS' Hall of Fame.

Outworlds Interview

Robert Shea was interviewed twice by the late writer Neal Wilgus, and they are the longest, best interviews with Shea that I'm familiar with. Wilgus was the author of The Illuminoids: Secret Societies and Political Paranoia, which featured an introduction by Robert Anton Wilson. I'm grateful to his son, Warren Asa Wilgus, for giving permission to reprint the two interviews featured in this book.

23 Questions for Robert Shea, posed by Neal Wilgus.

ONE: I know you're co-author with Robert Anton Wilson of *Illuminatus!* and presently a senior editor at *Playboy* and editor of your own anarchist journal, *No Governor*. Could you fill in some details on your life and present activities?

SHEA: I lead an almost eerily quiet life in a small suburb of Chicago. We are not far from Waukegan, which produced Ray Bradbury and Jack Benny, and Chicago, of course, is where Buck Rogers originated, so it's not an alien place for me. I was born and raised in New York, though, and as Nelson Algren wrote, nobody ever moves to Chicago except to make money. The day I was born – Valentine's Day 1933 – Herbert Hoover told Congress that gold was still a sound basis for currency. This may have influenced some of the favorable references to gold in *Illuminatus!* I remember the day the Hindenburg blew up and crashed – it was raining and I was riding a Fifth Avenue bus with my mother when we heard the news. I also saw the world's first commercial television broadcast, the opening of the New York World's Fair. But this only gets us to 1939, so maybe we better move on to the next question.

TWO: All right. Could you tell us something about the authors and ideas that have influenced you? Are you a longtime science fiction/fantasy fan? An HPL fan? A Neo-Pagan or occultist?

SHEA: I am not now, nor have I ever been, a member of the Communist Party. Jesus, yes, I've been a science fiction fan as long as I can remember. I was reading *Buck Rogers* before I could read. At the age of 11 I graduated to magazine science fiction when my Uncle Ernie bought me a copy of *Captain Future*. Soon I was reading all the science fiction mags. The first story in *Astounding* I read was Isaac Asimov's *Dead Hand*, part of the Foundation series, and it was a thrill to meet Isaac Asimov when I grew up and became a magazine editor. For some reason I've never cared as much for fantasy as I have for science fiction. I have a basically materialistic point of view that also seems to go back to my childhood, although I was raised as a Catholic (as was Wilson by the way – I don't know if he mentioned that in your interview with him – but I think it's significant.) I ceased to believe in magic while I was still a child, and I really don't enjoy a story – or I should say I enjoy a story less – when the basic premise seems, to me, impossible. There are exceptions, of course. I liked *The Lord of the Rings* and I do accept stories about telepathy and teleportation and telekinesis and whatnot as long as these psionic powers are presented by the author as somehow "natural."

I've read very little H.P. Lovecraft. The use made in *Illuminatus!* of Lovecraft's material is largely Wilson's contribution. I do like what I know of Lovecraft, but for some reason he's not one of those authors who have turned me on and made me want to read everything he's written.

I've pretty much ceased to believe in the supernatural and so am not into Neo-Paganism or the occult. I am very interested in Zen Buddhism. That isn't very fashionable any more, but I think most of the Americans who took up Zen in the 50s and 60s barely scratched the surface. Zen, as I understand it, doesn't involve any belief in the supernatural. It's more like a kind of psychotherapy. All religion is psychotherapy, I think. Human beings have been on this earth for four million years. During that time the human mind has developed into a very sensitive instrument. However, as life has been lived on this planet, that sensitive instrument has constantly been subjected to shock and pain. Something to stabilize and comfort the mind is a necessity. Thus, religion. But most religion is psychotherapy gone astray and instead of easing human misery has caused more of it. Mysticism as practiced in Zen seems to me to offer the benefits of a religion without the drawbacks. So I have been meditating every day for the past two years – the zazen method of meditation – counting exhalations up to ten and then starting over again. This has been a profound experience for me and one that has greatly enriched my life.

I am also an adherent of Discordianism, the worship of the goddess Discordia – known in Greek as Eris. We believe that the fundamental principle in the universe is chaos, and that there is so much chaos around, somebody must have put it here. Trying to impose order on chaos is a disastrous error – it's one of the fundamental errors of the Illuminati. My chief duty as a Discordian, other than to praise the Goddess and her doings, is to partake of no hot dog buns.

THREE : Dell's marketing of *Illuminatus!* as a trilogy rather than a one-volume novel and its hard-sell advertising of the book seems designed to make it a cult book like *Stranger in a Strange Land* and *Dune.* Do you think the book should be promoted this way? Do you think it will succeed?

SHEA: Actually, Dell didn't start advertising the book until it began to look like the first printing – without the help of advertising – was selling out. Anyway, promotion can only do so much for a book. It has to succeed, finally, because enough people read it and like it.

FOUR: I understand that 500 pages – close to 40 percent of the original manuscript – was cut from *Illuminatus!* before it was published. Do you think this helped or hurt the novel?

SHEA: The original manuscript was about 1,200 typewritten pages, and we were asked to cut about 200 pages, which we did, screaming in agony all the while. This didn't do any mortal, structural damage to the novel. It did cost us some good writing and some funny bits. A lot of what was cut was occult information in the appendices. Also *When Atlantis Ruled the Earth* was originally a complete screenplay-within-a-novel. Now it's down to a summary.

FIVE Any chance that the uncut version will ever see print?

SHEA: If the book catches on enough so that a hardcover or quality paperback publisher wants to produce the uncut version as a service to literature. But printing and paper costs so much nowadays, it's doubtful anyone will want to take a chance. No, the more I think about it, the less likely it seems.

SIX: Does it seem strange to you that Dell cut as much as they did and then used larger type in *The Golden Apple* (volume II) to fill it out to book length?

SHEA: I didn't notice that till you called my attention to it. According to my calculations, they get 44 lines on a page in volumes I and III, but only 40 a page in volume II. If they had used the same type in that volume as they did in the other two, *The Golden Apple* would have been about 250 pages long, instead of 272. But *Leviathan* is only 253 pages, so it would seem to me that a 250-page volume would have been viable. Sure, it seems strange to me, but publishing is a strange business. It is almost impossible to be logical in publishing. It's been my observation that the more logical a publisher's decisions are, the more likely he or she is to succeed. Publishers who fail are logical only five percent of the time. The average publisher is logical 15 percent of the time and manages – just barely – to survive. The successful publisher manages to get the logic quotient up to around 25 percent. The other 75 percent is spent acting like a witch doctor or just ignoring the business altogether.

SEVEN: Since you and Wilson were both editors at *Playboy* at the time *Illuminatus!* was written, I'm wondering why *Playboy* Press didn't publish it. Or was that too close to home?

SHEA: At the time we got the idea for *Illuminatus!* Playboy Press wasn't publishing original novels, and a very good friend of mine, Bob Abel, was an editor at Dell. I was looking for an opportunity to write paperback fiction, so I wrote Bob a letter briefly sketching about half a dozen ideas for books, of which a book about the Bavarian Illuminati was one. He thought that one had the most possibilities, so Wilson and I did three sample chapters and an outline and sent it in. On the strength of that we got a contract and began writing the book.

EIGHT: *Illuminatus!* touches frequently on anarchism and you edit an anarchist magazine. I'm curious about your ideas on the subject. Does the right-libertarian versus left-anarchist spectrum seem important to you?

SHEA: The anarchist philosopher with whose views I most agree is Max Stirner. He said that the individual is all there is, and any claim that anything is bigger or more important than the individual is sheer bullshit. I believe that the cause of most human misery is people's efforts to impose the rule of state and organized religion on one another. A society without coercion, in which individuals were guided by their own conception of their own best interests, would be a happy, harmonious society. I would like to abolish government, and I define government as any attempt to use force to impose the will of one person or group of people on others. When an armed robber takes your watch, he is doing the same thing a government does when it collects taxes. The fact that the government seems to be doing the will of the majority doesn't give it any special rights in my book.

I'm not a pacifist, but I think anarchists should not talk about armed revolutions, because such a revolution would be, in effect, a government – imposing its will on others by force – regardless of whether it called itself anarchist. So anarchists should work toward a society without government by means of nonviolent resistance and education.

As for the right vs. left split in anarchism, I think those people are wasting too much time arguing about economic arrangements. After the state is abolished, people will operate as capitalists or collectivists, whatever suits them best. The important thing, though, is to get rid of government. First things first.

NINE: *Illuminatus!* is dedicated to Gregory Hill and Kerry Thornley, and we learn in Appendix Nun, (Volume III) that Thornley was a friend of Lee Harvey Oswald and author of an epic poem called *Illuminati Lady*. Would you tell us more about Hill and Thornley? Was *Illuminati Lady* ever published?

SHEA: They are two of the most creative people I know. They invented the religion of Discordianism after having undergone a visionary experience in a bowling alley in Whittier, California, which also happens to be the birthplace of Richard M. Nixon. Subsequently, or shortly thereafter, they discovered the existence of the Bavarian Illuminati and what they had to say about Discordianism got all mixed up with what they said about the Illuminati. They were in correspondence with Wilson and me and turned us on to all these ideas. Because they introduced us to the subject of the book, is why we dedicated Volume I, *The Golden Apple,* to them. The golden apple refers to the apple with the word *Kallisti* – "to the prettiest one" – engraved on it, which Eris tossed in among the gods and goddesses while they were partying on Mount Olympus. This led to the Trojan War.

Anyway, Kerry Thornley was in the Marines – I don't have the exact dates in front of me – and met and conversed with Lee Harvey Oswald. Oswald was a Communist and Thornley was an Objectivist. By the time they parted company, Oswald wasn't speaking to Thornley. Kerry was quite shocked when his old barracks buddy was arrested for the assassination of John F. Kennedy. He testified before the Warren Commission and wrote a book and some articles about Oswald. Subsequently he went to New Orleans to try to help the Garrison investigation, but when he wouldn't say what Garrison's people wanted him to say – that is, help them nail the people they had decided to nail – he found himself named one of the assassination conspirators. It was a real nightmare and he's very fortunate that Garrison's efforts came to nothing. Kerry continues to write a bit, and his long epic poem *Illuminati Lady* was published in installments in The St. John's Bread Wednesday Messenger, a literary magazine out of Venice, California. Kerry is still deeply concerned about the Kennedy assassination and has a new theory about the mastermind behind it.

Gregory Hill and Kerry were high school friends. Greg is by vocation an artist, and one of his works of art is the Paratheoanametamystikhood of Eris Esoteric – P.O.E.E., which is his personal movement within the Discordian Society. The Discordian Society is for everybody, but P.O.E.E. is – or was – Greg's personal voice. Greg has lived in California most of his life. He recently spent a couple of years in New York, where he experimented with various new forms of conceptual art. Conceptual art is where the real creation is the idea or the process it generates rather than anything concrete or technical. A religion like P.O.E.E. is conceptual art; a correspondence or a newsletter can be conceptual art; a character can be conceptual art. As examples of the latter, Greg has created a number of personae for himself who sign his various writings and bulletins – Malaclypse the Younger, Doctor Ignotum P. Ignotus, Reverend Dr. Occupant and Mad Malik. Greg has now returned to California. He stopped off at my place and we discovered a new Discordian Society information leaflet, for those who find the address of Green and Pleasant Press in Volume III of *Illuminatus!* and write for information.

TEN: Bob Wilson said that the When-Atlantis-Ruled-the-Earth sections of *Illuminatus!* were 99 percent Shea. Are you a longtime Atlantis buff? Do you think an Atlantis-type civilization in prehistory very likely?

SHEA: For a while, as a kid, I was fascinated by the idea of Atlantis. I even kind of liked the Shaver Mystery stories in the old *Amazing*, edited by Ray Palmer. Atlantis is one of those mythological entities like the Illuminati – it's a kind of esoteric, colorful, dramatic explanation for how things got to be the way they are today. Actually, the archeological and geological evidence, as far as I know, indicates that no such place ever existed. I used it in *Illuminatus!* to present my own pet theory of the *Genesis* story. The Atlanteans are a kind of mythical golden age of humanity, living in peace, prosperity, freedom and happiness. They have a highly developed technology, no morality and no government. Then Gruad introduces the idea of good and evil and that leads to people using force on one another, and the whole Atlantean society collapses. The original sin, you see, was the invention of the idea of sin.

ELEVEN: How about the theories Erich Von Däniken has made popular in recent years? Do you think extraterrestrial "ancient astronauts" might have once colonized Earth?

SHEA: Von Däniken's notions only satisfy people who have a very low opinion of humanity. He takes a primitive carving which distorts human features for artistic purposes and says, "Look, there are no people like this on Earth; therefore this must be a portrait of an extraterrestrial who landed here." This denies that the primitive artist had the capacity to invent forms; he must have copied exactly what he saw. And Von Däniken takes some marvelous piece of ancient architecture and says, "Man couldn't have done this by himself. Ancient astronauts must have done it." Finally, he gets to the point where he no longer believes that any of human civilization was created by people like ourselves. All the basic inventions were given to us by higher intelligences. Von Däniken is just catering to the wish some people have to grovel before imagined higher powers. *Illuminatus!* was written, in part, to make fun of such wishes.

TWELVE: While reading *Illuminatus!* I checked a map and was surprised to find there really is an island named Fernando Poo. Was there really an historic explorer who discovered it in 1472 as Simon Moon implied?

SHEA: Yep, and his name was Fernando Poo. You can find him in the Encyclopedia Britannica, along with the Illuminati. When he discovered the island, he called it Formosa, which means "beautiful" in Portuguese. Later the Portuguese named it after him. His last name is often spelled Po, rather than Poo, but we like Poo better, and it is an acceptable alternative. The incorporation of Fernando Poo into *Illuminatus!* is a good example of how we worked. A friend of mine, Marion Shea, no relation, told me one of her kids had found an island called Fernando Poo in his geography studies. I said "Hey, we can use that" – we'd already started work on *Illuminatus!* Soon Fernando Poo had become an integral part of the structure of the novel. We were always keeping ourselves open to vagrant, random discoveries like that. Art is stumbled over, as much as it is created. The recent international crisis over Angola just shows you how dumb governments are – they can't come up with a script any better than what a couple of nutty satirists did years before in a science fiction novel.

THIRTEEN: Do you have as strong an interest as Wilson does in such things as immortality, colonization of space or Timothy Leary's mind-expanding Neurologic and Hedonic Engineering?

SHEA: In 1960 Eisenhower and Nixon were saying that space exploration was crazy Buck Rogers stuff. Then Kennedy made it a national goal to put a man on the Moon, and nine years later we put a man on the Moon. What this proves is that technology doesn't just happen. It has to be imagined – perhaps by people who have no idea how to do it

– and promoted, and the particular form has to be foreseen and shaped. Unquestionably our society is developing the means to send ever-larger numbers of human beings into space, it's finding ways to extend life expectancy, and it's developing a technology for controlling the human mind. Wilson and Leary are putting forward a particularly sane, humane, libertarian vision of how to develop these things so that they will enhance human life rather than become new ways of oppressing us. I think this is necessary and I take a friendly interest in it. But my personal priorities are such that I'm not actively involved.

FOURTEEN: Are you really a time traveler from the 23rd century, as Wilson has implied?

SHEA: Yes, the 23rd century B.C.

FIFTEEN: What's your view of the Bavarian Illuminati and of conspiracies in general?

SHEA: I thought you'd never ask. Since the publication of the book, Wilson and I have been billed as experts on conspiracy and *Illuminatus!* as a conspiracy book. Actually, *Illuminatus!* began with the idea of satirizing conspiracy mania. We were amused by the way the John Birch Society and other anti-Communists were finding Reds behind every tree, and we were even more amused when we learned – through Gregory and Kerry – that the right-wingers of this country were scaring themselves with the notion of a super-conspiracy behind all other conspiracies. Our thought was, "We'll write a book about it and blow their minds." There is also, of course, a conspiratorial mania on the left which is not quite as grandiose. There's a man in Chicago who keeps charging that the Chicago Seven were agent provocateurs sent in 1968 by the CIA to disrupt the Democratic convention in Chicago. There are other left-wingers who believe that Nelson Rockefeller really runs the country.

From time to time it turns out that somebody's conspiracy theory is true. I used to laugh at left-wingers who claimed the CIA and the FBI were spying on all of us. If somebody in the early 1960s told me the CIA and the Mafia were conspiring to have Castro assassinated with the tacit support of the president of the U.S., I would have hooted. But there's a qualitative difference between investigating allegations of individual conspiracies and conspiracy theory. The true paranoid conspiracy theory ties things together until everything happens as a result of one gigantic conspiracy. This is the state of mind we were trying to satirize in *Illuminatus!* Even the bad weather in Chicago is the work of the Bavarian Illuminati. Our entire civilization is the product of a conspiracy.

The thing is, of course, that conspiracy mythology is a cop-out. It's a way of evading our responsibility for history. We, all of us, the people, if you will, have made our world the way it is. If we don't like it but don't do anything about it, it will stay that way and we're responsible for that, too. A conspiracy didn't get us into World War II. The people of the U.S., most of them, wanted to fight the Germans and Japanese. Most people supported American intervention in Vietnam. When they stopped supporting, the U.S. got out. To realize that you can affect historical events and that you, as an individual, are responsible for what happens is the opposite of conspiracy mythologizing. The big historical events are the result of countless individual decisions, and it is those individuals, not some conspiracy, who are responsible for the course of history.

SIXTEEN: Do you think the frank sex and unconventional shifting of viewpoints in *Illuminatus!* will alienate a significant part of your audience – or is this where readers' heads are presently at?

SHEA: Of all the reviews I've seen – and there have been over a dozen at this point – not one has complained at all about the sex scenes in *Illuminatus!* Most haven't even mentioned that there is a lot of explicit sex. This leads me to conclude that people who read books regularly – that is, book reviewers – tend to take such things for granted. On the other hand, many people have mentioned the shifts in time, space and viewpoint – some admiringly, some to complain. The structure and texture of the book certainly makes it more difficult to read. But they also will help the conscientious reader to get a gut-level realization of the ultimate truth behind space, time and the human personality. Readers who have kept up with – and experienced – the discoveries of the last decade or so in psychology, philosophy and religion will enjoy the way the book is put together.

SEVENTEEN: How is *Illuminatus!* doing so far? Are you satisfied with its critical reception and sales?

SHEA: Delighted. There was always the possibility that it might sink without a trace. I knew we had written a good book, but would anyone pay attention? Original paperback fiction gets virtually no reviews, as a rule. But *Illuminatus!* has had at least a dozen reviews, all of them excellent. One of the things that still amazes me has been the positive enthusiasm of everybody who reads this book. The one thing I'm sorry about is that none of the professional science fiction magazines such as *Galaxy, Analog* or *F&SF* has vouchsafed to review *Illuminatus!* Granted, the novel isn't simply science fiction. Still, it is science fiction among other things and I'm sure it will have enormous appeal to people who read science fiction. There is a certain insularity in the professional science fiction world which is detrimental to the genre. As for sales, Dell tells me that they've gone back to a second printing, which means it's doing pretty good. Yes, I'm happy.

EIGHTEEN: Have you ever seen a fnord?

SHEA: One just won the Republican primary in New Hampshire.

NINETEEN: Wilson says *Illuminatus!* was communicated to you telepathically by intelligent beings from Sirius, the dog star. What's your story?

SHEA: It frequently helps an artist to imagine that the work he is creating has a separate life of its own and is being transmitted to him. I found over and over again that a certain alert passivity, a receptiveness, was valuable in writing *Illuminatus!* Much of the effort of creation should take place unconsciously. Nabokov says he sees his novels as already existing in another universe, and he has to reconstruct them in this universe by putting together the fragments that come into his mind. Stravinsky said, "I am the vessel through which *The Rite of Spring* passed." Keats said that an imaginative writer needs "negative capability," which is the ability to remain comfortably in a state of "uncertainties, mysteries, doubts, without any irritable reaching after fact and reason." Charles Rycroft, a British psychoanalyst, wrote an essay on the imagination in which he says:

"I must, however, state my impression, my conviction, that people who possess negative capability to a high degree seem not to conceive themselves as opposed to an environment which they have to master by 'irritable reaching after fact and reason,' but rather as a part of the universe which is capable of absorbing the whole into itself and then re-creating it by distillation in imaginative works; in other and psychoanalytical words, their relationship to 'external reality' remains identificatory, without any drawing of impermeable ego boundaries between themselves and other people and other things."

TWENTY: Are you a party to or supporter of Wilson's suit against the Neo-American Church for $1,000,000? What's your reaction to Art Klep's accusation in a recent High Times that *Illuminatus!* was really written by Tim Leary and only credited to you and Wilson in order to avoid Leary's contractual obligations?

SHEA: Whenever I am attacked – verbally at least – I always remember three things: The Buddha's maxim that nothing bounces back faster than hostility. King Charles II's saying, "The more you stir a turd the more it stinks." And the sad fact that Alfred Kinsey wasted years and shortened his life by taking seriously and attempting to respond to all the vicious attacks on him that followed publication of the Kinsey reports. Nevertheless, Wilson and I devoted years of our lives to *Illuminatus!* and are rather proud of the result, and it hurts to have some asshole come along and fabricate – out of an old grudge against Timothy Leary – the charge that we didn't write it. Wilson's reaction, treating the accusation as if it were worthy of attention, is most kindly. My own reaction is to be less kind, and ignore the whole business.

TWENTY-ONE: What are your own publishing plans? Any new books coming up?

SHEA: I'm working, very slowly, on a novel. It's not like *Illuminatus!* It's about a young man who slowly goes crazy in a typical American big city and commits acts of violence. In other words, the archetypal story of our times. I'm also trying to do a non-fiction book which will be a kind of general statement of the philosophy I've arrived at after 43 years of knocking around on this planet. The novel is about twenty percent finished. The other exists in the form of enough notes to fill a book, but they have to be pulled together. I'm also doing articles, essays, book reviews, things like that. If you'd like to know what I'd like to be when I grow up, I'll tell you. I'd like to be an old-fashioned man of letters, the sort of writer who was common in the Nineteenth Century but who has all but disappeared in our age of excessive specialization. The man of letters felt comfortable turning his hand to anything – fiction or nonfiction – articles, essays, poetry, short stories, novels, plays, pamphlets. Just a master of the craft of writing. George Orwell and Aldous Huxley are examples. I think you could call Wilson a man of letters.

TWENTY TWO: Will 1976 be the year we finally immanentize the Eschaton?

SHEA: It would be, if everybody reads *Illuminatus!* and takes it to heart. The Eschaton is always imminent. It's just a matter of seeing it.

TWENTY THREE: Who really did kill JFK?

SHEA: We all did.

Ⴚ

The Principle of the Good Soup

By "Alexander Eugenspiegel"

["Alexander Eugenspiegel" is a pseudonym that Robert Shea sometimes used – The editor.]

About two years ago a friend whom I see occasionally but, for logistical reasons, had not been in close touch with, got into pretty bad shape. I only learned about what happened after it all happened.

He had always been a heavy drinker, but he had always managed to get his work done, give time and love to his family and spend satisfying hours with hobbies and friends. Now he was in trouble. He didn't increase his intake of booze, but it seemed to be affecting him more severely. One martini would leave him slurring his words and staggering. He was often unable to work after lunch. He would come home from work, take a drink, go to bed and sleep until the next day. When sober he was surly and uncommunicative. He neglected the people close to him. His wife considered divorce.

Nobody considered hospitalizing our friend. Everyone who knew him and liked him – a considerable number – worried about him. But if he was intent on ruining his life by drinking too much, how could anyone stop him?

But one afternoon a friend who hadn't seen him for a long time ran into him in a bar and found him to be incoherent. Not just drunk, but literally unable to communicate. This person, who has a capacity for making decisions quickly and acting upon them, became alarmed. He even became angry that so many people had watched our friend deteriorating without doing anything about it. He called our friend's wife and some other mutual friends, got the necessary papers and by that evening they had all bundled our friend off to the detoxification ward of a good local hospital.

He didn't protest or resist. As he told me later, he was too muddled to understand what was happening to him.

The ward he was admitted to is a locked ward. The people held in it have been using alcohol, drugs or both to the point where somebody thought they ought to be hospitalized whether they wanted to be or not. They are, as I learned when I visited my friend, treated almost like criminals. Some of them are even facing criminal charges. Their rooms are searched and they are required to undergo individual and group psychotherapy.

Now any good anarchist would have to disapprove of this. Here is a man being deprived of his liberty, treated without his consent, imprisoned. That all this was done with good intentions may make it even more reprehensible from the anarchist standpoint. The most dangerous infringements on liberty are those which seem benevolent. As I said, I didn't find out about this until after it happened, but if I had been in on it I might well have protested that each of us has a right to ruin his life if we choose to, that psychotherapy administered under coercion is unlikely to do any good and that mental problems should not be treated as if they were physical illnesses. I like to think I might have tried to suggest some alternatives involving voluntary treatment, but the fact is I don't know any that would be likely to be effective in a case like this.

Our friend had been in the hospital for several days when I called his home, not having talked to him for months, and his wife told me what happened. I visited him, bringing a carton of cigarettes at his request, and found him shaky, tired, accepting the idea that being in the detoxification ward was a necessity. He mentioned that he was going to undergo a number of tests, including a CAT scan of his brain.

A few days later he told me the doctors had discovered that there was a tumor the size of a plum growing in the middle of his brain, actually pushing his brain out of shape. He showed me the X-rays. Soon after, they took out the tumor, which was benign.

He now leads a more-or-less normal life. He is still recovering from the operation in some ways. He still has serious emotional problems, but he doesn't get drunk any more. He still drinks, but not heavily, and it doesn't affect him much. It turns out that booze was not his problem, or at least not his main problem. The destructive behavioral changes that everyone attributed to alcoholism was actually caused by the tumor.

The person who instigated the hospitalization saved our friend's life. And he did it by taking an action I think most anarchists would condemn – involuntary commitment.

This isn't the first time I've encountered a situation in which people's acute needs seem to have come into conflict with libertarian principles. James Harris, in *Frefanzine* #50, raises the dilemma of a libertarian who sees his neighbor torturing a dog in his yard. Does the libertarian respect his neighbor's personal and property rights, or does he go to the aid of the dog?

Then there is the question that is asked of pacifists in various ways. What if your loved ones were about to be killed and you could save them by shooting the would-be murderer? Would you hold your fire and let the people you love be slaughtered?

It has been said that hard cases make bad law. But then, anarchists are not lawyers.

Every ethical or political system produces its hard cases. In religion classes in the all-male Catholic schools I attended we repeated worries about the question of the woman in labor who can be saved only if her infant is destroyed. We were told that if ever our own (future) wives were in that situation, and the doctor asked us what to do, we would have to tell him to save the baby and let the mother die. If we wanted to be good Catholics.

If you want to be a good pacifist, you let the murderer kill your family. If you want to be a good libertarian you let your neighbor torture his dog.

If you want to be a good anarchist you let your friend die slowly rather than force him to go to the hospital.

But it seems to me if you want to be a good human being you demand that the doctor save your wife, you shoot the people menacing your family, you rescue the dog and one way or another you get your friend into the hospital.

I have come to feel that sticking to religious, philosophical or ideological principles in situations like this is a kind of insanity. There are times when an immediate need must be met.

The many Zen stories about enlightened people who do un-Zenlike, but just right, things in moment of crisis have provided me with some guidance here. But my favorite commentary on this kind of situation – well, not exactly this kind of situation but something like it – comes from Meister Eckhart:

> "If someone is in such a state of ecstasy as Saint Paul, and knows a sick person who needs a good soup, it is far better that he suspends his raptures and serves God in a greater love."

For a mystic nothing can be more important than direct contact with God, and yet Eckhart says one who breaks his communion with God to bring soup to a sick person shows an even greater love of God.

Perhaps the key word in Eckhart's statement is "love." In the late 60s a school of thought called situation ethics attracted the attention of people interested in religion and morality. It was mostly advanced by Anglican clergymen, such as Bishop John Robinson in England and Father Joseph Fletcher in the U.S. There is only one absolute moral commandment, the situation ethics philosophers claimed, and that is always to act out of love. They quoted Augustine: "Love, and do what you will." They thought that no moral system could cover every situation; therefore, what the good is in any situation can only be determined by the person who is in that situation and must do the choosing. That person cannot fall back on some well-established moral rule to justify his or her act. It is possible, according to situation ethics, that a person could go impeccably by the book morally and still commit an evil action.

Situation ethics was denounced by conservative moralists as permissive, as another example of humanistic liberalism invading the theological sphere and undermining our moral codes. But its advocates pointed out that it actually held people to a more rigorous moral standard than traditional morality. Only rarely will a person's judgment of the situation lead to an action at odds with traditional ethics. Moral rules may only be guidelines rather than absolutes, but they are still very important guidelines, to be respected, not neglected.

Gradually the controversy died down, and one stopped hearing about situation ethics and its companion movement, the new morality.

Personally I am not attracted to anything that presents itself as religion or morality, but I think the situation ethicists had a point that applies to any code of conduct, even the non-supernatural principles that many anarchists adopt and by which they judge their own behavior and that of other anarchists. Situation ethics might also be a good basis for interpreting those puzzling Zen stories in which the masters merrily flout Buddhist principles. Although Zen teachers would probably say that even situation ethics is an attempt to reduce the ineffable to a formula and therefore must fail in the end.

I recently heard a Zen talk by Roshi Philip Kapleau in which he said that once one has arrived at the Buddhist insight that there is no distinction between self and other, it may be hard to see a reason for acting, since doing something for another may seem like taking money from one pocket to put it in another (my humdrum simile, not Kapleau's). Kapleau said that the motivation for acting is always there. The Buddhists call it compassion. Many others call it love.

The need to act out of compassion or love is what ties together all the hard cases I've mentioned. If love for a sick person, for a dog, for a family, for a mate, for a friend is strong enough, one will go ahead and violate principle. It could be argued that one is only following a higher principle, but I feel such actions transcend principle and go into a realm where words are perforce left behind.

But perhaps we must give a name to this ultimate sanity so we can talk about it. How about calling it the Principle of the Good Soup?

Ǥ

Big and Cool for Peace in Chicago

By "Alexander Eugenspiegel"

The radio on the morning of Saturday, April 5, informed me that Mayor Daley had decided to let us march. This despite the fact that there had been small disturbances on the South and West sides marking the anniversary of Martin Luther King's murder and the National Guard was in town and Daley and Governor Ogilvie were congratulating themselves on having prevented a riot.

Feeling in no wise grateful to Mayor Daley-Doody (as my friends are amused to call him) I put on my marching clothes – white shirt and navy blue suit – and headed downtown.

It was just cold enough to keep one from getting sweaty, but sunny and not very windy. You never know in Chicago, either how the weather will be or how it will go with a demonstration: will all be cool, or will you get scarfed? This demo turned out almost too good to be true, a day of smiles, minimal friction, massive numbers, events going down cool and smooth as Carvel ice cream. We assembled on the south bank of the gray, green, greasy Chicago River, opposite the corn-cob towers of Marina City, last word in urban alienation. There came Vets for Peace in Vietnam, masses of signs, hundreds of little American-Legion-type hats, rumors of real servicemen in their ranks (in civvies, of course). Behind the vets came Women for Peace, led by a double rank of mothers pushing babies in strollers, the best possible defense, one imagined, against Mace, missiles, clubs and other troubles.

Thousands of little plastic toy police whistles had been distributed among the marchers by some unknown agency. A couple of evil friends of mine who like peace and quiet as well as peace in Vietnam surreptitiously pocketed dozens of the whistles to keep down the noise level around themselves; but the whistles were good theater reminiscent of the ululations of Arab women in *The Battle of Algiers* and *Lawrence of Arabia*, adding a much-needed freak dimension to the event. The mood of the crowd was that of jaundiced good feeling, which has marked the moratorium on activism following Nixon's election. A good rage against the present administration has yet to develop.

The cops were cool, too. The Chicago papers had made much in advance of the written psychological test used to screen the police on duty during the march for "restraint, emotional stability, friendliness and cooperativeness." From the *Chicago Seed*, however, came dire warnings of mass arrests scheduled for the night before the demonstration with the aim of decimating our ranks by busting everybody the cops could reach with pot charges or whatever could be trumped up. The arrests hadn't happened; we'll never know if the *Seed* people were freaked out by rumors or whether their timely warnings prevented a calamity.

Personally, I had been expecting the trouble to come from our local right-wingers. Righties have recently disrupted two public meetings in the Chicago area, once driving Bernardine Dohrn of the SDS right off the stage with their heavy heckling, which is a shame since SDS so staunchly upholds the right of any speaker to have his say. The rightists did show up at the peace march, but there were only about two dozen of them, it seemed to me (next day's papers said 60). When we passed under the El tracks and entered the north end of the Loop, they were over on the sidewalk on the east side of State Street, big American flag leading the way, a bunch of little, vibrating baby flags following like baby geese behind their mother. Under the flags, angry faces with gaping, shouting mouths. There were thousands and thousands of us and not enough of them to provide a single platoon for the war in which they demanded "Victory Now." Most of them appeared to be teenage boys, and I remarked to fellow marchers that since they were under 30 their opinions must be sound. They were welcome, as far as I was concerned; one needed something to get the old adrenalin up.

More amusement was offered by a grim-faced man in a black leather jacket who stood in front of Woolworth's holding up a large, neatly-lettered sign reading "This Parade Is Communist Inspired." And in front of Marshall Field's a little band of patriots yelled imprecations and waved flags from behind a big "America – Love It Or Leave It" sign. One man in this group kept shouting something which was drowned out by replies from the marchers, so that I could only hear the word "Kill . . ." repeated over and over again.

On our side, some signs were adorned with bumper stickers reading "Support Mayor Daley" with a picture of a jock strap, a tiny Mayor Daley peering out of the cup. One kid carried a hand-lettered sign that said, "The Draft Is A Gas – Stick It Up Your Ass." People carried copies of an underground paper with the big headline, "Stop the Goddamn War," and a page from *Moderator* with a picture of Nixon captioned "Would you buy a used war from this man?" One man held up a papier-mâché skull decorated with "Nixon's the One." And one loquacious sign declared, "An Authority That Ceases to Speak the Truth Is No Longer An Authority to Be Obeyed."

Besides the predictable chants – "No more war!" and

"Whaddaya want? Peace! When do you wannit? Now!" – there were people chanting "So-so-so-society" and the new slogan promulgated by the Bavarian Illuminati of Chicago, "Kick out the jams!" The Illuminati did not march as a unit, but Mordecai the Mad and Josh the Dill, as well as others, had joined various contingents. Some of the militant kid types chanted "One more war – Revolution!" a sentiment that was neither picked up nor appreciated by those demonstrating for peace pure and simple.

We marched down State Street through alternate patches of sun and shadow; the Loop has many low buildings (remaining from the era of decay that preceded the Daley-promoted building business boom) which permit some sunlight to fall on State even in the late afternoon. Passing under the southern El tracks, we moved into the northern fringe of the South Side. State Street here becomes a black skid row, bars alternating with pawn shops, and black winos made the V-sign at us as we passed.

When we got to 14th Street, final turning point from which the marchers were to enter the Chicago Coliseum for a rally, my friends and I left the march and stood on the sidelines to watch the rest of the parade. We stood on the edge of a big parking lot at 14th and State. Suddenly, here came the right-wingers again with their bunches of American flags, still marching on the sidewalk beside the demonstration route. They turned into the parking lot, where they may have held a brief rally – I don't know, all I saw was a bunch of milling around and yelling. I was talking to anarchist poet Kevin O'Flaherty McCool, who figured the march had come to an end, since there didn't seem to be any more people coming down State Street, and guessed that there had been about 5,000 people in the demonstration. Suddenly, in the parking lot, a uniformed cop and a plainclothesman were dragging a kid by his ankles and wrists, his body sagging down between them, and his ass almost dragging on the ground. When they were almost out of the lot a big ring of demonstrators surrounded them, and a medic wiped the kid's face with a damp cloth – I thought of the day before, Good Friday, and Veronica's veil. The kid had masses of kinky, curly hair and a thick gray sweater on which the uniformed cop kept a tight grip. Some of the demonstrators were yelling "Let him go!" while some rightists in the crowd yelled, "Throw him in the lake!" More cops appeared and pushed everybody out of the parking lot, and the cops who had the kid got away with their prey. Sunday's papers said that Edward A. Schultz, 17, had been arrested in the parking lot after he swung a stick. He swung first at Marcia Wilson, 21, who had tried to grab a Vietcong flag from a demonstrator. Then he swung at a plainclothes cop. Miss Wilson was also arrested, in a display of impartial justice or something.

New masses of marchers, including large contingents from local high schools and nearby Midwestern universities, now came down State Street. There was also a float made to look like a gigantic helmeted skull labeled "The War Machine." This was surrounded by guerilla street theater people, some wearing wound makeup, others tall black hoods, and still others with red, white and blue papier mâché eagle heads. A bass drum was beaten slowly and solemnly while the wounded screamed and groaned and the eagle-heads made simulated attacks.

Several big black anarchist flags appeared in this part of the parade, and McCool, still standing on the sidelines with me, applauded gleefully and happily shouted, "Viva anarchy!" a cry taken up by other bystanders. McCool and I had revised our estimate upward to over 10,000, and there we rested as the sanitation trucks came doing a zig-zag waltz down the street. Police estimates in the papers ranged from 10 to 20,000, and the Chicago Peace Council claimed a clearly exaggerated 35,000. But the numbers were definitely bigger than those at the demonstrations of last summer and fall, when feelings were running high. It looks as if the peace movement in the Midwest is still growing.

Nobody I know went to the rally. Max Primach, co-chairman of the Chicago Peace Council, who spoke at the rally, said it well for all of us: “I am not a person who likes rallies, anyway. They’re too long and the speeches are too repetitious.”

G

Jebu meets Lady Taniko

This excerpt is from Shike: Time of the Dragons, Robert Shea's first published novel, set in Medieval Japan, around the time the island was invaded by the Mongols. The novel's hero, Jebu, has been dispatched to serve as a bodyguard and escort for Taniko, a young woman who is going on a journey to marry an important lord. Jebu is a monk in the order of the Zinja, a fictional philosophical warrior order which serves as a vehicle for many of Shea's ideas. Much of the novel, which features plenty of action, takes place in China as well as Japan. The Mongols, the most feared military force of their day, feature in many scenes.

Jebu was awake long before sunrise. He washed in a bucket of cold water and passed an hour in seated meditation in a corner of the yard. He made his mind blank by counting his exhalations up to ten, then starting over again. As the edge of the sun appeared at the top of the bamboo palisade that protected the Shima grounds, Jebu stood up and began his calisthenics, a series of movements from position to position that looked like – and in fact, was – a vigorous, complicated dance. Next he drew his sword and performed his sword drill.

Now he could hear the sounds of the household waking up. An attendant in a grey cloak took him to the stable and showed him the horse Bokuden had chosen for him. Jebu examined it closely. It was a brown stallion with no outstandingly good qualities, a little past his prime, but with no serious defects either. He was called Hollyhock. Jebu was to return Hollyhock to the Shima town house in Heian Kyo. The selection of Hollyhock as his mount showed typical Shima parsimony, Jebu thought.

Lady Taniko's party was beginning to gather. Two porters loaded large, heavy packs on the backs of two ancient, wheezing mares. Those jades would be lucky if they survived all the way to Heian Kyo. Servants in grey robes led three more horses out of the stable. Jebu went and fetched Hollyhock. He stood beside the brown stallion, holding his reins. The maidservants, wrapped in identical peach travelling cloaks, appeared on the porch of the women's house. They looked at Jebu, whispered together and giggled.

Apparently the plan was for the women to travel on horseback. No self-respecting lady of Heian Kyo would ever ride in anything but an ox-drawn carriage. Of course, no lady of Heian Kyo would ever venture more than a few miles outside the walls of the capital. It was a good thing the Shima ladies, like most samurai women, were able to ride horseback. A carriage could not negotiate the whole Tokaido Road from Kamakura to the capital.

At last the Lady Taniko came out on the porch of the northern building, the women's house, followed by a group of children and a blubbering, middle-aged woman, doubtless her mother. Lord Bokuden emerged with stately pride from the central building and joined his family on the porch of the women's house. All bowed low to him.

Jebu studied the girl he would be escorting half-way across Honshu. She wore a lavender travelling cloak over a dark red trouser skirt. She had a fine, pale complexion, a tiny, rounded nose, a wide mouth and a pointed chin. Her gaze swung round to Jebu, and he felt as if the claws of a cat had raked his face. It was a surprisingly mature, candid look for a pretty thirteen-year-old girl. There was something ruthless, even cruel, in Taniko's eyes. Her look raised Jebu's hackles and excited him all at once. This baby chick could grow up to be a dragon.

"Is that gangling, ugly monk to be my sole escort?" Her voice was light and slightly metallic.

Bokuden said, "It is well known that one Zinja is the equal of ten samurai."

"If I know my family, it is more likely that ten Zinja are the equal in price of one samurai."

"I would not send you with this monk if I were not sure you were absolutely safe."

"It might serve your purpose better if I were raped and murdered by a gang of bandits on the way to Heian Kyo. Then you would have made the gesture of offering your daughter to the elderly and influential Prince Horigawa and be saved the expense of a wedding."

Jebu chuckled to himself, amused at the way she bore down on the words "elderly" and "influential." By the Willow Tree, the girl was shrewd. She might even be right. Perhaps the two of them were both being thrown to the sharks by this son of pirates.

Bokuden's seamed face was white with anger. "Keep up this disrespect towards your father before his household, and there will be no journey to Heian Kyo and no wedding. You will spend the rest of your life in a convent telling your troubles to the compassionate Buddha."

Taniko fell silent, her cheeks burning red. She has gone as far as she dares go in baiting her contemptible father, Jebu thought. Many times further than most daughters would have the courage to go. He liked her. She was brave. She was intelligent. She was witty. Indeed, she was destined to be a dragon, quite a beautiful one.

Servants helped Taniko and her maids to mount their geldings. The women rode side-saddle. Jebu in the lead, the three women next, and the two porters on their baggage-laden old horses last, the party clattered out through the gateway. The Shima gate shut on the weeping mother, the impatient father, the cheering children, the waving servants.

The Tokaido passed north of Kamakura, and they rode out of the city in that direction. From here on, five lives were in Jebu's hands. He reminded himself that a Zinja acts for the sake of action and does not concern himself with the outcome of what he does. Whether the party got to the capital or was massacred by Mutatomo hirelings within the next mile should be as one to Jebu. Should be, but in fact he was nervous.

The horses' hooves thudded on the packed dirt street. The smell of fish – fresh fish, cooking fish and rotten fish – pervaded the air of Kamakura. Every so often as they rode out of the city, Jebu looked back to see if they were being followed. There was no sign of it. Evidently the third daughter of Lord Shima no Bokuden was not of enough interest in Kamakura to attract even the hint of a threat.

As their road climbed into the hills, Jebu looked back at Kamakura. It was a city dominated by the sea; the heart of the city was clearly the collection of wharves and warehouses at the crescent-shaped water front, and its pulse-beat was the arrival and departure of its big fishing fleet. Ringing the dock area were humble houses of the fisherfolk and those who worked on the wharves. Beyond them were the larger houses of the owners of ships and warehouses and of those who had grown wealthy trafficking in each season's catch. But at the outermost edge of the city, rising into the hills and far from the docks, were the newly built mansions of the great lords who were moving into Kamakura from the north, great landowners like Lord Bokuden, whose estate, as befitted the first family of Kamakura, was visible from a long distance, the red Takashi banner standing out against the dark green trees growing near it.

Jebu noticed that Taniko was riding beside him. She never glanced back at her childhood home but kept her face resolutely turned forward. Perhaps the long journey ahead frightened her. Jebu turned to her with a smile and said, "Kamakura is as important in this part of the country as Heian Kyo is in the south."

Taniko's piercing black eyes glared at him. "Of what interest is the opinion of a ragged monk of an obscure order who has doubtless never poked his long nose out of the monastery before? Keep to yourself and do not speak to me again. I have troubles enough."

"In my Order we say, he who thinks himself a victim, makes himself a victim. But if you choose to consider yourself a person of many troubles, my lady, I wish you joy in your choice. And I respect your wish to brood over your sorrows in solitude." He spurred Hollyhock up the path ahead.

He felt not the least bit angry; he still liked the girl. In fact, that had been a rather neat touch, the business about his long nose. She was a keen observer; the nose was one of the things he'd inherited from his foreign father. Jebu felt pleased with himself that his Zinja training enabled him to remain calm and cheerful in the face of hostility from others. He hoped Taniko would not fret constantly about her grievances, though. That would be a heavy burden to carry all the way to Heian Kyo.

That night they stopped at the country home of one of

Lord Bokuden's allies. From her baggage Taniko took the pillow she had slept on ever since she was a little girl. Its paint worn, its corners chipped, the wooden headrest gave Taniko a warm, safe feeling, just as a cherished doll or a favourite sleeping robe might give to another girl. In the pillow was a concealed drawer, its edges made to look like ornamental carving. Taniko opened the drawer and took out a notebook, its carved wood covers bound with decorative red and gold string. Also in the drawer were a brush, an ink stick and an ink stone. Using water she had brought with her to the bedchamber in a soup bowl, Taniko began to rub the stick on the stone to make ink.

From the pillow book of Shima Taniko:

People who cannot think for themselves are in the habit of saying autumn is the most beautiful season of the year. I think it is too sad to be beautiful. I do not, like so many silly young girls, think sad things are beautiful. I see the lines of ducks flying overhead and think to myself that they are deserting us. They fear the coming of the cold that kills. I hear the murmuring of the insects in the woods and think to myself that soon they will all freeze to death.

And for my life, too, the summer is over. I am to become the wife of a man whom I have never seen, but who, I have heard, is old and cruel. Like winter, he will chill me through and through. But this also means I leave the rustic backwater of Kamakura to live in the city I have always longed to see, the capital, Heian Kyo. To see and walk among the exalted people who rule this Sunrise Land! It has always been my dream to move among the great ones. If I must suffer a misconceived marriage in order to climb above the clouds, I am willing to pay that price.

My father, it seems, is unwilling to pay much to ensure that I travel safely, judging by the strange youth he has hired to protect me. One hears dark tales about this sinister Order of Zinja, that their warriors are aided by evil spirits and that no one is safe from them. One also hears interesting things about the goings-on between the Zinja monks and their temple women. I wonder if this one has ever been a lover. He is so huge and of such an odd colour. I would be afraid to let him near me. But if he were near me I would be afraid to refuse him whatever he wished. There is something pleasurable in the thought of a man who makes one feel helpless. The Zinja monk's presence makes this journey far more interesting.

– Seventh Month, twenty-third day
YEAR OF THE DRAGON

• • •

The white cone seemed to block out half the sky. Every time Jebu looked at it, he gasped again. He had never seen a mountain of this size. No one had warned him that on this journey he would behold such a marvel.

He had seen it from a distance as they rode into the hills above Kamakura, but then it was small and far off. As they crossed the neck of the Izu Peninsula he began to grasp its size. Its simple symmetry astonished him; the way its snowy peak reflected the colours of the day, from rose to white to gold, brought tears to his eyes. But it was only today, approaching Hara, that he had a full sense of the silent volcano's immensity. Yesterday he had spoken to no one of his feelings about the mountain. Today, as it happened, the Lady Taniko was riding beside him. He overcame his hesitancy and addressed her.

"Please, my lady, what is the name of that magnificent mountain?"

She turned to him slowly, her face a mask of exaggerated surprise and contempt. "You mean you've never heard of Fuji-san? Truly, the Zinja are ignorant as well as poor and miserable."

She lowered her head so that the brim of her circular sedge hat hid her eyes. She pulled her horse's head around abruptly and trotted back down the road towards her maids. The sudden movement startled two cranes in the near-by reeds, and they flapped upwards until they were two tiny silhouettes in the sky above Mount Fuji.

The journey down the coast was slow. No one spoke to Jebu. Taniko and her maids apparently considered him beneath their notice, and the porters were afraid of him. The days were punctuated only by frequent rainstorms and the necessity of passing innumerable toll barriers. Every so often the road would disappear altogether, and they would have to pick their way along boulder-strewn beaches or through pathless woods.

The baggage included a small tent, which the ladies used for sleeping outdoors and as a shelter in wet weather. Jebu and the two porters took turns standing watch when the party slept out of doors. When possible they stayed at monasteries or at the homes of Lord Bokuden's friends, several of whom had built castles overlooking the Tokaido.

One sunny afternoon, eight days after they set out, they were riding single file along a hillside that rose sheer out of the sea, when the porter leading the way suddenly threw up his hands. He fell from his horse, rolled over and over down the hill, arms and legs flailing, and disappeared with a great splash amid the brown rocks and blue-white breakers. Jebu got a glimpse, as the man fell, of the grey and white feathers of an arrow protruding from his chest.

Jebu clenched his fists and ground his teeth with rage. He had failed. Because he had chosen this particular afternoon to bring up the rear, he had let the porter ride to his death. A life that had been in his keeping was lost. He shut his eyes momentarily and reminded himself that a Zinja is aware at all times of his own perfection, regardless of circumstances. Then, shaking his head angrily, he spurred Hollyhock up the path to put himself between the rest of the party and the attacker.

Blocking the road was a big samurai in box-shaped, many-plated leather armour, mounted on a black roan horse. In one hand he held his longbow – a bow that must have required three men to bend it for stringing. Beside him stood three tsuibushi, each holding the foot soldier's favourite weapon, the long-handled naginata.

Jebu estimated that the samurai was not quite as tall as he was. Bareheaded, he wore his greasy hair pulled back tightly and tied in the round black knot of hair by which the samurai identified themselves. His beard was raggedly trimmed. He had the pink eyes and permanent flush of the heavy sake drinker. Jebu recognized the type at once: a rustic bully, too in love with fighting and drinking to settle down to farm work. Doubtless the terror of the neighbourhood when young, enjoying his pick of the girls. One who might easily have become an outlaw but who, through some accident of birth or social connection, was made a local official and could legally prey upon the peasants. Growing more cruel, more dangerous, more unpredictable as he got older and the futility and boredom of his life began to eat at him. At bottom, most samurai were like this man, though some were born to greater wealth, were more competent in the arts of fighting, travelled farther and did better for themselves than others. The samurai saw themselves as noble and redoubtable warriors. The Zinja saw them as destructive, dangerous and stupid, like small boys whose parents have foolishly permitted them to play with knives.

Jebu reined up Hollyhock a short distance from the samurai and his men and said, "You have murdered an unarmed man. You will answer for it to the oryoshi of this district. We will demand justice."

The samurai laughed and struck his leather-armoured chest

with a gauntleted fist. "Then you must demand it from me. I'm the oryoshi here. I enforce the law in this place."

The words and the man's bearing made it clear: they would have to fight. Jebu began to compose himself in the Zinja manner. Your armour is your mind. A naked man can utterly demolish a man clad in steel. Rely on nothing but the Self. Here it was, his first combat, the moment towards which his life had pointed for the last seventeen years. The bottom of his stomach felt hollow. Yet, for a Zinja, every combat was the first, and the first was like every other. So they said in the monastery.

Now he would see. Now he would have to try to kill a man. He had been trained to do it. He knew ten thousand ways to kill. But could he really do it?

He heard hoofbeats on the stony road behind him. Taniko's metallic voice said, "That man you killed was a servant of Lord Shima no Bokuden of Kamakura. You will answer to Lord Bokuden and his allies, oryoshi."

Jebu kept his eyes on the samurai. "Get back, my lady, back behind everyone else."

"I am responsible for my father's servant."

"And I am responsible for you. Back. Now." He admired her courage. It was what he expected, having seen her confront her father.

The samurai smiled broadly. Several of his front teeth were missing; others were yellow. "Your father's name means nothing here, my lady. This is Muratomo territory, and I am their ally. We are the only true warriors in the land, living and dying by the sword. We're not effeminate courtiers like the Takashi. How typically Takashi for your father to send you this way with no more escort than a monk armed with a sewing needle. Armed monks are fit only to clean fish. I'll kick this monk into the sea where he belongs, and then I'll take charge of you, little lady."

Jebu said, "If you force me to fight, one of us will die. Perhaps both of us. Perhaps others, too."

"Either kill him or be killed yourself," Taniko said. "That's what my father hired you for. Don't sit there and argue."

"I'm obliged by the rule of my Order to warn him."

The samurai laughed, threw out his chest and squared his shoulders, his armour creaking and rattling. "Warn me? Warn me? I am Nakane Ikeno, son of Nakane Ikenori, who put down the Abe in the land of Oshu and slew Abe Sadato, their champion. I am the grandson of Nakane Ikezane, who fought against Takashi Masakado, captured him and sent his rebellious head back to Heian Kyo. I am the great-grandson of–"

Jebu, sitting easily in his saddle with his reins loose and his fists on his hips, interrupted. "You are an ape and the son of an ape and the grandson of an ape. As for me, I am nothing. I have no family name. My father was an unknown in the Sunrise Land. I have done nothing. I come from nowhere and I go nowhere." Jebu touched the Zinja emblem on his chest. Ikeno's eyes flickered to the blue and white circle of silk and widened slightly. Jebu went on, "I want nothing and I fear nothing. If you kill me you will have accomplished nothing, and no one will care. Let us pass."

"Am I supposed to be terrified because you're a Zinja, boy? The Zinja are cowards who kill by stealth. And you're a coward, or you'd challenge me like a man. Why should I give way before someone who calls himself nothing?"

"Air is nothing. Yet a windstorm can destroy a city. Stand aside, ape." Even as he spoke, Jebu repeated to himself the sayings that quieted his mind and filled his body with the power of the Self. Rely on nothing under heaven. You will not do the fighting. The Self will do the fighting.

Ikeno bellowed, "You dare call me an ape and insult my ancestors? I'll see you die a shameful death. You will not be burned or buried. Your body will lie above ground to be eaten by dogs, and your bones will be bleached in the rain and the sun."

"The lickspittles of the Muratomo can kill only unarmed porters." Now Jebu was deliberately goading Ikeno.

Ikeno's long, heavy sword flashed out of its scabbard with a hiss, and he spurred his horse. Jebu remained where he was until Ikeno was upon him. Then, as Ikeno's sword came around, he threw himself flat on Hollyhock's back, hugging the horse's neck, and the samurai sword whistled through the air above him. Jebu heard the screams as Ikeno's horse hurtled on towards the remaining porter and the three women, who all turned their horses and fled from him. Ikeno was far down the narrow path, still waving his sword over his head, before he could stop his horse, turn around and come back for a second try at Jebu.

Jebu glanced at Ikeno's three tsuibushi. They stood open-mouthed and staring, showing no interest in joining the fight.

With a rattle of hooves Ikeno was on him again. Jebu jerked his horse to one side and Ikeno thundered harmlessly past, the sword slashing through empty air. I told you I was nothing, thought Jebu.

Cursing, Ikeno jumped down from his horse and threw the reins to one of the tsuibushi. He ran at Jebu, reaching with leather-gloved hand to pull him down from the saddle. Without any prompting from Jebu, Hollyhock reared back on his hind legs, and Ikeno had to halt his rush and jump back to avoid the flailing front hooves. Jebu felt waves of pleasure rising within him and radiating out to Hollyhock, to Ikeno, to the mountain, to the ocean. They were all part of one stately dance, and time seemed to slow so that he was able to turn his head and look for Taniko. As he expected she was looking at him at the same instant, just as Hollyhock had known exactly when to rear up and check Ikeno's attack. Taniko's eyes, wide with awe and fascination, looked straight into Jebu's, and he saw what Taitaro meant when he said that the eyes are more beautiful than any jewel. And he knew that the Self was looking at the Self. They both turned away at the same moment and he found himself looking into Ikeno's bloodshot eyes, full of anger and befuddlement. Jebu felt compassion for Ikeno. You do not know who you are, he thought.

He drew the short Zinja sword, which Ikeno had called a sewing needle. It was small indeed, compared to Ikeno's sword. He swung his leg over the saddle and dropped lightly to the ground. Ikeno gripped his sword with both hands, holding it before him in the samurai attack stance, and took a step towards Jebu.

"I'll slice that smile off your face and your head from your body, monk."

Ikeno lifted his great sword over his head to bring it down on Jebu. At that same moment, taking three quick steps towards Ikeno, Jebu drew his own blade back, one-handed, then whipped it around in an arc completed so quickly the sword seemed at one moment to be poised over Jebu's right shoulder and at the very next to be beside the left. Jebu relaxed, dropping his hands to his sides. He knew he had killed Ikeno.

Ikeno stood silent and motionless, the long, gleaming blade raised to shoulder height, still tightly gripped in his gloved hands. The anger in the samurai's face faded, became horror, then agony. The mouth fell open. The eyelids fluttered. The sword fell from the hands with a clang, and the hands dropped limply. The whole body began to lean forward, falling from the feet. A thin ring of bright red appeared around the dirty brown neck.

Then, suddenly, the head separated from the shoulders and fell to the dirt and stones of the path. Blood fountained up, hissing, from the stump of the neck. The body stood like a pillar for a moment longer, then collapsed with a crash of steel and leather on top of the severed head.

The three tsuibushi dropped their naginatas, screamed and ran. Unhurriedly, Jebu strode back to Hollyhock, took his small bow from its saddle mount, nocked an arrow with a willow leaf head and fired. One of Ikeno's men fell with the arrow between his shoulder blades. Jebu dropped a second man with another willow-leaf arrow. The third man turned at the edge of the pine forest, fell to his knees and raised his hands in supplication.

Jebu took a coil of hempen rope from his saddlebag and strode up the hill to where the trembling man knelt.

"Please don't kill me, shiké," the man quavered. He was cross-eyed, and Jebu couldn't hold either eye with his own. What would Taitaro say about these jewels?

"Come over here." Jebu motioned towards a big maple. When he stood under the tree, he cut off a length of rope with his sword and tied the man's hands behind him.

Taniko rode over to them, her horse's hooves thudding softly on the mossy hillside. "What are you going to do to him?"

"Cut his head off."

The man screamed and fell to his knees again. "Oh, no, shiké, don't kill poor Moko. I have five children. I meant you no harm. Ikeno made me come with him. Moko's no soldier. He's just a poor carpenter."

"A cross-eyed carpenter?" said Taniko. "I'd like to see what sort of houses you put up."

Moko tried to grin. His two upper front teeth were missing. There was a rare beauty in his ugliness, Jebu thought. In the space of a minute he had gone from thinking of this man as just another enemy tsuibushi to seeing him as a likeable person. I'd really rather not have to kill him at all, Jebu thought.

"I'd surprise you, my lady," Moko said. "I'm a good carpenter. Please ask this great shiké to have mercy on me. Compassionate lady, you wouldn't want my six children to starve."

"Do spare him, Jebu. He's harmless."

"Harmless? He'll be back tonight with a gang of cut-throats." Good, she's on Moko's side, too, he thought. I'll let her talk me out of it.

"No, I won't, shiké. Lord Nakane Ikeno was the only real fighter around here. That's why he was the oryoshi. He forced the rest of us to follow him. None of us men would go out to fight if he hadn't threatened to kill us. I promise you, nobody will come to avenge Lord Ikeno, may his soul inhabit a nightsoil jar – begging your pardon, compassionate lady."

"Jebu, I'm going to be married. I don't want the memories of my wedding marred by an act of cruelty."

"I thought you considered your marriage to the prince a cruelty in itself," Jebu said dryly.

"You are impertinent, monk. I do not want this man's ghost haunting me."

"Why should he haunt you? You will not do him any harm."

"You are my escort. Therefore I am responsible for what you do."

"I am impressed by your sensitivity, my lady. To spare you any pain, I shall spare this man's life." He turned to the kneeling carpenter. "All right. You may live. But you must transport Lady Taniko's baggage to Heian Kyo, replacing the porter that samurai murdered. If you run away, I'll track you down and kill you."

His hands still bound, Moko threw himself flat on his face at Jebu's feet. "Thank you, shiké, thank you. I'll go anywhere you say. To China, if need be."

Taniko said, "What about your five children? Or is it six? Surely they would starve if you went to China."

Moko raised his head and gave Taniko a gap-toothed, cross-eyed grin. "No children, my lady. I'm so ugly no woman would have me. So, no children. A man like me, a mere carpenter of no honour, will say anything to save his life."

Jebu kept his face severe as he cut Moko's hands free with his sword. This man was going to be a blessing from the kami. A man who could be amusing in the face of death was bound to be a better travelling companion than any of the members of the Shima party had so far proved to be.

Thanking Taniko and Jebu many times over, Moko ran off to join the surviving porter and the maids.

"I hope your kindness doesn't bring trouble down on us later on," Jebu said to Taniko.

Jebu was so tall and Taniko so tiny that even though he was on foot and she on horseback, their eyes met almost on a level. She smiled at him for the first time.

"You are a remarkable fighter, Jebu. I've never seen anything like the way you killed that Muratomo lout. When you were fighting him your eyes met mine and I felt something – I cannot describe it. Perhaps some day I will be able to express it in a poem. For now, I want to apologize for my rude words to you. I didn't want you to spoil my new appreciation of you by killing a helpless man."

Jebu was pleased, but he kept up the pose of the stern warrior. "An egg is helpless, but it may hatch a deadly serpent."

"One thing the Zinja taught you well."

"What?"

"How to be a windy bore." She whirled her bay gelding and rode off, calling mockingly over her shoulder, "Shiké!"

Ǥ

Worlds Without Government

Ever since More's *Utopia*, science fiction, or speculative fiction, has been an obvious vehicle for those who want to present a vision of an ideal society. In view of this, it's surprising that it isn't used more often in this way. There are a number of outstanding examples of political speculation in science fiction, but aside from these the field as a whole has tended to be politically unimaginative.

Most science fiction writers seem to accept the notion that the present U.S. system of government is as good as the human race is ever likely to do. Also, most science fiction writers are primarily interested in scientific or technological change rather than in political change. So they tend to describe the political systems of future societies as similar to – or even more primitive than – our own.

Thus, Isaac Asimov's *Foundation* trilogy is a rerun of the decline and fall of the Roman Empire. *Dune's* Paul Atreides is a combination of Mohammed and Genghis Khan. Many specimens of grown-up science fiction are no more sophisticated politically than *Star Wars* (which I loved, but would have loved even more if the good guys had been anarchists instead of a princess and her followers trying to restore a Galactic Republic.)

A great many SF writers seem to be would-be historical novelists who don't like to do historical research. So they set their stories in future worlds whose trappings resemble those of the past societies that attract them and fill in the blanks with science fiction details. There was a period when every other cover of *Analog*, it seemed, portrayed a man dressed as an ancient Roman or a medieval Crusader or an Elizabethan sea dog, only when you looked closely his costume turned out to be a space suit.

Many SF writers, including those who most firmly believe in the possibilities of scientific and technological progress, apparently don't believe in the possibility of political progress. Others, like Huxley in *Brave New World* and Orwell in *1984,* appear to believe that change is likely to be for the worse. (But see Huxley's *Island* for another view.)

It is sometimes argued that there can be no progress in political systems because the basic forms of political organization are limited in number and were all discovered long ago: monarchy, aristocracy, anarchy, republic, democracy, oligarchy, dictatorship. But the basic ideas of science and the basic forms of technology are also limited in number and were all discovered a long time ago. The Greeks had the atomic theory. Canoes and nuclear submarines are both boats. Arrows and rockets are both missiles. For that matter, the fact that the Cro-Magnon cave painters are some of the greatest artists this world has ever seen makes Larry Rivers no less interesting.

Naturally, anarchists would like to see more anarchist science fiction; everybody would like to see their favorite kind of fiction reflect their favorite political ideas. There are many kinds of anarchism; at least one novel could be written about each sort. Anarchist ideas raise a great many problems to which a variety of solutions can be offered, all of which could be examined in a speculative way in fiction. Nearly every anarchist I know is also a science fiction fan, and science fiction fans always want to write the stuff themselves, so there should be enough writers to take care of all the available anarchist science fiction ideas.

Of course, the effort to impose any sort of political or moral tendency on literature is poisonous to creativity. But on the other hand, as George Orwell put it, "All art is propaganda." Even the silliest situation comedies and even the art-for-art's-sake novels of Vladimir Nabokov, whether they are intended to or not, present a view of the human condition. Therefore, every artist needs to be aware that the work will carry a message no matter what, and should accept responsibility, up to a reasonable point, for that message.

The worst kind of propagandizing in fiction, it seems to me, is that in which the author slavishly follows a party line or church dogma. Better, usually, is the story which preaches a point of view that, at least, is the product of the author's own thinking. Ayn Rand's novels, for instance, besides being good stories, are obviously the work of a writer who thinks for herself. Their weaknesses arise from the fact that Rand is often more interested in getting across her ideas than in telling a good story. Where the demands of fiction are subordinated to the requirements of propaganda, which happens most frequently in *Atlas Shrugged*, of all Rand's novels, the storytelling falters.

I agree with John Gardner's view expressed in his most recent book, *On Moral Fiction*, that the best fiction is that which puts ideological and moral propositions through a kind of laboratory analysis. An author takes a particular idea and as honestly and painstakingly as possible tries to show how that idea works itself out in everyday life. For example, an author may believe that all politicians are schmucks and want to say so in the book. But honest storytelling and good characterization demand that any politician in the story be presented, not merely as a schmuck, but as a many-sided figure, as all of us are. The author who meets this challenge will tell us more about politicians than the one who sticks to a superficial, one-sided view.

In the work of the greatest artists, like Shakespeare, the analysis is so thoroughgoing that the moral propositions dissolve altogether. When this happens, fiction does not just give us some generality that we can carry away with us as we would the advice in a *Readers Digest* self-help article. It gives us, instead, the effect of having gone through an actual experience. As we do with our own experiences, we can derive many different ideas and generalities from good fiction. We can go back to *Hamlet* or *War and Peace*, as we can go back to an important event in our own lives, and mull it over again and find new meanings and new lessons in it.

One reason for Robert A. Heinlein's success is that he doesn't set out to prove propositions in his writing but subjects them to an honest test. He writes stories to discover what the logical outcome of such-and-such a premise would be. It is a tribute to Heinlein's craftsmanship that in *Stranger in a Strange Land* he developed a philosophy so plausible and persuasive, with a terminology so attractive, that it was adopted wholesale by many in the hippy movement. Heinlein himself is in most ways as far from being a hippy as you could get.

Indeed, the teachings of Michael Valentine Smith were so convincing that Charles Manson announced, after his arrest, that *Stranger in a Strange Land* was a major influence on himself and his family. Heinlein was so revolted by this that he has consistently refused even to discuss the matter publicly.

Similarly, the picture of an anarchist society on the Moon in *The Moon Is a Harsh Mistress* is equally believable. This is one *sort* of anarchism, at any rate, in which each person acts as his or her own self-defense force and the antisocial eventually get kicked out of an airlock without a space suit by some self-appointed executioner. Reasonable people treat each other with great politeness. Unreasonable people don't last long. This Wild West anarchism wouldn't appeal to all anarchists, but it does give us a chance to experience one way that a society without a government might work. Many anarchists like it so much they suggest it to non-anarchists as introductory reading.

Yet, Heinlein is definitely not an anarchist. He made that massively clear in a commencement address he gave at the U.S. Naval Academy a few years ago in which he praised patriotism as one of the highest human virtues. Which only goes to show that an honest non-anarchist can do as good a job as writing about anarchism as any anarchist.

I do not know whether Ursula K. LeGuin is an anarchist, but *The Dispossessed* is the most convincing, coherent, carefully worked out picture of an anarchist society I've seen anywhere. Here again, one gets the impression that the author did not set out to make a case for anarchism, but rather wrote a work of fiction to test anarchism's propositions. Anarres is a believable world because LeGuin has subjected it to fiction's demands for honesty, logic and probability.

Cecelia Holland's *Floating Worlds* is not anarchist propaganda either, but it, too, presents a persuasive picture of an anarchist society. The episode in which Paula, the heroine, gets back the flute stolen from her by a drug addict is an appealing and funny instance of the way crime might be dealt with in a totally free society. The testing to which Holland subjects her anarchist community is so severe that it is finally destroyed by invaders. But not before we have learned to love it and to mourn its passing – 4,000 years in the future.

To take an example of preaching as testing from my own experience, *Illuminatus!* by Robert Anton Wilson and myself started out simply to satirize the boobs, mostly John Birchers, who believe that the world is secretly ruled by the Bavarian

Illuminati. As we wrote and researched, though, we became fascinated by the history of esoteric illuminism and discovered that while the Illuminati may never have ruled the world, their ideas deserved serious consideration. We ended up writing something that, whatever its literary merits, goes way beyond simple satire of the espionage thriller genre. It is, among many other things, a work of anarchist science fiction.

This, by the way, is something some purists would not accept. One editor of a prominent SF magazine refused to have *Illuminatus!* reviewed in his pages because, he insisted, it was not really, truly science fiction. Many science fiction writers, editors, fans and critics tend to be closed-minded in their views of what constitutes SF. This narrow mindedness frequently includes an unwillingness to entertain unorthodox political ideas, such as anarchism. That is why so much science fiction, even today, gives us the same dreary round of galactic empires fighting galactic republics.

But it is not surprising that science fiction people are not more open-minded. Scientists themselves are far from being as open-minded in practice as they profess to be. In earlier times the battles for academic freedom centered around the right to teach new scientific ideas – the Copernican system, evolution, Freudian psychology – in the face of religious opposition. Today, there is a move afoot among science-oriented university professors to suppress the teaching of subjects such as creationism, reincarnation, astrology, UFOlogy and other paranormal phenomena, which Modern Science, they say, has found to be false. So much for freedom of thought, which I had always imagined was the basis for science.

Most people don't consistently live out what they profess to believe. And most people believe political progress as a matter of increased control, organization, law and order. Few are really dedicated to increasing the degree of freedom all of us enjoy. Even many anarchists and libertarians aren't as thoroughly committed to freedom as they'd like to think they are.

Even so, there are enough lovers of freedom around to make a difference. And anarchist science fiction can be a most effective device for bringing the vision of freedom to concrete life. Those fans, critics, editors and writers to whom the ideal of freedom is congenial can, by each working a little harder at his or her own thing, make more room in science fiction for anarchist ideas.

G

"We Came Here for a Blow Job and Got Screwed"

Cavalier magazine, September 1966

Before he went to work for Playboy magazine, Shea was the editor from 1965 to 1967 of Cavalier, a men's magazine not unlike Playboy.

So widespread, both throughout history and at the present time, is the dissemination of, and belief in, utter crap, that it is frequently impossible to tell whether the originators thereof are clever charlatans or are merely themselves the first to be taken in by their own fabrications. Such is the case with Andy Warhol, silver-haired boy of Pop Art, underground movies and the Jet Set.

Fortunately, there is an antidote to crap: skepticism. Students, as a class, seem to have a corner on this antidote, their sensitivity to snow jobs apparently being much greater than that of the population at large.

For instance, there was the reaction of an audience of Columbia University students to a presentation of Andy Warhol's underground movie, *Blow Job.* You have to get the picture. Here is an auditorium on the Columbia campus, pretty well packed with students and a few fringe types like myself. We have all come to see a movie called *Blow Job.* We have come, certainly, partly out of Prurient Interest, but Warhol's reputation in the art world lends the occasion Redeeming Social Importance.

On the screen appears the head and shoulders of a young man. For thirty-three unrelieved minutes, all – *all* – we are to see is the head and shoulders of this young man. The entire action consists of various blinkings, squintings, eye-rollings, head-shakings and facial contortions.

Now, were this film being displayed to the usual *après moi, le déluge,* status-hungry, Jet Setty, sleek, know-nothing crowd of East Side Establishment sophisticates, all this would be – and on other occasions doubtless has been – greeted with reverential awe and silence. But this, as I have said, is an audience of students fortified with a healthy skepticism.

Ten minutes after the start of the film, a voice from the orchestra seats announces in portentous tones:

"In 1936, in Madison Square Garden, Alf Landon said, 'Everywhere I go in this country, I meet Americans.' " There is a moment of thoughtful silence, then laughter and thunderous applause. More minutes pass while the face on the screen stares out at the audience, which stares back. Then the same heckler declares:

"And in 1954, Dwight David Eisenhower said, 'If there's one thing the Russians can't stand, it's ridicule.' " The audience also applauds this sentiment.

From this point on, as it becomes more and more apparent that nothing new is going to happen on the screen, the students proceed to fashion their own entertainment by spontaneously inventing a game. Anyone who feels he has a comment that will amuse his peers makes that comment. The peers indicate their pleasure with laughter and applause, their approval with boos and hisses.

"The book was better." (Laughter and applause.)

"Don't go off half-cocked." (Loud hisses).

Someone singing: "We shall never come." (Laughter).

Girl's voice (after a particularly violent wince on the screen) "Where does it hurt?" (Silence.)

"Go down, boy." (Hisses).

"He's faking it." (Laughter).

(After about twenty minutes of the film has elapsed): "Don't give up, tiger!" (Laughter).

"He's just getting it up for the first time." (Loud laughter).

"What do you mean, Rockwell couldn't come?" (Loud laughter and applause. Some weeks before, there was to have been a lecture by George Lincoln Rockwell at Columbia. But he was arrested by the New York police the minute he set foot in town and so never showed up.)

And, as the last of the picture's three-minute reels flickers across the screen: "We came here for a blow job and got screwed." (Loudest laughter and applause of the evening).

So it was that Andy Warhol, anti-art hero of our time, at last assisted in the creation of a work of art. His Blow Job engendered a Happening.

The Unhappy Writer

Is anxiety a distinct cause of writer's block, apart from rebellion against self-regulation, or are anxiety and rebellion somehow linked? Working daily at writing can be painful when one is anxious about how good the work is or how well it will be received. The more painful it is to work, the more effort it takes to get oneself to work. My libertarian approach to self-regulation is meant to show how to get oneself to do what one wants to do despite the discomfort involved. But, of course, reducing the discomfort makes self-regulation a lot easier. Anxiety, depression and pessimism are all sources of discomfort to a writer.

I maintain that writing is enjoyable in itself; you don't have to make yourself enjoy writing; you have to eliminate what prevents you from enjoying it. The less one is able to enjoy writing, the more one is likely to succumb to writer's block.

The basic guideline for self-regulation is to try to do in any situation what we think we need to do to take care of ourselves. Libertarians believe that people should only act in their own best interest. I believe that we don't simply do what we think we should do, because living in an authoritarian society in which we have to take orders – and in which we are expected to be willing to sacrifice our interests for the sake of some entity bigger and more important than ourselves – has led to our developing psychological mechanisms that thwart the direct expression of our thoughts and feelings. As a libertarian, I believe that freedom is the natural human state, and that growing up in an authoritarian society therefore distorts character and is the cause of much inner conflict.

We are used to having our faculty of self-control work in the service of the authorities – parents, politicians, clergy, teachers, bosses. If we try to take charge of our own lives, we sometimes act like a newly independent nation that collapses into disorder because it doesn't know how to govern itself. There's nobody to tell us to clean the house, so we let the house turn into a garbage dump. We tend to forget that we are in control of our own lives, and we rebel against our efforts at self government. To become a free-lance writer for instance is to take charge of our own work. But if we haven't yet learned how to get the different parts of our psyche to work together, the experiment in self-employment may have disappointing results.

However, people don't refuse to do things they think they ought to do just to be ornery, although a sense that what one is doing is obligatory can dim the enjoyment of even the most pleasing activities. Usually there has to be some other reason for not wanting to do the desired activity, such as that it's uncomfortable or inconvenient. If an activity is accompanied by a lot of anxiety, that makes it uncomfortable and therefore a likely focal point for an inner rebellion.

What is the anxious writer anxious about? Just doing a bad job, or doing a job that is scorned and rejected by the authorities? For most writers, I think, the two concerns are mixed, in that the writers are trying to do a good job by their own lights but also trying to produce something that will pass muster with important others. But I don't think the writer's own criticism of his or her work is the main culprit in writer's block. I believe that the conviction that one must achieve extrinsic goals is what has a paralyzing effect.

In an authoritarian society, we learn that the only important thing about any task is whether it pleases the bosses. We learn that what's worthwhile about our own ability to judge our work is the degree to which we can foresee what the bosses want and win their approval. We learn to do things for extrinsic reasons like approval and money rather than for qualities intrinsic to the work that please us.

Extrinsic goals should be made secondary or eliminated altogether. Possibly the writer should suspend the critical faculty and just rely on unconscious growth processes.

Or it might be more interesting and enjoyable to try to achieve one's personally chosen intrinsic goals, where both the choice of goal and the judgment of the result is something the writer has full control of.

Linked to anxiety about their work, for many writers, is a tendency to be pessimistic about how successful it will be. From this pessimism arises depression. Depression delivers a double whammy to the unhappy writer: First, it makes them more sure that the writing is no good and will be received with scorn and rejection. Trying to write in the face of this belief is hard and painful. It's just like when I speak and feel the audience is bored or hostile, I enjoy speaking less and tend to dry up. If they look eager and interested, I enjoy talking to them and I warm up and expand.

Second, the depressed writer doesn't believe his or her efforts at self-regulation are worthwhile. Why bother to force oneself to do this painful thing – writing – if it isn't going to get me published and make some money for me?

Not every creative person who writes to please an audience or to make money is afflicted with inner rebellion, anxiety or depression. Mozart wrote music which followed accepted forms, and he wrote what was popular and what would showcase the singers he was writing for. In effect, Mozart was what we would call a hack. Perhaps because he had confidence in what he was doing, this seems not to have kept him from writing beautiful music, from enjoying composing and from doing a lot of work.

Similarly, Balzac was enormously prolific, spent most of his waking hours writing and seems to have been sure that his work was the product of genius. He was driven by anxiety to work his way out of debt, but his inner unity, confidence and optimism protected him from writer's block.

So, you can write to please others and still not be anxious, if you expect to be successful in pleasing others. But it is hard to be optimistic about accomplishing something that is more or less out of your control.

Increasing hopefulness works on two levels: it makes it easier to follow the regimen directed by self-regulation, because we believe it will work; and it makes it easier to enjoy the writing itself, because writing is enjoyable when done in a hopeful spirit. When I write with optimism and enjoyment, the flow of ideas is swift and abundant.

Optimism and confidence can be increased, pessimism and anxiety decreased, through cognitive therapy methods. What these boil down to is inner discussions and conversations. Similarly, to overcome inner rebellion we have to have regular self-meetings and internal conversations – parleys between the new independent government and the guerillas. By a process of self-education, we have to commit ourselves to the belief that we are best expressing our freedom and individuality when we do what we think we should do. We have to dispute and reject the belief that when we decide not to do what's in our best interests we are somehow being more true to ourselves.

Our inner peace conferences have to make certain: a) that we are, in fact, employing our faculty of self-direction entirely in our own best interest, that what it proposes is truly what we need to do to take care of ourself in this situation; b) that we have contemplated all the things we want to do, each of which is probably good in itself, and we have made a decision about priorities.

If I've made my inner peace, then I will no longer act to defeat myself. I will no longer divide myself, alienate parts of myself. If I'm right in thinking that one who has adopted the libertarian approach to self-regulation will have more success, more inner unity and more energy, then these successful experiences and good feelings will make them more optimistic.

In Alcoholics Anonymous they solve the problem of getting themselves to do what's best for them by turning their will over to the directions of a Higher Power. If you think you're just getting directions from yourself, then you may try to rationalize yourself out of doing what you think you should do, and you won't respect the side of yourself that argues for what you should do. This is especially true if you are used to needing an authority to tell you what to do. Whereas if the spokesperson in your mind for what you should do represents the will of a Higher Power, you will be able to distinguish more clearly what you should do from all your other impulses (you know good and well that your Higher Power isn't going to tell you to go out and get drunk) and will be less inclined to resist it, having made the commitment to follow the directions of the Higher Power.

If one is a libertarian and believes in God, then one would believe that God is a libertarian. A libertarian God would want us to govern ourselves, not take orders from him or from people claiming to be his representatives. So whether the libertarian is theist or atheist it would seem to come down to the same thing, they will want to maximize their ability to regulate their own lives.

When I discover some promising new writing method, I always work with more enthusiasm, because the notion that I've found a magic secret increases my optimism. However, I have learned from experience that no magic secret is going to make me a better writer or make writing easier for me. In the past when I've realized that, I've tended to get discouraged. I see now that the only thing I can change is how I think about the process of writing, about the quality of my writing and about the hardship involved. If: a) I believe I'm truly doing what's best for myself and therefore what I want – even love – to do; b) I am optimistic about how good my writing is and about my ability to handle hardships, then I can truly enjoy my writing.

To enjoy our work, to enjoy life in general, we need to place our ability to judge our work at the service of what we like and don't like. And we need to place our ability to control our behavior at the service of what we believe we need to do to take care of ourselves. And if we believe in God, we need to believe that this is what God wants us to do.

The Martin Gardner Challenge

From issue No. 9 of *No Governor*, Robert Shea's anarchist zine.

A number of comments on *No Governor* have raised questions about whether an anarchist society can protect its members from crime, and I have promised that I would write something on the subject. This, with a bow to Benjamin Tucker is offered, "Instead of an Essay, by a Man Too Busy to Write One."

Several years ago, in the hope of provoking a constructive discussion in the *Bulletin of the Social Revolutionary Anarchist Federation*, I sent a letter published in issue #88, asking for people's opinions on how antisocial behavior would be handled in an anarchist society. Here's a slightly condensed version of that letter:

> *Dear SRAFriends: There are some very basic questions about anarchism which hardly ever come up in contemporary anarchist writing but which are invariably the first questions asked by non-anarchists when we try to explain the idea to them. Questions like: How does the tiny anarchist minority propose to bring about a worldwide revolution? What's to stop some other group from seizing power after such a revolution? How would a totally free society deal with antisocial behavior?*

Why don't we discuss these basic questions more often? I suspect it's because we think we have the answers and don't need to think or argue about them any more. But, if these are answers we arrived at years or decades ago, will they still stand up to scrutiny?

A question that interests me very much is that of anarchism and antisocial behavior. Years ago I wrote, along with a group of co-authors, a little pamphlet called The Anarchist Solution to the Problem of Crime. *I still have copies and will be happy to send one or more to anyone who writes asking me for one. I'm not sure my ideas today would be the same as they were when I worked on that pamphlet.*

Recently, in a book of essays by Martin Gardner called The Whys of a Philosophical Scrivener, *I ran across one entitled "Why I Am Not an Anarchist." The core of Gardner's argument seemed to be in the following passage:*

"As things are, there simply is no way a modern industrial society can flourish without a strong government to enforce the law. This means, of course, a system of police, courts, lawyers, judges, jails, and, given the absence of a world community, a military establishment. You cannot even enjoy your humblest possessions unless a government supports a vast system that prevents thieves from taking them. Regardless of whether altruism is genetically based (as anarchists like Prince Peter Kropotkin argued, and some modern biologists believe), or entirely acquired after birth, there is not the slightest reason to suppose that humanity can, in the foreseeable

future, eliminate what Christians call original sin."

Martin Gardner is a mathematician, an author and a professional skeptic. He's written a couple of books debunking what he considers to be delusive belief systems, such as dianetics and astrology. My point in quoting him is that this seems to me an articulate statement of what many a reasonable, well-educated person says when confronted with the ideas of anarchism. Anarchists have been saying for over a hundred years that crime can be controlled, perhaps even eliminated, and that police, courts, lawyers, judges and jails are not only unnecessary but harmful to society. Most people seem never to have heard what anarchists have to say.

So, my question to anarchists and libertarians is, how, today, would you meet this perennial challenge? What would you have to say, in response to the above, that is new and persuasive? Not persuasive to those already converted to anarchism, but to all the other people who aren't – which I am sorry to say is most of them.

How would you answer the Martin Gardners?

After this letter was published, I followed it up with another in which I offered my own answer to the question. The first draft of my letter turned out to be too long for the *SRAF Bulletin*, which has an upper limit of one page for letters. So I sent them a shorter version. Since in my own magazine I can let my writing jolly well run as long as I want, this is the longer version, somewhat revised:

Dear SRAFriends: In issue #88 I suggested, as a theme for a general discussion in the Bulletin, Martin Gardner's challenge to anarchism: "You cannot even enjoy your humblest possessions unless a government supports a vast system that prevents thieves from taking them." Here's my own response:

Gardner's critique of anarchism contains an unquestioned assumption: That the present system of governments and governmental law enforcement is effectively preventing robbery, rape and murder. But there is much evidence that law enforcement really isn't working. Crime is on the increase. For every hundred crimes of violence committed in this country, only one criminal is caught and sent to jail. And even with this low rate of punishment, prisons are terribly overcrowded. The use of legalized force to prevent or to punish crime appears to be failing. Just as this country's efforts to protect itself from foreign enemies has led to an arms race which may eventually cause the destruction of the planet, so efforts to make police more effective against crime are moving our society in the direction of a totalitarian police state in which we'll all be so spied upon, harassed, frustrated, taxed, ordered about, circumscribed, controlled and punished that we'll be as miserable as if we did live in a society in which thievery, rape and murder flourished unchecked.

What is it that really keeps people from stealing Gardner's, and our, possessions? I suggest it is not fear of the police, but the simple, natural fact that participation in human society is intrinsically rewarding.

The law enforcement approach to crime essentially fights fire with fire. It assumes that since robbers, murderers and rapists use force to impose their will on others, the way to deal with them is to use force on them. Thus government comes into being *in imitation of* robbers, murderers and rapists, legitimizing antisocial acts for the supposed benefit of society.

Government is the continuation of crime for other ends.

Force begets counterforce. This is a process that started thousands of years ago with the invention of warfare. If it continues it seems likely to lead the human race to environmental catastrophe, a permanent and universal totalitarianism or nuclear obliteration. This is protection?

Side by side with the evolution of the state, which threatens to destroy us all, has evolved culture, which may yet save us. Science, the arts, philosophy and technology have developed over the centuries in spite of the destructive intervention of the state and its perversion of the products of culture to violent uses. The greater part of human transactions are carried out in a context of trust and benevolence. Culture is nonviolent. It can't flourish in an atmosphere of rampant violence. The more people share in the benefits of culture, the less inclined they are to sacrifice the possibility of enjoying those benefits by attacking one another. In the U.S. it is the poor who most frequently commit crimes and the poor who are most frequently victims. Nations go to war hoping through violence to obtain a greater share of the world's goods, or to defend what they have.

To fight violence with violence is simply to oppose one government with another. To renounce violence is to renounce government. Gandhi knew this; it was why he called himself an anarchist. As more and more people come to see that accepting the legitimacy of violence must lead to total destruction, we are coming closer and closer to anarchism. The anarchist revolution will necessarily be nonviolent. If it were violent it would not be anarchist.

It follows that when an anarchist community is created, its method of dealing with antisocial behavior will be nonviolent. Individuals may sometimes need to use force to protect themselves or their loved ones in extreme situations. To deny individualists this freedom would be to attack the very basis of freedom. But individuals using force would be answerable to the community, and for a society to call itself anarchist the community would have to make nonviolence a settled principle in dealing with all antisocial behavior.

Many of the benevolent functions of today's police would still be performed by members of an anarchist community – from directing traffic to rescuing people in danger. Detection of those responsible for antisocial acts and judgment of their responsibility would still occur. People might not want to use force on those who do harmful things, but they would certainly want to know who they are. Nonviolent sanctions against crime, including boycott and ostracism, would be powerful deterrents.

The inequities and frustrations of today's society are maintained by legitimized force. In the absence of such force, greater participation in human culture and greater sharing of its benefits would be available to us all. The basis for creativity is freedom, and creativity is the basis for the prosperity humanity is enjoying today as never before, paradoxically at the same time as we are threatened, as never before, with extinction. When we liberate humanity from government we will unleash a creativity so fertile that the most imaginative science fiction writers would have a hard time envisioning its benefits and delights.

In such a society the ultimate deterrent to crime will not be punishment but quite simply that the antisocial person will cut himself or herself from others. The antisocial person will create his or her own prison, and the only escape will be through restoring the bond with other men and women by whatever process of reconciliation or restitution may be called for. In a free society the platitude that virtue is its own reward will become a fact.

A Note on Anarchist Tactics

For many people, myself included, non-violence is the preferred strategy for achieving worthwhile social changes from peace to anarchy, and Gandhi is the great model. But when we think about applying Gandhi-like tactics to problems in the U.S., it's important to remember the differences between Gandhi's situation and ours. First, as far as we can tell, the majority of the people of India wanted the independence Gandhi was working for. Judging by the results of the last election [1984], we'd have to say that at least half the people in the U.S. favor a continuation of the arms race. Second, the people of India had no legal means of rejecting British rule. They couldn't vote the British out. They had to resist. The question was whether to resist violently or non-violently. In principle, at least, if a majority of Americans wanted to end the arms race or make any other progressive social change, they have the political machinery available to them to do it. In practice, of course, the people can be deceived, as when they have elected leaders who promised peace but were secretly planning to start or expand a war.

The position of anarchists is even grimmer than that of the peace movement. The prospect for anarchism in this country is analogous to what Gandhi's might have been if he had been advocating that Indians take up a diet of beef and pork. For most Americans the existing political system is indeed a sacred cow.

I don't conclude from this that anarchists should turn to violence or to electoral politics, either of which would not just be self-defeating, but self-negating. I think we need to recognize how big the job is, particularly the educational job, and how intelligent and imaginative we will have to be to do it.

The Inner Game of Sex

From *Playboy* magazine, October 1978

Americans do not enjoy sex totally. We are a driven people. There is a post-New Testament God keeping score on our bedroom games, and the newest version of the Protestant ethic is, "Thou shalt pursue a full, active, regular, frequent, satisfying, varied, exciting, healthy, normal sex life." We have had our sexual revolution, but we are still governed by the style, if not the rules, of Puritans and Victorians; we are compulsive, anxiety-ridden, competitive, relentlessly self-improving, perpetually self-critical. The morality has changed but not the habit of moralizing. Sex, of all human activities, should be the one we enjoy most freely, yet it is one of the most ruled and regulated. The old regulations made people feel guilty; the new ones make them feel inadequate.

Is there an antidote to the American way of sex? Perhaps. Japan is admirably free of sexual hang-ups. One reason for this is the pervasive influence of Zen in Japanese life. Now Zen has become popular in America. We've had Zen in archery, drawing, flower arrangement, judo, karate, aikido, motorcycle maintenance, tennis, skiing and creative management. With all this, there should be a Zen approach to sex.

There is. People have been putting Zen into their lovemaking for ages. The word Zen means meditation, and meditation means turning off the verbalizing mind and letting what is be. So the essence of Zen in sex is to function naturally and pleasantly without bugging ourselves.

Anything and everything we do can be a means of meditating, of doing Zen. Timothy Galwey's *The Inner Game of Tennis* has applied this idea to Western sports, turning tennis into an opportunity to meditate. We will enjoy tennis more, he says, if we will do four things: Abandon self-criticism; rely on spontaneous learning processes; concentrate on here and now; shift our goal from outward success to inner growth.

These four principles can just as well be applied to sex. The first rule of the inner game, and maybe the most difficult for anyone raised in this culture, is to give up the habit of judging ourselves and everything we do in terms of positive and negative – good or bad, right or wrong, success or failure. We all know that in any skill when we are self-critical, we become awkward, stumble and fall, lose touch with the sources of information. It's as if we had two selves that might be called the player and the spectator. The player is pure action; it does not think in words and it needs to concentrate. The spectator observes and intellectualizes. When the spectator gets out of hand, starts hollering out criticisms from the sidelines, giving unnecessary advice, trying to control the player's actions, calling attention to the score, the player develops two left feet. If the spectator starts acting up like that at a sexual performance, it will spoil that performance.

For instance, a man may find that when he is making love, especially to a woman he doesn't know well, he seems to be two people. One of them is in bed doing things to and with a lover. We might call this person the Player. Pure action. In contrast, the Second Self, the Spectator, is standing back, criticizing, like the director in a pornographic movie – a very anxious director, who says things such as, "You've played with that nipple long enough, idiot. Go on to the other one, quick." Or, "She doesn't like the way you're stroking her. Too mechanical. She's losing interest. Think of something else to do."

Whenever you have to make a move – strike up a conversation, make a romantic gesture, display your expertise in bed – the Spectator feels somewhat nervous. Whenever your self-esteem depends on the outcome of some effort, there is stage fright. That terrible paralysis. That pounding of the heart, trembling and clamminess of the hands, draining hollow in the stomach. The mind goes blank, speech and gesture turns to wood. You feel terrified of making a fool of yourself. It strikes when you are in bed with someone you badly want to impress. It can ruin an experience. Liberating yourself from stage fright is what Zen is all about.

You are so in the habit of labeling everything either good or bad that it's hard to imagine any other way of thinking. There *is* another way though: being completely aware without judging. Stop classifying what you see as good or bad and simply look at the facts as they are. *I am a camera.* For example, if a woman doesn't have an orgasm when a man makes love to her, he doesn't have to blame himself or her, or treat the incident as a calamity. He can simply note the fact, recognizing that the explanation for it is not yet known.

Millions of American women worry about their breast measurements. Millions of American men worry about their penis size. Such concerns only measure the national insanity. If a man's erect penis is four inches long, he needn't say, "My penis is four inches long and that's a disaster." Nor should he try to use positive thinking and say, "My penis is four inches long and that's marvelous." That would be just as much a distortion of reality. He just says, "My penis is four inches long." Period. Or maybe, "So what?" Scientific fact. No praise, no blame.

Americans are obsessed with numbers. Poor Alfred Kinsey. He wanted to free us from guilt. He wrote that there was so much variation in our levels of sexual activity (he found one man who regularly had 30 orgasms a week and another who'd had only one in 30 years) that we should stop using words such as normal and abnormal, much less good and bad. Everyone has ignored that statement and remembers only that Kinsey counted everything that can be counted. And Kinsey's statistics have given us a new way to feel guilty. Four orgasms a week is above average, therefore good. One a week is below average, therefore bad. How many of you keep count of how often you get laid? Hands, please. Quite a few, we see. How many of you try to count the number of orgasms your women have per night? Still a great many. How many worry when either number falls below a certain level? That's what we suspected.

But if we don't criticize our performance, how are we ever going to improve? How do we learn anything? Most of us think we are taught the right way to do things by hearing a lecture or reading a book. Then we practice while observing our performance carefully for mistakes. If the mistakes are too numerous or seem insurmountable, we go to a teacher, coach or therapist. Or we read a dozen more how-to-do-it books.

The instructions in *The Joy of Sex* are so detailed and complicated that any couple who wanted to follow them would have to have crucial passages printed on the sheets or lettered on the bedroom ceiling. And a man would need the coordination, reflexes, strength and endurance of an astronaut to make ideal love. But also like an astronaut, he would always be working from a checklist.

It is possible to improve a skill without consciously trying. In fact, it seems to be the better way. When you are trying to do something, the Spectator frequently talks too much, filling your mind with confusing instructions that are hard to follow. When the Player takes over, however, it will sometimes perform virtual miracles, moves that are brilliant and instantaneous and could be achieved only through inspiration. You've had moments when you were on or hot and did something memorable, a clever conversational comeback, a skilled bit of driving that got you through an emergency or an inspired move in lovemaking that sent your partner to a new height of ecstasy. Left to do its thing without a lot of nervous chatter from the Spectator, the Player will find ways to grow and improve that surprise you. For instance, you might suddenly and spontaneously introduce a new kind of sex-play in a relationship. The first time a man goes down on a woman, he may not know (unless she asked for it) how she will take it. She might see him as a nasty pervert or – much more likely – she might love him all the more. Sometimes a woman will react both ways at once. After all, she has a Spectator and a Player on her side of the net, too.

There are two aids to learning with a quiet mind. One is the use of mental pictures instead of words. If people watch good golfers or tennis players in action, or movies of them, their own game improves afterward. If you want to be better in bed, you should read pornography, which provides images rather than instruction, and go to sex movies. Pornographic movies are being exhibited with sound, color and wide screen in most of our big cities these days. Sex therapists have also recognized the value of visual images. Couples now spend weekends sprawled on cushions and watching both pornographic films and movies made especially for sex education.

The other way to learn is through practice. From the strange point of view prevalent in this culture since at least the fall of Rome, getting lots of practice in games, the arts or business is praised as diligence, but getting lots of practice in sex is denounced as promiscuity. In sex, as in most things, the more you do it, the better you get at it. Some people think it intensifies the pleasure of sex to save it for special occasions. Not necessarily. Sexual malfunctions are more likely to arise in people who enjoy sex only rarely. Nor is there any reason to fear running out of steam. Most of us have a lot more sexual energy than we generally use.

To keep the Spectator quiet and the Player practicing, you have to concentrate, which means keeping the mind in the here and now. Gallwey writes, "Concentration is the supreme art, because no art can be achieved without it, while with it anything can be achieved." He suggests that tennis players concentrate on the seams of the ball as it flies back and forth. You might try concentrating on your lady's navel.

Sex in the Western world is like an O. Henry story; the whole point is in the outcome. India developed tantric yoga, the use of sex as a means of meditation, in which the last thing anybody wants is to get it over with. In his book on tantric yoga, Philip Rawson writes, "Indian eroticism always focused on the inner state of erotic possession." The ideal of lovemaking "is a protracted ecstasy of mind and body, whose fires are continually blown by long engagement and stimulation of the sexual organs, not mutual relief."

Keeping the mind in the present means not worrying about how things will eventually turn out. A future-oriented man can be greatly troubled if he sees a good-looking woman on the street. There he is at five minutes to nine on Monday morning and all he can do is look. He sours the pleasure of looking by not being satisfied. It's no good, he thinks, unless he can have more. Or he is having dinner with a lady and finds himself worrying about whether or not he'll be able to get her into bed in an hour or two. What he should do is bring his thoughts gently back to the food and the wine and the conversation or here and now. If he doesn't keep his mind on now, there may not be anything happening later.

A friend had an experience that illustrates the rewards of being unconcerned about the future. In his early 20s, he'd had only four bed partners in his life and he had learned that, except on rare occasions, he was capable, at most, of two orgasms a night. Then he started an affair with a woman who, for most of her married life, had had sex about once a month. She thought anything her partner might do would be prodigious. The man didn't care whether or not he impressed her in bed.

He found himself making love with his friend three times a night just about every time they went to bed. His low-key attitude relieved him of the pressure to perform, and that put him in touch with feelings he hadn't been aware of. He never planned or even expected his improved performance. It simply happened, like inspiration. "We'll just be lying there after the first time," he told me, "maybe talking or just petting a little bit. And all of a sudden, I'll be ready again. And even then, I'm not sure I'm going to come. But I always do. Again and again."

Masters and Johnson call our habit of focusing on climax the "end-point release orientation." As an antidote, they recommend "sensate focus." You should direct your awareness toward the pleasant sensations you're experiencing now, without having a goal in mind. Sensate focus has cured impotent men and non-orgasmic women. Told by the therapist to let the partner stroke and massage him or her – not touching the genitals and not trying to have sex – many a man, no longer wondering whether he will or will not get a hard-on, and many a woman, no longer anxious about whether or not she will come, finds new life in a body that hasn't felt anything in years. The chill becomes a tingle again. It's almost as good as high school back in the greasy Fifties, when the height of a Saturday night's pleasure was to spend hours necking in a parked car till our lips were lacerated and swollen. Those were inhibited times, but concentrated. One squeeze of a breast, one fingertip contact with a nipple under a partly-unbuttoned blouse was emotional capital that could be invested in a week of fantasies. Screwing was out of the question. We were thus spared the blight of goal-oriented sex. There were some men, Masters and Johnson have observed, who did their sexual basic training in whorehouses, where the ladies were always telling them to hurry it up. If they took the lesson too much to heart, they became premature ejaculators, another malfunction from worrying about what's going to happen instead of appreciating what is happening.

A man who tries to retard his orgasm is thinking too much about the future. Holding back, by doing mental arithmetic, thinking about business worries or simply stopping all movement when orgasm feels near, has long been considered the height of male sexual sophistication. But sometimes the result isn't as satisfying to either party as it is supposed to be. Going with the flow often works better; sometimes the man's vigorous thrusting will bring on a woman's orgasm. Sometimes he will have a second or third erection and will take longer to reach his second or third orgasm, thereby greatly extending his partner's pleasure. Nature has a way of taking care of us when we don't try to fool her.

Playing this kind of inner game in which the obstacles to be overcome are one's own mental states, Gallwey explains, "frees the player from the fruits of victory; he becomes devoted only to the goal of self-knowledge, to the exploration of his true nature as it reveals itself on level after level." In the Orient, the idea of sex as a means of self-awareness is not as strange as it might seem in our own culture, in which sex is often seen as a manifestation of our animal side, which is thought to be lower than our mental side – as if the mind were not as much a product of animal evolution as the hand or the stomach. One of the sacred stories of India tells how the god Krishna made love to 16,000 girls in one night. Hindu and Buddhist holy pictures frequently show the gods and goddesses in sexual union.

Janwillem van de Wetering, a Dutch man who went to Japan to study Zen, tells of a Zen monk called Bobo Roshi – a title that translates literally as Master Fuck. Unable to achieve satori after years of meditating on his *koan*, he climbed over the wall of his monastery and wandered through the streets of Kyoto. A prostitute in the Willow Quarter took him in. Having lived as a monk for so long, he didn't realize what was happening until she started to undress him:

"Then she took him to her bath, that's the custom here. Your shoulders are massaged and you are dried with a clean towel and they talk to you. Slowly you become very excited and when she feels you are ready, she takes you to the bedroom. He must have been quite excited after so many years of abstaining. At the moment he went into her, he solved his *koan*. He had an enormous *satori,* one of those very rare *satoris* which are described in our books, not a little understanding which can be deepened later but the lot at once, an explosion which tears you to pieces and you think the world has come to an end, that you can fill the emptiness of the universe in every possible sphere. When he left the woman, he was a master."

Sex for the sake of illumination may make it sound like a sort of spiritual masturbation. Actually, the view of sex we're exploring makes it impossible to be self-centered. The stage fright that spoils sex comes from too much concern about one's standing in the game. With the Zen approach, you stop asking "How am I doing?" And when a man stops seeing his lover as his judge or competitor, he can enjoy sex all out. That will make him a better lover, because a person who thoroughly enjoys doing something is good at it. He is free of the feeling that he has to control or impress his partner: he is playing *with* her, not against or upon her.

We already have the capacity to enjoy sex fully right now. We don't need any improvement: we need only to get out of our own way. Toward the end of The Inner Game of Tennis, Gallwey explains that the book should not be taken as a manual for self-improvement: "Admittedly, much of this book may seem that way, but speaking as a man who was once a compulsive self-improver, I want to make it clear that the last thing I wish to do is encourage any notion that you should be any different from what you are right now." From this point of view, we are already perfect just as we are. If sex seems to lack something, the solution is not to try harder but to remove whatever is blocking it. Many people complain that their sexual experiences seem unreal to them. They've pushed their thinking, worrying Spectator between themselves and the wordless, thoughtless realm of the player. That is sad, because sex should be enjoyed in all of its here and now glory, fun, playfulness and profundity. A change in attitude can help restore delight.

Ɠ

The Joy of Baking Pie in the Sky

"Maybe anarchy is 'pie in the sky' but it's good pie."

– Dave Johnson

Early in 1990 a developer (around our way developers are as revered and respected as child molesters) bought the lot next to mine and staked a claim, based on a 90-year-old surveying error, to a sizable strip of land running along the south side of my yard. I turned the problem over to a lawyer and tried to forget about it.

Then one Saturday morning in June the developer sent an earth-moving machine that looked like a small Brontosaurus with caterpillar treads to tear down my fence.

I did what I think any good anarchist in such a situation would do. I called the police.

Mike Gunderloy's call for papers on unresolved questions in anarchism asks for "points of view anchored in everyday life," and what's more everyday than a land dispute? But, you might be asking yourself, how can a self-proclaimed anarchist call the police? How come he even *owns* property?

I wonder that, too.

Having decided nearly two decades ago to call myself an anarchist, I feel obliged to believe certain things and live by certain principles. But I find that reality, the hard stuff, gets in the way.

When I first read Mike's article, "Closing the Gaps," I found that answers to most of the questions he raised sprang instantly to mind. But they were recorded messages, the answers I've developed over nearly 20 years of discussing these issues with anarchists and nonanarchists.

Mike is quite correct in pointing out that most anarchists talk to each other and tend to ignore, rather than face and grapple with, the big holes in anarchist theory that people who are not anarchists keep pointing out. I think any individual anarchist or anarchist group that wants to be effective needs to tackle these questions, giving full weight to the difficulties, and come up with truly workable answers.

But I do not think it will ever be possible to arrive at a set of answers to these questions that most anarchists can agree upon. Indeed, if we put off proselytizing and organizing until we have a unified anarchist program, we'll still be arguing among ourselves when the universe ends with a Big Whimper.

Leaders often try to articulate a single set of ideas and impose it on their followers, but if you examine the history of any large political party or successful revolutionary movement you'll find coalitions of people of differing views and personal interests who have learned how to unite around a few common principles and work for certain practical ends – often very temporary ones. This ineradicable diversity is one of the ways in which all people, whatever their political views, are natural anarchists, and it is an observation that gives me hope. If anarchism ever gets off the ground it will be because anarchists have learned how to develop such a pluralistic coalition.

So, just reeling off my set of solutions wouldn't be a very satisfying way to respond to Mike's challenge. I see this as an opportunity to do some new thinking. Other questions occur to me: A lot of people have dropped out of the anarchist movement in the years since I came on board; why haven't

I? Conviction – or just habit? What about the gap between my personal life and my political and philosophical ideals? Am I actually doing anything that will move the world even a millimeter closer to an anarchist society?

These reflections are tangential to the issues Mike raised. In the course of my musings, I will get around to giving some of my answers to Mike's questions. But I hope my oblique approach will contribute a different perspective to the rethinking process he is trying to initiate.

I was originally drawn to anarchism because it seemed to me that the greatest threats facing humanity – nuclear war, destruction of the environment and the ever-increasing power of the state over the individual – had their source in government. Not just in abuses in government, but in the very essence of government. Therefore the abolition of government seemed the only solution that attacked the root of the problem.

From this starting point I derived a set of propositions that, it seemed to me, an anarchist would have to believe: A government is any person or persons who coerces others. Coercion is the use of force to compel or restrain, especially when the user of force claims legal authority. Since anyone who employs force as a matter of policy tends either to become coercive or to be eliminated by more coercive competitors, the soundest strategy for anarchists is to rely on nonviolent means to establish the government-free society and to maintain it. As Benjamin R. Tucker wrote in *Individual Liberty*, "The idea that Anarchy can be inaugurated by force is as fallacious as the idea that it can be sustained by force. Force cannot preserve Anarchy; neither can it bring it. In fact, one of the inevitable influences of the use of force is to postpone Anarchy."

But because anarchism requires nonviolence as a general strategy, we have to admit it's a pie-in-the-sky ideology. One only has to riffle through a newspaper to see how far humanity as a whole is from general nonviolence.

By pie in the sky I mean that – unless life extension becomes a reality – I do not think any of us now living will see an anarchist society emerge on this planet, not even see any great number of people converted to anarchism. Whenever and wherever anarchism has enjoyed great popularity in the past, its supporters have not understood how demanding anarchism really is. Sure, it means the abolition of government, but government is so insidious that frequently anarchist programs have coercion built into them under another name.

Some anarchists, asked how they would deal with murder, rape or robbery in the absence of courts or police, answer that the community will punish people who do these things. But then "the community" is using coercion to punish violators, and "community" is just another word for government. This type of "anarchist justice" exists even now, and is known as lynching.

Or take the property question. The big division between anti-government people has been between those who advocate retention of private property rights and a free-market solution to all of society's problems and those who support communal ownership of property and collective solutions to social problems. How are these differing property arrangements going to be maintained and defended? Not by governments, we're told, but by private defense agencies or people's militias.

But when does defense become coercion? No one would call a person using a shotgun to defend his or her home against invading thugs a government. But from Attila the Hun on down, everybody who has ever resorted to force has claimed to be acting in self-defense. Certainly there's a gray area here. But the more anarchists try to stay safely deep within that gray zone, the less anarchism looks like a practical possibility. And the more anarchists try to be practical and to venture out to the edges of the gray area, the more anarchism tends to resemble laissez faire Republicanism or democratic Socialism. Which are simply other flavors of pie in the sky.

Because anarchism is pie in the sky, the first thing a bunch of self-proclaimed anarchists seem to do when they get together – I've been present on a few such occasions – is look at one another at a loss and say, "What do we do now?"

Most of my anarchist activity is intellectual and motivated by self-interest. I'm an anarchist, on average, only a few hours a month. Most of my time is devoted to my family and to my chosen work, writing novels. By my current standards, writing this essay is a major project. I'm just as happy to remain in this armchair as Albert Jay Nock was, getting up only to go to my desk where I edit magazines like my sporadic *No Governor* and write essays like this one. I sometimes talk about anarchism to interested groups. I've identified myself as an anarchist in print and on television and once even debated anarchism on cable TV with the mayor of a nearby suburb, Arlington Heights.

Writing novels led to my becoming a member of the Libertarian Futurist Society. Michael Grossberg's work in organizing the society is a model of innovative anarchist activism. (As far as I'm concerned, "libertarian" and "anarchist" mean the same thing. I refuse to allow the term "libertarian" to be misappropriated by crypto-Republicans.) And I like to think I would be just as enthusiastic about the L.F.S. if they hadn't given an award to myself and Robert Anton Wilson.

Other anarchist groups I have participated in have mostly been discussion groups, some of them face-to-face and some of them amateur press associations and correspondence publications like *FreeFanzine, The Connection* and the apparently-now-defunct *SRAF Bulletin.* The most anarchists I ever saw in one place was an assembly organized by the

Social-Revolutionary Anarchist Federation (SRAF) in the summer of 1977. About two hundred of us, if I remember rightly, from all over North America gathered for two days in tents and around campfires on Wildcat Mountain in Wisconsin, near the spot where the Sauk war chief Black Hawk, who was something of an anarchist himself without knowing it, was captured in 1832.

In the Chicago area the highest-profile anarchist group is that centering around *Nomos,* an eclectic magazine. Most of these people are anarcho-capitalists, which as I've already indicated is not my flavor, but at least they don't make you feel guilty for owning a car that runs, so I enjoy hanging out with them.

Clearly I'm the model of a modern armchair anarchist. Do I sometimes feel sheepish about this? Sometimes. Anarchists are always criticizing one another for lack of action, meaning physical action, and this criticism hits home. But then I notice that the criticism itself is an intellectual activity, delivered from other people's armchairs or barstools, and I take heart.

And I strongly believe in the long-range power of intellectual activity: articles, books, lectures, meetings, demonstrations, even letters to the editor. Around the ideas spread in these ways, I believe, considered institutions and activities will eventually develop.

Since that pie up yonder seems so far away sometimes, inevitably one gets drawn into this-worldly politics. If you were to label me on the basis of the political things I do, you'd probably call me a (hiss!) liberal. However, one conventional political area where I've been quite active in recent years is the peace movement. And if I'm right in thinking that anarchism and nonviolence are virtually identical, then anything that furthers nonviolence also furthers anarchism.

The striking thing about contemporary anarchism is how un-contemporary it is. It seems to have had little to say to those working for sexual, reproductive and racial freedom, for freedom of expression, for protection of the environment, for peace, for the elimination of poverty. I've noticed a strong anti-feminist tendency that seems to have developed, largely unopposed, among Right-wing anarchists. Anarchists write cranky attacks on the New Age, seemingly unaware that not everything that goes under that rubric is about crystals, UFOs and channeling. Few anarchists know much about quantum theory, the holistic paradigm, Asian philosophy or the relationship among those fields of knowledge. I've seen more than one anarchist ignorantly use "mysticism" as a synonym for superstition, apparently never having bothered to find out what the term really means. A lot of contemporary anarchist writing seems to convey the sense that anarchists have the answer, and everything else is cow pies.

I can't seriously believe that the anarchists have the only answer to humanity's problems – or that anyone else does, either. The anarchist answer, as I've already suggested, is pie in the sky. Whereas cow pies, at least, can help a few flowers to grow.

Anarchism is a philosophy as well as a social movement; it teaches that one's self is the supreme value in life and that no "higher" or "larger" entities have any moral claim on us. This view is congenial to me as a worker in the arts because I believe that individuality is the – so to speak – fountainhead of creativity.

Developing a moral code from the idea that each of us is a law unto ourselves, I've been working out a psychological theory that much self-defeating behavior is the result of inner moral divisions. I think people may do things to hurt themselves because they see this as the only way to rebel against what anarcho-philosopher Max Stirner called "spooks," which they are carrying around inside themselves. I am interested in the possibility that by unifying themselves internally people can make positive changes in their lives as dramatic as those we hear of arising from religious conversion, but without submitting their wills and destinies to some supposed higher power.

I've been testing this theory in my own life with some success and some failure and in 1988 announced it to the anarchist world with an article called "Liberating Morality" in *Nomos* (Volume 6, Number 2.) I haven't heard that reading my article cured anyone's alcoholism or smoking habit, but maybe they haven't gotten around to writing me yet.

I continue to advocate anarchism, even though it's pie in the sky, because we need some people to envision and uphold distant, utopian ideals. As a lifelong science fiction fan, I feel comfortable playing that role. The quality we need above all is patience, the patience to be willing to work for an end that may not be realized for hundreds of years. And the patience to use means, such as nonviolence, appropriate to the end of a noncoercive society.

And I have a few ideas about how to work for such a society. Before anything else can happen, people, a lot of people, have to learn what anarchism is and persuade others that it is a worthwhile ideology. I know that we ourselves don't agree what anarchism is, but that's a detail. One way to educate people is to organize more small, autonomous groups. Some could be local, others could be regional correspondence or electronic networks. As monasteries did during the Dark Ages, these groups, in a largely government-oriented world, could function as think tanks, centers for education and for the practical development of new ideas.

But anarchism, for me, always attaches more importance to the individual than the group. As individuals we need to continue to educate ourselves. Each of us, I think, should regularly and frequently turn to our shelf of basic anarchist texts, the writings of such as Kropotkin, Bakunin, Max Stirner, Benjamin Tucker, Emma Goldman, Paul Goodman, David Friedman, Murray Bookchin – add your own favorites. Not necessarily to get the answers. Just as much to wrestle with and reject in the search for one's own answers. And we should be reading the most interesting non-anarchist thinkers and try to apply their ideas to reinvigorate anarchism.

I am skeptical about all isms, including anarchism; that goes with being a professional writer. I've seen how the barricade mentality – the need to propagandize for a doctrine and defend it against its critics – frequently stultifies thought. My values are the wellspring of my creativity, but I would hope that I'd be ready to give up any value, if reasoning and creative thinking lead me in that direction. Thinking for myself may or may not be good for anarchism, but it will certainly be good for me.

Paradoxically, my efforts to keep my mind free of orthodoxy seem very anarchistic to me.

For example, I thought for myself, rather than trying to do the correct anarchistic thing, when that developer threatened to tear down my fence. I produced a survey map which showed that the fence was on our property, right where it was supposed to be, and our village police officer told the developer there's to be no digging until the thing is settled to everyone's satisfaction. It isn't settled yet, but it's back to lawyers writing letters to each other, and I'm still in happy possession of my yard. I have no regrets about asking the police for help. Dark times call for dark remedies.

For anarchists, these are indeed the dark ages. But maybe, just maybe, we can shed some more light.

And maybe that pie in the sky will turn out to be tomorrow's sun.

Ǥ

Science Fiction Review Interview

This interview by Neil Wilgus was published in 1985 in Science Fiction Review, a popular fanzine of the time. The introduction is by Mr. Wilgus. This is reprinted with the permission of the Neal Wilgus estate.

The son of a doctor, Robert Shea was born in New York City on St. Valentine's Day, 1933. He attended Manhattan College, where he worked on the college newspaper, yearbook and literary magazine and helped found a fraternity that dispensed with blackballing and pledging. Drafted in 1954, he spent most of his two years in the Army doing public relations writing. After earning a master's degree in English literature at Rutgers University and writing the first draft of an autobiographical novel (as yet unpublished) about his college years, Shea returned to New York, where he tried freelance fiction writing for a time. His first professional short story was published in *Fantastic Universe* by Hans Steffan Santesson, who invited Shea to join the Hydra Club. At a Hydra meeting, Shea met Larry T. Shaw, editor of *Infinity*, who hired Shea to work on *Custom Rodder* and *Car Speed & Style*. (Shea was not to pass a driver's test for another seven years.) In 1963 he joined the editorial staff of *True* magazine and in 1966 he was appointed editor of *Cavalier.* In 1967 he was asked by *Playboy* to become one of the editors of "The *Playboy* Forum" letter column. As a "Forum" editor he represented *Playboy* in many lectures, panel discussions and debates. By 1977 he was solely responsible for editing "The *Playboy* Forum." He lost his job at *Playboy* in an economy drive in September 1977.

Throughout his career as a magazine editor, Shea continued to write. His work included occasional science fiction short stories and a couple of novels (he tends to be vague about how many there were) that never saw the light of day, as well as other pieces that did. He had better success with nonfiction, his articles and essays appearing in magazines as diverse as *Today's Health* and *The Los Angeles Free Press.* In 1968 he was one of a group who put together *Law and Disorder*, a one-shot magazine sponsored by the American Civil Liberties Union in the aftermath of the 1968 Democratic National Convention in Chicago. The publication attacked Mayor Richard J. Daley and the Chicago police and supported the peace demonstrators. Shea writes mostly about subjects related to the behavioral sciences, such as psychology, sex, religion and politics. As his novel-writing schedule gets heavier, his articles become less frequent. An important article was his "Women at War," a critique of the women's anti-pornography movement published in the February 1980 *Playboy.* Lately he has taken to doing travel pieces on hotels and restaurants in the Midwest for *Travel & Leisure*. His most recent published article was "Nobody Else Can Do It For You," in *The Writer,* November 1984.

During his years at *Playboy* Shea met Robert Anton Wilson, also an editor on "The *Playboy* Forum." Together they wrote *Illuminatus!,* published by Dell in 1975. The three volumes of *Illuminatus!* have been described as "the anarchist/acid rock answer to *The Lord of the Rings*" by David Harris, one of the editors who worked on it.

Illuminatus! is still in print, unusual for a paperback original; it has been produced on the stage in England, the Netherlands, Germany and the U.S., and a small, antic cult has grown up around it. It was republished in a one-volume trade paperback edition in 1985 and has since appeared on a couple of science fiction and libertarian best-seller lists.

Shea continues his career as an editor by getting out his own amateur magazine, *No Governor.* He claims it has a circulation of a little over 100.

Shea's novel *Shike* (pronounced she-kay), set in medieval Japan, was published by Jove Publications in June 1981. It has come out in eight foreign editions and is now in its seventh printing.

His newest novel, *All Things Are Lights*, a novel about a troubadour and the women he loves in the time of the Crusades, will be published by Ballantine Books in the summer of 1986. He teaches part time for the Department of Communications at Loyola University, Chicago.

Shea lives with his wife, Yvonne, and his son, Michael, in a small yellow house surrounded by evergreen shrubs in a suburb of Chicago on the shore of Lake Michigan. It is a surprisingly conventional setting for a man who writes science fiction and calls himself an anarchist. The choice is probably explained by a quotation from Flaubert Shea has tacked to the bulletin board of his office: "Live like a bourgeois and think like a god." He says, "We bought this house because we needed room and it was cheap and pretty, and now the price of houses has gone up so much that it's even cheaper to live here. In fact, we probably couldn't afford to move."

Shea works in a room in the back of the house which has a pleasant view of green fields. Crammed with books, the room is papered with a black and white design of heraldic lions. The walls are decorated with framed posters advertising performances of the stage version of *Illuminatus!* There is also a small portrait of Shea and Robert Anton Wilson side by side, each with his head enclosed in a pyramid surmounted by an eye, the symbol of the sinister Bavarian Illuminati. There is a bulletin board on which, Shea says, he changes the items once a month. This month's items include a calendar of his own devising (the weeks begin on Monday), a schedule of the editing course he is currently teaching at Loyola, the above-mentioned line from Flaubert and several odd-looking photographs without captions clipped from newspapers. On some shelves the books share space with what Shea calls "my collections of tacky souvenirs," cheap, gaudy objects purchased in gift shops in various parts of the world. There is a gilt replica of the Eiffel Tower, a China pig from Louisville, Kentucky, a Space Needle pencil sharpener from Seattle, a dinner bell from the Sherlock Holmes Hotel in London, a pincushion from St. Louis, Missouri, and a replica of New York City in a bottle. The centerpiece of Shea's workroom is an Apple IIe computer which he calls "Mr. Chips."

Shea is about six feet tall, slightly overweight, and has a full head of wavy, greying hair and a brown mustache that droops over the corners of his mouth. He wears gold-framed bifocals. His manner is calm and pleasant. He speaks with a slight New York accent in a nasal voice that tends toward loudness, he says from years of trying to talk above subway noises.

SFR: After the publication in 1975 of *Illuminatus!*, which you wrote with Robert Anton Wilson, your opus enjoyed a remarkable career on the stage. How did that come about?

SHEA: A mad English showman by the name of Ken

Campbell discovered the *Illuminatus!* books and decided to try to produce a theatrical version. Campbell's Science Fiction Theatre of Liverpool production of *Illuminatus!* opened on Nov. 23, 1976, in a coffee shop called the Liverpool School of Language Music Dream and Pun on Mathieu Street, almost next door to the site of the Cavern Club, where the Beatles got their start. After that it played the National Theatre in London, and later in Amsterdam and Frankfurt. Then the Empty Space in Seattle got wind of the British production and arranged to do their own, halfway around the world, which ran from September to December of 1978. Campbell and his co-playwright, Chris Langham, an illuminated comedian who used to write for the Muppet Show, originally set up *Illuminatus!* as a cycle of five plays, one to be performed each weekday night, followed by a Saturday marathon performance of all five plays lasting from noon to midnight, with pub breaks at suitable intervals. For the National Theatre they trimmed that to eight and a half hours. The Empty Space turned it into a cycle of three plays, and their marathon performances last about eight hours.

SFR: What did you think of the stage productions?

SHEA: What greater delight can a writer experience than to see real people taking the trouble to bring his work to life? When what began as a vague shape in the mind takes on solid form in a theater before an audience, it's a thrill that can't be duplicated. It was one of the most sublime experiences in my life, second only to being with Yvonne when she gave birth to our baby. Novelists are often displeased with adaptations of their works to other media. But Wilson and I were delighted with both the British and Seattle productions. They were ingenious in handling problems of staging and special effects, and they were faithful to both the text and the meaning of the books. The actors were passionately dedicated and gave brilliant performances.

SFR: How were the plays received by the public? Did people have trouble sitting there for eight to twelve hours?

SHEA: Audiences at the marathon performances seemed even more enthusiastic than those who saw only one play at a time. *Illuminatus!* achieves some of its best effects through sheer size and all-inclusiveness. In Liverpool, London and Seattle the house was always full for every marathon performance.

SFR: What did the critics have to say?

SHEA: There were dozens of reviews of the various stage versions, nearly all of them favorable. The few negative reviews were invariably aimed at the material rather than the actors. I'm glad we got a few hostile reviews.

SFR: Why?

SHEA: *Illuminatus!* was intended to outrage, disgust, disturb and bewilder many sorts of people. When two anarchists write a long novel filled with satire aimed at everything from conspiracy theories to government to organized religion, somebody better be offended, or the authors are not communicating very well. The novel is replete with favorable references to drugs and rebellion, it presents a series of pornographic scenes of progressively increasing complexity and perversity, and it is peppered with obscene and blasphemous imagery and language. If nobody is turned off, it means nobody is paying attention.

SFR: In addition to its science fiction and anarchist aspects, *Illuminatus!* displays a strong preoccupation with the occult and the paranormal. Has your interest in this area grown, or are you more skeptical these days?

SHEA: I've always been pretty skeptical about the occult and the paranormal, but in an open-minded way, if you take my meaning. I think magick, witchcraft and paganism have value as alternative pathways to what the mystics call illumination. I am willing to believe that occult or paranormal phenomena really exist, if ever I'm presented with conclusive evidence. I think that it is a betrayal of science that some so-called scientists are trying to use institutional sanctions to discourage research in these areas. But I don't think anything has been proven yet. And don't ask me to take things on faith. I was a believing Catholic until I was 30, and it was difficult enough to get away from that. No more spooks for me, thank you. Meanwhile, however, in *Illuminatus!* and elsewhere I'm willing to use such concepts as story material without worrying about whether they're real or not.

SFR: What about the Ancient Illuminated Seers of Bavaria? Don't you believe in them?

SHEA: At the time the book was written, I thought the legend of the Bavarian Illuminati was a silly, paranoid myth. We were simply using the Illuminati legend and the related plethora of conspiracy theories about the Sixties' wave of political assassinations as a launching pad for an extended flight of black humor and political satire. In the years in which we wrote *Illuminatus!* the country was awash in paranoia, and we were hoping to exorcise some of it by poking fun at it. It has not been that long since Senator Joe McCarthy had the whole country in the grip of Communist conspiracy mania. It was not that long since a harmless couple named Julius and Ethel Rosenberg were sent to the electric chair as atomic spies. The evidence against them was pure shit, if you look at it today, but it was convincing at the time because of the prevalent hysteria. At the time we were writing, the John Birch Society had magnified that conspiracy mania by connecting the Communist conspiracy to the Illuminati conspiracy, which Robert Welch had now discovered, and they were blaming that conspiracy for sex education, fluoridation, rock music, the peace movement and the popularity of marijuana. And they were being believed. It was in that climate that Wilson and I took up our pens to tilt at the windmills of political madness.

SFR: Have you changed your mind at all about the existence of the Illuminati since the book was published?

SHEA: You, yourself, having written and researched *The Illuminoids,* and which I consider to be a very sane and scholarly study of the Illuminati myth, are in a better position to say whether they actually exist than I am. I still think the John Birch Society picture of the Illuminati – which is also now being put about by a Birch-like group led by an extreme authoritarian named Lyndon Larouche – is sheer nonsense. Of course, there are secret deals among world leaders and dastardly criminal acts are committed by government agents. Still, I don't believe in a single, worldwide, age-old conspiracy that explains All of the Bad Things That Are Happening.

There is also the tradition of philosophical research whose initiates are sometimes known as Illuminati, a tradition that includes the heretic-martyr Giordano Bruno, Aleister Crowley, and Robert Anton Wilson, my co-author. But members of this tradition have not tried to take over governments or the world economy, only to turn on more light in their own – and others' – heads.

SFR: So you wrote *Illuminatus!* purely as political satire?

SHEA: Our intentions kept changing all the time. At first we saw it simply as an international espionage thriller, with the Illuminati as arch-villains, giving us, as I said, an opportunity to satirize current paranoias. As the book developed, it rolled along like a blob-monster, absorbing everything in its path. We came to consider it what the literary critic Northrop Frye calls an anatomy, a long work of prose fiction that incorporates everything that interests the author – ideas, opinions, curious facts, canny stories. *Moby Dick* is a good example of an anatomy. We wanted to outrage authoritarians of left, right and center, so we made the book subversive, blasphemous and pornographic. We threw in generous helpings of anarchist propaganda and our notions about the theory and practice of mysticism. Eventually, we dared to hope that *Illuminatus!* might be a more-than-literary experience, might actually have psychotherapeutic or mystically enlightening value, make readers feel as if they were participating in some magical or religious rite. Only, the aim of this rite would be to liberate people, rather than confirm their current programming. I think the stage versions of *Illuminatus!* really did have this magical quality. The marathon performances reminded me a bit of the long Catholic services for Holy Week that recapitulate the trial, crucifixion and resurrection of Jesus. Of course, *Illuminatus!* is a good deal more entertaining than any religious ceremony I've ever sat through. Maybe this was what religion was like before somebody decided it had to be boring to be good for your soul.

SFR: You wrote *Illuminatus!* while an editor at *Playboy.* Did you find working there an enjoyable or a stultifying experience?

SHEA: It was a very lively, creative place to work, especially during my earlier years there. My work on "The *Playboy* Forum" gave me lots of material for *Illuminatus!* Later on, though, the corporation started to run short of money, so the staff got smaller, and I had to take on most of the work that had formerly been done by a group of people. It took all my time just to do the "Forum" well, and there was nothing left over to develop new ideas or new directions, so the job became something of a treadmill. Then there was an economy drive. On a single day in September 1977, about 150 employees were axed including several editors, and I was one of them.

SFR: Was that traumatic for you?

SHEA: No matter how much they tried to tell me I was a swell person and my work was first-rate, I couldn't help but feel I had been weighed in the balance and found expendable. Also, Yvonne and I had some family tragedies at the same time that made things worse. Less than two months after I was fired my mother, who died in 1979, became an invalid, and Yvonne's 22-year-old brother was killed in an accident. So the end of 1977 was a bad time for us, not just because of my being kicked out by *Playboy.*

SFR: How did you get through it?

SHEA: I was buoyed by Yvonne's unshakable confidence that I'd find worthwhile work to do. Years of studying Zen helped a lot, too. It's a bounce-back philosophy. When fears of not being able to support my family plunged me into anxiety or depression, I reminded myself that my family needed someone who could stay calm and cheerful more than they needed someone who had a job. That helped me out of a lot of funks. Besides, *Playboy* didn't exactly cast me adrift without a life raft. There were 15 weeks' severance pay, my profit-sharing and several freelance editing and writing assignments.

SFR: How did you manage to strike out on your own as a freelance writer?

SHEA: I'd always intended to leave *Playboy* – on my timetable of course – and try to write for a living. I didn't feel ready to do that when I was unexpectedly fired, but while I was job hunting a substantial amount of freelance writing came my way. At the same time, I gave some short outlines for novels to my agent, Al Zuckerman. One of them turned into *Shike*, the medieval-Japanese novel which was published by Jove in 1981. That's a publishing company, not a Roman god. Once Al landed a writing contract for me that would pay enough to support us, there was no question about going back to the old office-job-and-paycheck routine.

SFR: What is life like out on your particular limb?

SHEA: When I had a regular job I used to observe the freelance writers I knew and say it must take nerves of steel to live like that, but I had no bone-deep understanding of how frightening it really is until I started to do it myself. It is very difficult to be creative while worrying about when my next check is going to come in. I've learned to put thoughts of money firmly out of my mind, as much as I can. It helps a great deal that Yvonne now has a fulltime job and I can ditch that old role, so destructive to men, of being the sole support of my family. Work is much more of a pleasure than it was when I was a magazine editor. It's hard at times and lonely at times, but what could be more fun than spending all day in a quiet room watching and recording the doings of the creatures of my imagination?

SFR: Have you always had a creative bent?

SHEA: As a kid I constantly drew and made models of dinosaurs, spaceships, robots and horrible monsters. I made my own toy soldiers out of paper. They were usually supposed to be Martians. I built fleets of paper rocket ships. I staged great battles on the living room rug. At the same time, I was making my own newspapers. Before I knew how to write I would fold pieces of paper and decorate them with regular rows of squiggles, which I would then "read" to any interested adult, making the news stories up as I went along. I made up a long epic about my teddy bear, which I told in daily installments to my mother. As I grew older I developed the ambition to write and draw my own science fiction comic strip. This grew out of my fascination with *Buck Rogers*, which I began reading in 1938. I feel about *Buck Rogers* the way my son now feels about *Star Wars.* I drew my own comic strips and passed them out to friends.

SFR: How did you get started as a writer?

SHEA: Just as reading *Buck Rogers* made me want to do my own comic strip, reading SF made me want to write the stuff. I started reading science fiction – a *Captain Future* story called "Magic Moon" – when I was 11. Since the magazines didn't come out fast enough for me, I started patronizing a back-number magazine store in my neighborhood, and pretty soon I had built up a big collection of SF magazines. About the time I got the urge to write sf stories myself, I discovered that this store had stacks of back issues of *Writer's Digest, The Writer* and *Author and Journalist.* These magazines fed my ambition, and they also taught me that there are principles in the construction of fiction, techniques for telling a story, methods of going about writing. I started reading how-to-write books. Those by Jack Woodford were among my favorites. By the time I was in high school I was turning out short stories pretty regularly. As a senior in high school I wrote a long pseudo-history of the future, which I called *The March of the Martians.* It leaned heavily on a book I loved, *The March of the Barbarians* by Harold Lamb, a history of the Mongols. I had a couple of short stories published in *The Manhattan Quarterly,* the college literary magazine. I had finished college and done two years in the Army and was in graduate school when I had my first professional publication, a short story called "Brave Feast," which appeared in the January 1958 issue of *Fantastic Universe,* edited by Hans Stefan Santesson.

H.L. Gold published a story of mine called "Mutineer" in the July 1959 issue of *IF*. I wrote fiction and articles frequently during my days as a magazine editor, but it wasn't until 1975 that Bob Wilson and I came out with *Illuminatus!*, which was the first time I had my name on a book.

SFR: Can you remember the first novel you ever read?

SHEA: Not for sure, but the most important was *The Wind in the Willows.* One of the great books of all time. Yvonne and I took turns reading it aloud to each other a few years ago, and I recently read it aloud to Michael, and I still think it is a beautiful and delightful book. *Swiss Family Robinson* is another favorite. I read *Moby Dick* and *Huckleberry Finn* when I was seven or eight years old, but I didn't understand them very well until much later.

SFR: What books did you like most when you were a teenager?

SHEA: I read more magazine science fiction than anything else. When I was in my teens there were no publishers regularly bringing out SF books. I was enchanted by Leigh Brackett's *Shadow Over Mars* and by Asimov's *Foundation* series. Among novels I loved Robert Penn Warren's *All the King's Men* and Ayn Rand's *The Fountainhead.* I also liked big gaudy historicals like *Gone With the Wind* and *Anthony Adverse* and the many novels of Frank Yerby and Thomas B. Costain.

SFR: You must do a lot of reading as part of your work. Do you read for pleasure as well?

SHEA: A writer who doesn't read for the sake of reading is doomed to lose all sense of what writing is all about. I do most of my leisure reading either for pleasure or for self education. Recently, for pleasure, I have read *Lincoln* by Gore Vidal, *Heretics of Dune* by Frank Herbert, *The Warlord* by Malcolm Bosse, *The Gate of Worlds* by Robert Silverberg, *The Tomb* by F. Paul Wilson and *Pet Sematary* by Stephen King. For enlightenment, in the last few months, I've read *The Time Falling Bodies Take To Light* by William Irwin Thompson, *The C Zone* by Robert and Marilyn Kriegel, *Intimate Connections* by David D. Burns, *The Holographic Paradigm* edited by Ken Wilber, *The Turning Point* by Fritjof Capra and *Prometheus Rising* by my good buddy Robert Anton Wilson.

SFR: What contemporary authors do you get the most out of reading?

SHEA: The list is continually undergoing revision as my taste changes and my reasons for reading change, but John Fowles, Romain Gary, Norman Mailer, Yukio Mishima, Vladimir Nabokov, George Orwell, Thomas Pynchon, J.R.R. Tolkien and Robert Penn Warren seem to have taken up permanent residence in my literary pantheon.

SFR: As a former magazine editor, you probably read a lot of magazines.

SHEA: Dozens, though I don't have enough time to read as many magazines – or books for that matter – as I'd like to. My favorite is *The New Yorker,* which I think is the best magazine published in the U.S. today. I also love *Natural History*, especially the column on evolution by Stephen Jay Gould. *The New York Times Sunday Magazine* and *Scientific American* are other favorites.

SFR: Could you describe your working habits?

SHEA: I'm always experimenting with new ways of going about writing. The habits of the moment are not the habits I had last year and may not be those I'll be using next year. Right now, though, I try to follow a routine that varies little from one day to the next. Monday through Friday I get up at six a.m. I start writing between eight and nine. I eat a light lunch and go for a long walk. Then I continue working till six. Those may seem like long hours, but there are interruptions, because I have to be available to our twelve-year-old Michael, though he doesn't need me as much now as he did when I started freelancing. From six to eight is free time, then I read till around ten, and so to bed. That's my ideal schedule, you understand. The reality is punctuated by all sorts of vicissitudes.

SFR: Is it boring to follow a daily routine?

SHEA: I like it. Many teachers of mysticism recommend a daily schedule. By not having to worry about what you're going to do next, you keep your mind on a higher plane. That's why monks the world over follow a regular routine. It encourages the growth of the inner life and of creativity.

SFR: How much planning do you do before starting to write a novel?

SHEA: To get an advance from a publisher you have to submit an outline of your proposed novel. So I write an outline of forty pages or so. But I don't necessarily follow that outline when I write, and I plan the finer details of a chapter or scene when I'm ready to write that particular section. I go along with John Fowles' rule, "Follow the accident, fear the fixed plan." I try to look at my original idea as nothing more than a springboard, with the real creative process happening as I work along.

SFR: Do you work through a piece of writing from beginning to end, then, or do you hop around, writing sections as they occur to you?

SHEA: I've tried hopping around, but the results are confused and don't seem to fit together too well. For me, the most natural way to write is the way I read most novels, straight through from start to finish. But I often do get ideas for parts of the book other than the one I'm working on. I make notes of those ideas and use them when I'm ready.

SFR: When you're writing fiction, do whole scenes appear in your mind, or do you have to make yourself figure out what happens next?

SHEA: I start by rereading what I wrote yesterday and looking at my notes or outline for the scene I'm writing. This gets my mind back into the story. The scene starts to unfold in my mind as if I were reading it in a book or watching it on a movie screen. Sometimes I'm a passive observer, and I simply write what I see and hear. The words and sentences come to me without much effort on my part. Sometimes, though, I have to take a more active role in shaping the scene, asking myself what the characters would probably do or say, what would the details of the setting probably be. Although I like my stories to develop spontaneously, I'm not above manipulating characters and events to push the story in the direction I think it should go.

SFR: Do you find that writing dialogue is easier than straight narrative?

SHEA: So much so that it's a problem. Once my characters start talking to one another it's hard for me to get them to shut up, so we can get on with the story. You know those monologues in Ayn Rand's novels that go on for pages and pages? Well, I could easily write *dialogues* that would go on just as long. Usually, I let my people talk as much as they want to in the first draft, then cut back on the conversation when I'm revising.

SFR: How much revision do you do?

SHEA: I try to keep it to a minimum. I try to avoid what I call "overfuss," which means tinkering with a piece for seven years or so before submitting it, something I have been known to do from time to time. I think two drafts is best. My first draft writing usually means that much revision. I did *Shike* in three drafts for the most part, typing several pages of first draft material, then rewriting that, then typing a final draft and moving on to the next clump of pages. I don't like to write a whole draft of a novel, then go back to the beginning and start over. But the novel I just finished, *All Things Are Lights*, was tougher to do than *Shike*. It took me six complete drafts over four years before I finally got it done. This is still not the way I prefer to work. Of course, I could go on revising my writing endlessly. There are always improvements that can be made. But I think the best way for me to develop as a writer is to get a lot of practice by producing a large quantity of work, rather than by perfectionistically polishing a few pieces.

Now that I do my writing with an Apple IIe computer and a word processing program called Apple Writer 2, revising is a lot easier. I just call up the old draft on the screen, type in my changes, punch a couple of keys and turn out a new draft on my Apple letter quality printer at a rate of about a page a minute. As you can see, I'm an Apple loyalist. I got the computer in 1983, and all those later drafts of *All Things Are Lights* were done on it.

SFR: What do you think is the strongest point in your writing?

SHEA: Story structure. Keeping the story moving in a definite direction without wandering away from it and without losing track of the various plot threads. I'm also good at imaging and describing pageantry and spectacle, big scenes, events on an impressive scale.

SFR: Do you think a work of fiction can satisfy the demands of an intellectual, educated elite and the larger general public simultaneously?

SHEA: First of all, the vast majority of people in this country don't read books at all, so as soon as you write a book you are already appealing to an intellectual elite. Within that book-reading audience, I think, it is possible to achieve both popular and literary success. If you go back and look at my list of favorite contemporary authors, you'll notice that they are all respected artists and they have all written best sellers. My ideal is to write about people and events that have popular appeal, yet tell my stories with a richness that will satisfy discriminating readers.

SFR: Do you have an imaginary reader in mind when you write?

SHEA: Much of the time I'm not thinking of any reader at all, just doing my best to put the right words on paper in the right order. At other times, all sorts of readers invade my mind. I imagine my agent or my editor, or some friend or acquaintance reading some passage I've just written. These readers over my shoulder tend to make negative comments. I would like to have an ideal reader to whom I could address my work, but I haven't been able to develop such a character systematically in my mind. In lieu of an ideal reader, I try to use myself as the touchstone. I try to write the sort of thing I myself would like to read. I try to write as my favorite writers do. I figure, if my writing pleases me, there must be some other people out there whom it will also please.

SFR: Do you think it's true that the writer is never the best judge of his or her own work?

SHEA: On the contrary, the writer is the only judge whose opinion is important. In order to work at all, I must be able to judge my own work and to assume that I am a good judge of it. I have to know when something I've written needs more work, and when it is okay and I can leave it as it is. If I couldn't make such decisions, I'd be writing in a vacuum. It is true that writers often can't predict how their writing will be received by others. Others may praise work of mine that I am unhappy with, or dislike something I think is fine. But other people's opinions are not really the important thing for a writer. Writers can't learn from what others think of their work.

SFR: Isn't it important for writers to follow editors' directions?

SHEA: If you encounter an editor who doesn't like your work, it's best just to go looking for another editor. The publishing business abounds with stories of writers who had a manuscript rejected by twenty two publishers, only to have it accepted by the twenty third and become a best seller. A high-ranking editor at *Playboy* once stated categorically at a staff meeting, "Isaac Asimov can't write." Now, Isaac has a strong ego and a huge following, and he could care less what any one editor thinks of his writing. But I wonder how many potential Asimovs may have been cut off at the beginning of their careers because they took some asinine editor's word for it that they couldn't write. In fact, when I was making my adieus at *Playboy* another high-ranking editor advised me to look for another editorial job rather than try freelancing because in his opinion I wasn't that good a writer. Thank God I didn't listen to him. The editor whose word you take as gospel today may be a public relations account executive – or a freelance writer – tomorrow. The only teacher you can rely on over a lifetime is yourself.

SFR: Are you very critical of your own writing?

SHEA: I try to be neither too severe nor too lenient. You can't fool yourself, and when you are a writer, you're working for yourself. You know when you're goofing off and not getting the work done, spending too much time sharpening pencils. You know when you're doing below-standard work. So there really isn't much danger of a person who is serious about writing being too lenient with himself or herself. The greater danger is paralyzing one's self with perfectionism. Aside from listening to too many other opinions, the factor that more than anything stifles would-be writers is an overactive critical faculty. The people who tell you that writing is agony for them are usually criticizing their work even as they try to turn it out. I try to avoid that. When developing story ideas or doing first draft work, I try to ignore the voice of my critical faculty. Get something on paper first. The critical faculty is more useful to me later, when I'm revising and polishing, but I need momentum when I'm trying to come up with ideas or get a first draft on paper.

SFR: Could you describe *All Things Are Lights* for us?

SHEA: The title comes from a medieval philosopher, Scotus Erigena, who said, "All that are, are lights." The main characters have an outlook that is as mystical as that statement, only their mysticism is not of the orthodox variety. The main character is a troubadour who achieves illumination in an adulterous affair with a countess through the rites of courtly love, which I portray as a Westernized version of tantric yoga. The troubadour is also in love with a woman minister of the heretical Cathar sect. Nowadays they tell women they can't be priests; in those days they burned them at the stake for trying. These people get caught up in the disastrous Seventh Crusade led by King Louis IX, known today as St. Louis. The crusaders are eventually defeated by the Egyptian Mamalukes. The survivors, including the King, are held as hostages by the Moslems and try to save their lives by paying an enormous ransom.

SFR: Sounds strangely familiar. What are you working on now?

SHEA: It's in the formative stages and I don't want to say too much about it, but it seems to be a sequel to *All Things Are Lights*. It will be a continuation of my dyspeptic view of the Crusades and of the Middle Ages generally.

SFR: Let's talk about *Shike* for a moment. How did that novel fare in the marketplace?

SHEA: Quite well, though it wasn't a best seller. That is to say, it didn't make the *New York Times* or *Publisher's Weekly* best seller lists. But it did make the best seller lists of several bookstore chains, such as B. Dalton's, Waldenbooks and Kroch's and Brentano's. It was listed as a best seller by the *Toronto Star*. And reprint rights have been sold in eight foreign countries. It has gotten good reviews and gone back for seven printings. All in all a respectable performance. And the people who like it, *love* it. That's the most important thing.

SFR: Did you learn anything in researching Oriental history for *Shike* that might be of interest to us in the twentieth century Occident?

SHEA: Many things. For instance, right wing libertarians often talk about private armies and private police forces as a necessity for a free society. I learned that the samurai, whom we look upon as the epitome of militarism, were just that, private warriors. They were not official government troops. They were armed retainers protecting the private property of local landlords. The word samurai means "one who serves." But only a few hundred years after the class first appeared, they became the government. Government is based upon the power to coerce, and as long as that power exists, there will be government.

SFR: Your outlook is both anarchist and pacifist. Did you have trouble writing with sympathy about authoritarian militarists like the samurai?

SHEA: Any writer of fiction who sympathizes only with characters whose ideas agree with his or her own is going to run out of material fast. I've always admired Japanese culture, and in particular the samurai. The samurai ideal is to develop oneself as a whole human being, to be an artist, poet and philosopher as well as a fighting man. The samurai often studied under Zen masters, and some who lived long enough retired and became monks themselves. I find this cultivation of aesthetic sensitivity side by side with martial ferocity to be most attractive. You have to go back to the knight-troubadours of Provence, the Vikings or the pagan Celtic warriors to find anything similar in Western culture, yet as recently as World War II Japanese officers were still writing poems in beautiful brush-and-ink calligraphy before charging into battle waving their beautiful obsolescent swords.

As far as my being a pacifist goes, paradoxically the martial virtues are not antithetical to pacifism. Gandhi remarked that many of his most steadfast nonviolent campaigners were men with military training and experience. In fact, both Gandhi and the Buddha were born into the Kshatriya, the Indian warrior caste. In the *Aguttara Nikaya*, a Buddhist scripture, we find, "Warriors, warriors we call ourselves. We fight for splendid virtue, for high endeavor, for sublime wisdom, therefore we call ourselves warriors." Bob Wilson had a nice little essay in *New Libertarian* several issues ago on the need for an effective pacifist to have the heart of a warrior.

SFR: Isn't historical fiction a rather drastic switch from science fiction?

SHEA: Well, *Shike* started out as a proposal for a science fiction novel which borrowed its plot from certain historical events – the War of the Roses in England and the Mongol invasion of Europe in the thirteenth century. An editor expressed interest in the story, but asked if I could set it in medieval Japan, since he was in the market for historical romances, not science fiction. This is not, by the way, the editor or the publishing house that ended up buying the book. Anyway, I did a little quick research and discovered that there was a Japanese civil war like the War of the Roses. The parallels were startling, even to the opposing sides using red and white as their official colors. I knew, of course, that the Japanese had suffered a Mongol invasion. Since the novel was in an embryonic state at that point, it was possible to do a little genetic engineering and program the organism to develop into an historical novel rather than a science fiction novel. This new novel is connected to my other work in other ways as well. My hero belongs to an order of warrior monks whose resemblance to the Illuminati is not coincidental and whose teachings suggest many of the ideas about mysticism, philosophy and politics expressed in *Illuminatus!* There are similar threads connecting *All Things Are Lights* with *Illuminatus!*

Generally speaking, there are many similarities between historical fiction and science fiction. A lot of science fiction is historical fiction set in the future. In both genres the writers must create in their imaginations a society and a way of life that they cannot know firsthand. Many science fiction stories describe future societies that existed in the past. Asimov, for example, drew on the history of the Roman Empire for the Foundation series.

SFR: What other writing have you done recently?

SHEA: The last piece published was an article in *The Writer* for November 1984 called "Nobody Else Can Do It For You." In it I said at greater length what I just told you, that a writer has to be his or her own teacher and critic.

SFR: Would you like to write more SF?

SHEA: Oh sure, but I could never be exclusively or even primarily a science fiction writer. There are too many other kinds of writing I want to do.

SFR: Do you have any advice for aspiring authors?

SHEA: Write the sort of thing you yourself prefer to read. Use your own taste as a guide to what to write and how to write it, and you are more likely to find a market for your work and to be happy doing it. Don't write what you consider trash just because it seems like a way to make a lot of money. Don't, on the other hand, try to write *belles lettres* because such writing confers prestige, if reading such literature puts you to sleep. Take as your models not the writers who make the most money or those who rank highest with literary journals, but the writers from whose work you personally derive the most satisfaction.

There's another word of advice I consider equally, maybe more, important: Don't listen to people who give advice to aspiring authors. As it says in the painting aboard the *Leif Ericson,* "Think for yourself, schmuck." OD'ing on advice produces confusion, stultification, discouragement. I mentioned reading how-to-write magazines and books when I started writing. After a while, though, I reached a point where too much reading about how to write messed me up. I was forever changing my methods to follow the latest how-to article or professional tip that impressed me. I even followed advice from writers whose actual novels and short stories I had never read. I kept fantasizing that I would discover the Secret and feeling depressed because my writing never seemed to get any better. When you are trying to learn to write, you usually go through a period of having your work rejected by editors, and during this painful time you're tempted to listen to any plausible character who comes along. All this advice hunting made my approach to writing much more erratic and inconsistent and hampered by discouragement than it would have been if I'd just figured out my own way of doing things and kept on writing and writing and writing. The kingdom of writing is within you.

SFR: Then you agree with the people who say it's impossible to teach anyone how to write?

SHEA: Even that notion is misleading, if it is taken to mean that writing is a mysterious ability that can't be studied rationally or developed methodically. People who believe so, if they're not happy with their first efforts at writing, may conclude that they don't have genius or talent or whatever it takes, and may give up. What I'm saying is that you have to *learn* writing by yourself. You can be quite rational and conscious about it, or you may just practice and allow your skill to develop – whatever suits you. You can learn a few things from other writers, but you have to be very selective. You have to invest your own ideas about writing, your own methods and techniques, your own goals. The kingdom is within.

SFR: Have you yourself followed this advice?

SHEA: Not all the time, and that's how I learned that the advice is good. Whenever I've tried to do some sort of writing I despise or dislike, I've been miserable and the result has been poor. Whenever I've uncritically adopted someone else's writing theories or practices, my development as a writer has been held back.

SFR: Looking over your writing career, you seem to have had more work published in the last ten years than you did before that. Why do you think you are accomplishing more lately?

SHEA: I've been gaining experience and I've learned my way around the publishing business. The fact that *Illuminatus!* was a collaboration helped me get that book done, too. I had Bob Wilson's encouragement and example to spur me on. Before *Illuminatus!* I produced several novels that I never finished.

Perhaps most important is that I started psychotherapy in 1963, when my first marriage was falling apart, and I went into full-scale psychoanalysis between 1967 and 1973. Before all of this professional help I had a lot of problems with sticking to projects that I started, with meeting writing commitments, with figuring out what I really wanted to do. Psychoanalysis taught me how to be productive.

SFR: What else besides writing are you working at?

SHEA: I'm teaching, among other things. I give courses in magazine editing and magazine article-writing at Loyola

University in downtown Chicago. It's great fun pulling all my experience together and trying to make sense of it. In my writing course I stress self-criticism and self-development as opposed to seeking answers from writing gurus.

Then, I irregularly publish an anarchist magazine called *No Governor*. I let this lapse between 1977 and 1984, but then I started doing a magazine for Arthur Hlavaty's *Golden APA*, and that got my editing and publishing motor started again. Lately, my apazine has turned into a revived *No Governor.* The magazine is now less purely anarchist and has strong mystical and fanzine components.

> *[Editor's note: An "APA" is an "amateur press association," an organization of fanzine writers who agree to have their fanzines published together as one bound volume. See the appendix about the Golden APA at the end of this book.]*

I write for other anarchist and far-out publications when time permits. I give talks when asked and occasionally attend meetings of anarchist and related groups. I'm a member of the Social Revolutionary Anarchist Federation, an umbrella organization for a number of anarchist individuals and groups. Several years ago I engaged in some anti-draft activity. For the past several years I've been much involved in the Freeze movement, working at the community level here in Glencoe. I write publicity and propaganda for them and do occasional computerized mass mailings. At the moment the Freeze isn't getting much publicity, but I still think it's the only practical alternative to the extinction of humanity in a nuclear war.

I'm deeply interested in the study and practice of mysticism, particularly Zen. I meditate. I try to regulate my life in ways recommended by mystical teachers. I have built up a large library devoted to mysticism. I sit now and then with the group at the Zen Center of Chicago.

SFR: What do you do for fun?

SHEA: Everything I do is fun.

SFR: Does your fiction have a political purpose?

SHEA: Naturally my writing reflects my ideas about politics, religion and whatnot. But I do not write to advocate my ideas. Not the way Ayn Rand – whose advice and Ideas I admire in many ways – did in *The Fountainhead* and *Atlas Shrugged*. My primary purpose in writing is to be a storyteller, not a preacher. The ideas in my stories are just more material out of which the story is built. A story, to be any good, must honestly embody the writer's values and beliefs. But the better writer you are, I think, the more those ideological elements will be absorbed into the creative process and become invisible. For over four hundred years people have been arguing about the meaning of various characters and events in Shakespeare's plays. If Shakespeare was trying to get some ideological message across, he failed abysmally. And he is too good a writer for that, so I have to conclude that he did not intend his plays to be vehicles for messages. We admire Shakespeare because he created events that enthrall us, people that live for us, language that dazzles us. Many other fine writers who do have messages, we admire *in spite* of what they are saying. Milton's Puritanism, for instance.

SFR: Do you feel a need to take a public stand on political questions, or do you think you should just stay in your study and work?

SHEA: I try to participate when I can find time for it. But I think I may be doing my most important work for humanity when I stay home and write. So I have no qualms about letting my involvement in public issues take a much smaller share of my time than writing does. In any case, whatever I do in public, it is not political but anti-political, since politics is the art and science of government, and I advocate the abolition of government.

SFR: Insofar as you believe in political – or anti-political – activism, what do you think is the most libertarian thing a person can do? What approach would be most likely to hasten the advent of a totally free society?

SHEA: Government will never be abolished as long as most people think there is no alternative they can live with. So the first step is education: explaining anarchism to people. Showing them that it is not inimical to basic human needs and values, as it has often been portrayed. Offering evidence that it is not utopian thinking either, but a way of reorganizing society that can work in the real world. Helping them to see that, far from being a practical necessity, the institution of government is leading the human race to the brink of extinction. We can do this educating by whatever means are available: Talking to people on the job or in the local tavern. Making speeches. Writing pamphlets and songs. Drawing cartoons. Making anarchist paintings, novels and symphonies.

SFR: Wait a minute. You previously praised writing that doesn't have any message.

SHEA: True, but Blake said that all poets are of the Devil's party, whether they know it or not. I would say that all novelists are anarchists, consciously or unconsciously. All art that affirms life encourages anarchism.

SFR: Do you consider yourself a left-wing anarchist or a right-wing anarchist?

SHEA: The argument between left-wing and right-wing anarchism makes about as much sense as the argument between socialism and capitalism makes in a world which is tending more and more toward a single hybrid economic system. The more important question is not what kind of economic system we ought to have, but whether our economic system will develop freely, by voluntary participation and voluntary observance of the rules of the economic game, or whether it is going to be enforced and imposed by a government. I was appalled the first time I heard an anarcho-syndicalist declare that in an anarchist society nobody would be *allowed* to practice capitalism. I'm equally appalled by people who call themselves anarchists and envision armies of Pinkerton types protecting their real estate and industrial holdings. I imagine a free society as one in which many different communities will undertake many different kinds of economic experiments, with the blessing of humanity as a whole.

SFR: Many anarchists think violent means are necessary in the struggle against government. Why do you insist on pacifism?

SHEA: Because as I see it, violence is what makes any organization a government. A government is any person or organization which uses force to coerce people into obedience. When anarchists use terrorism, revolutionary violence or military means, they are no longer advancing the cause of anarchism. They have become another government, regardless of what they may call themselves.

SFR: You mentioned that you were a believing Catholic until you were thirty. Has anything taken the place of religion in your life?

SHEA: Mainly my own philosophical speculations. I am thinking for myself, as I have learned I must do, trying to decide on a meaning for my life, to work out a satisfactory explanation for the world around me and my place in it, to select values that will help me chart my course. I want a philosophy that will do for me what religion does for a person, but with me in control of it.

SFR: How is your philosophy turning out?

SHEA: It's a mixture of mysticism, anarchist individualism and scientific materialism, elements that are somewhat difficult to blend. One of my key convictions is that we have to cease to be guided by the ideas of good and evil. The origin of human misery, as the *Book of Genesis* tells us, lies in the adoption of our ideas of good and evil. Oddly enough, no preachers seem to have drawn the logical conclusion that we ought to stop thinking in terms of good and evil. However, that is what both mysticism and the philosophy behind psychoanalysis seem to suggest. I also think, and this somewhat contradicts the above, that people have a natural moral sense that transcends their own culture. So that a sensible Aztec might feel there is something wrong with human sacrifice, for example. I make it possible for the contradictory elements in my thinking to coexist by keeping my philosophy aphoristic rather than systematic. You may have noticed that I've contradicted myself several times in this interview already. Don't worry, I'm not going to quote Walt Whitman or Ralph Waldo Emerson.

SFR: How did you get interested in mysticism?

SHEA: I mentioned how I sedulously read writers' magazines. One very influential article I read, published in *The Writer* in 1958, was "Zen and the Art of Writing" by Ray Bradbury. Bradbury's advice was "Work. Relaxation. Don't think," which is not a bad encapsulation of the Zen approach to the arts. As I said, I was constantly fussing over my methods and techniques of writing in those days, and I was getting in my way. Later, I read Herrigel's *Zen in the Art of Archery* and many books by Alan Watts and D.T. Suzuki, and they all helped my creative development. Practicing an art in the Zen way gradually turns you into a mystic.

SFR: And, I take it, mysticism to this day continues to satisfy some need in you?

SHEA: By 1968 I had gone through a radical change in my own point of view, and mysticism, especially Zen thought, was the only outlook that made sense to me. I met Alan Watts several times and was one of his many admirers. I learned a lot about mysticism from Bob Wilson. The countercultural revolution of the Sixties, in which I participated, was inspired in part by the impact of mystical Oriental ideas on a number of Western minds. By the beginning of the Seventies I was meditating regularly and had adopted a number of mystical practices. I started to treat my work, everything in my life, as a Way. I started to treat everything that happens to me as a lesson or a problem presented to me by life, the true sensei. To me, mysticism has nothing to do, necessarily, with theology or morality. It's simply a means of making direct mental contact with the ultimate, indescribable reality, thereby achieving a state of peace and euphoria. This is an utterly inadequate description of what mysticism is.

SFR: So are you both a mystic and an atheist?

SHEA: Yes. One of the important threads in my thought derives from the existentialism of Sartre and Simone de Beauvoir who teach that the universe is not ruled by a god and is meaningless and amoral in human terms, that there is no hereafter and that life on this planet is a chance event which has no significance. This is, so far as I know, what science appears to have learned about the human condition. Nevertheless, the existentialists assert that it is possible for human life to have value, meaning and dignity, if we realize that we can create these things for ourselves. The universe doesn't have meaning – we put meaning into it.

SFR: I'm curious about your outlook on lifestyle as it affects long life and vitality. Do you engage in activities like jogging or running? Yoga or Tai Chi? Is nutrition important in your daily life? Are such concerns likely to extend our life spans and enjoy life more?

SHEA: I used to lead a determinedly unhealthy lifestyle. I was a heavy smoker, drinker and eater. I preferred high cholesterol foods like beef and cheese. I got no exercise. I liked to stay up half the night and often worked or played through two days straight without sleeping at all. Sounds like fun, doesn't it? Gradually I got the message that it's a fun way to shorten your life. So I've been whittling away at these self-destructive habits. Studying and emulating the practices of mystics has helped. I try to follow the Buddha's rule of walking a middle path between harmful asceticism and self-indulgence. I have to say, though, that I am repelled by fads. A couple of the things you mention have become fads to the point where I wouldn't do them even if they would double my life span. When I see a jogger coming down the street in his hundred-dollar Adidas warm-up suit, I want to reach for my revolver.

SFR: I note that you and I share the unique distinction of having become fathers for the first time at forty. Isn't it great? Do you think it's better than becoming a father in your thirties?

SHEA: Fatherhood is rather like its necessary precondition, sex, in that the older you get, the more grateful you get that something so nice can still happen to you. And, as with sex, parenthood is an area of life in which our cultural evolution has outstripped our biological evolution. Though it is physically possible for us to become parents in our teens, the cultural tendency seems to be to put off actualizing this potential until later and later in life. In their twenties, and even in their thirties, people are still finding themselves. In the old days, if you hadn't found yourself by the age of sixteen, you were dead. But now, people have more time and need more time, because life is more complex and there are more options. So it's often not until their thirties or forties that people have a sense of who they are and where they are going, have mellowed out somewhat and have the matured values that enable them to enjoy parenthood. Parenthood is like any other task – you've got to enjoy it to do well at it.

SFR: Many vital and creative people extol the virtues of will power in making life more than just one damned thing after another. Is will an important part of your approach to life?

SHEA: For a long time I dismissed will power as an obsolete Victorian notion. I thought Freudian psychology had established that people have no control over the way they act, that it's all determined by the structure of their subconscious. Then I learned that Freud never held any such view. He, and modern psychoanalysts, hold that people can direct their behavior rationally and should try to. Freud even admired those great exponents of will power and character the English Puritans, so much so that he named one of his sons Oliver, after Oliver Cromwell. All the important varieties of psychotherapy, even the non-Freudian ones like behavioral therapy, agree that for the therapy to be successful the patient must have a strong will to change. This is a *precondition* of therapy. Psychotherapy doesn't replace will power, it depends on will power to be effective. In my own case, I thought my bad habits, smoking and the like, were neurotic symptoms that would go away automatically when I completed my analysis. Not so. I still have the same struggle to direct my behavior rationally that I did before. The only difference – and it *is* a crucial difference – is that I'm a more together person and can struggle more intelligently with my self-defeating tendencies. There is no substitute for will. We must take responsibility for our lives. We can't just go on blaming the silly things we do on our parents or the economic system or the devil. Unfortunately, this doesn't seem to have gotten through to the public at large, which is still looking for miracle cures. All that being said, please understand that I don't consider myself a very strong-willed person. I try to use the power of habit. I'm very conscious of my habits, and I try to strengthen the helpful ones and gradually chip away at the self-defeating ones. I also think that will depends a lot on attitude, and that one's attitudes can be improved – and one's will strengthened – by constantly reminding oneself of the attitudes one wants to have. For instance, if you like to smoke, you have to keep reminding yourself that tobacco is a poison and smoking is slow suicide. This is what is meant by reprogramming yourself. In this connection I also like Gandhi's advice, that you should never give something up just for the sake of giving it up, but only make a sacrifice when you can see it as a way of gaining something else that you value more. Good health, say, or mystical illumination. That is what will is, in a sense – a zeroing in on what you value most. Through a process extending over many years I've become a somewhat more disciplined person. I behave more intelligently than I once did. But I still have a long way to go.

SFR: Thank you, Robert Shea.

Ǥ

Hasta La Vista, Chicon

A Report on the 49th World Science Fiction Convention

The 49th World Science Fiction Convention, i.e. the "Worldcon," was held in Chicago in 1991. Convention reports are a staple of science fiction fandom; this is Shea's contribution to the genre. It is reprinted from the Spring 1992 issue of Prometheus, the journal of the Libertarian Futurist Society, the group that gives out the Prometheus Award.

A Question of Legitimacy

During the week leading up to Chicon V, I discovered to my disappointment that many friends with whom I'd spent time at my two previous Worldcons – Chicago in 1982 and Atlanta in 1986 – were not coming to this one, mostly because money was short. No Discordian Business Meeting? No Libertarian Writers' Mafia? Alas! Alack!

So I was glad that I'd signed up for a lot of program events in the hope that if the con made money I'd be reimbursed the $115 I paid for membership. Now I saw another advantage in being fully booked: I wouldn't be wandering around at loose ends all the time and would have a way of meeting people apart from being introduced to friends of friends or – shudder! – talking to total strangers.

The week of the convention I got a call from Bill Ritch, one of the editors of Prometheus, the newsletter of the Libertarian Futurist Society. Since I live in the Chicago area, he asked me to make whatever phone calls might be necessary to arrange a time and place at the convention for the LFS to present the Prometheus and the Hall of Fame awards.

Every year since 1982 – Chicon IV – the two LFS awards have been presented at the World Science Fiction Convention. Every year there's been some kind of screwup. It has crossed the minds of LFS members that this is, as Josef Stalin used to say, "no accident."

Bill had previously called the con committee with inconclusive results. Brad Linaweaver had written them an unofficial "to whom it may concern" letter urging them not to give the LFS the same short shrift previous con committees had. Brad was worried that his letter might have provoked hostility among the committee members, but my guess was that it had simply slipped through some bureaucratic crack.

I began making phone calls. I really got worried when I talked to one committee member who said she'd never heard of the Libertarian Futurist Society and doubted its "legitimacy" and anyway everything was all set and absolutely carved in granite and why hadn't we gotten in touch with the con committee earlier? Fortunately, she relented from this hardline stance just enough to mention a few other names I could call.

On Thursday I talked about the awards to one K.T. FitzSimmons. She said she'd do what she could, but managed to sound icy and spacey at the same time.

The Libertarian Party was having its convention in Chicago over the Labor Day weekend, so I called Carol Low, the editor of the libertarian magazine Nomos, who said she was sure the LP would welcome our award ceremony. I hoped we could stick to tradition and do it at the SF con, but it was comforting to have an alternative.

Political Correctness. Threat or Menace?

The Hyatt Regency overlooks the south bank of the Chicago River, just where Lake Michigan flows into the river, this being one of the Engineering Wonders of the Midwest. A block or so from the hotel lines of brass plaques on the sidewalk mark the site of Fort Dearborn, built in 1804 in the midst of the original log cabin settlement of traders and farmers known as Checagou. I parked in an underground garage near the hotel.

At the convention registration desk I picked up my badge, which had a clever, useful feature pasted on the back, a computer printout of my schedule, listing times and places.

I checked the Voodoo Message Board, one of the services that Filthy Pierre, aka Erwin Strauss, provides at Worldcons. All con members are listed on bulletin boards. If there's a red sticker next to your name, it means there is a message for you filed alphabetically in one of the boxes by the bulletin boards. Pins formerly were used instead of stickers, whence the name "Voodoo." I found a message for me – from Filthy Pierre himself, suggesting that we meet at a later time near the message board.

I took the elevator to Bill Ritch's floor. Bill had also talked to K.T. FitzSimmons, who had not yet been able to find a room assignment for the LFS. Bill and I went to a panel on "Censorship from the left", one of a number of panels planned to deal with hostile pressures on SF, fantasy and gaming.

The first speaker at this panel was John Norman, author of the oft-deplored, much-read *Gor* novels. His example of censorship was an editor who had declared that he would not even look at a manuscript bearing the name "John Norman". He ended his remarks with a resounding call to arms. The panel's moderator, Michael Flynn, a Prometheus Award candidate, responded with a dry, "Kawabunga!"

The other panelists gave similar accounts of encounters with what have come to be called "politically correct" views. I tended to sympathize with the causes the panelists represented but the fact was nobody could point to an instance of censorship in the strict sense of the word – the use of force to prevent something from being published or distributed. The panel left me feeling that the Left – whatever that term might mean – is nowhere near as big a danger to freedom of expression as authoritarian conservatives, Fundamentalist Christians and George "Ban Flag-Burning" Bush.

Publish or Perish

In the Pocket Program an "m" next to a panelist's name meant that person was expected to be moderator. On Friday, August 30th, I discovered I was "m" for the "Cross-Bred Genre Writers" panel. The other panelists were Nancy Atherton, Ginnie Dazzo, Don Keller, John Maddox Roberts and Lillian Stewart Carl. At the last minute we added literary agent Donald Maass, who had endeared himself to me before I met him with an article in Science Fiction Chronicle entitled "Who'll Get Rich Writing Fiction in the '90s?"

I didn't think this panel would generate much controversy, but we did get an argument going over whether genres per se are a Good Thing or a Bad Thing. The conclusion seemed to be that they are bad for writers who feel imprisoned by them and good for writers who enjoy them (as I enjoy space opera, for example) or for writers who write whatever they feel like writing.

A SFWA meeting was scheduled right after the panel, and when I walked in they were arguing over something I'd always wondered about – whether people like me really belong in SFWA. People like me being those who've somehow gotten enough SF into print to qualify for active membership but haven't published any SF lately.

Under the current rules, originally proposed by Robert Heinlein, as long as one keeps paying dues (currently $60 a year for active members), once an active member, always an active member. Jerry Pournelle, who seems to be the point man for this particular movement, wants the rules changed so that to retain active membership status one would have to publish an SF novel once every three years or three short stories a year. Pournelle, who defended this proposal with vehemence and bluster, seems worried that SFWA will be taken over by amateurish neophytes whose policies would run counter to the interests of the practicing pros.

I've always felt grateful that SFWA granted me active membership, and as long as I don't write more science fiction I intend to hold my peace about its policies. Still, I resent Pournelle's implication that people who don't publish SF regularly are, ipso facto, fools who would run the organization into the ground, and I jolly well won't vote for a rule change that would deprive me of the right to vote from then on.

In the early evening I met Filthy Pierre, who sat with his breath-powered keyboard in his lap in the big hallway near the Voodoo Message Board. Filthy said that Timothy Leary had shown up on Thursday to register as a participant and had been asked to prove that he really was Timothy Leary. Probably by the same person who never heard of the Libertarian Futurists.

Bill Ritch and I approached K.T. FitzSimmons yet again; we actually met her in person this time. She finally came through with a slot for the LFS award: Sunday night at 6. Bill hurried off to get fliers printed.

I listened to some of the guest of honor speeches but around 8:30 was seized by a powerful urge to eat and left before Hal Clement spoke. I had supper in a Vie de France in the underground tunnels that radiate out from the Hyatt like tree roots. A woman at the next table had the nerve to – shudder! – speak to a total stranger asking me if I was having a good time and showing me a T-shirt she'd bought in the dealer's room depicting Arnold Schwarzenegger as the shotgun-wielding *Terminator 2*, with the legend, "Hasta la vista, Baby."

Back at the Hyatt I went with Martin Morse Wooster to the Fosfax party. Martin told me the editors had chosen to stop publishing one correspondent's letters because a number of other readers found them offensive. Seems he had murdered his girlfriend and was bragging about it. This had given rise to a pseudo-censorship controversy. I left with three recent issues.

At home Mike was waiting for me, having driven all the way home from Indiana State University in Terre Haute in his well-worn '84 Ford Tempo. I'd been worrying about him in the back of my mind all afternoon. A downer for me this weekend was that he'd be home but I wouldn't be able to spend much time with him. Mike and I had gone together to Confederation, and now I sat up for a couple of hours filling him in on Chicon.

Sound, Wholesome Americans

Saturday morning in the Green Room, where participants hung out between gigs, I talked with John Maddox Roberts about his S.P.Q.R. series of historical mysteries set in ancient Rome. He tries to write twenty pages a day, doesn't start until the deadline is almost upon him, writes the whole novel in about two months and does little or no rewriting. Since it has been taking me about two years to finish a novel, I am envious.

That afternoon I was on a panel entitled "High Weirdness Update" with Philip Jose Farmer, Timothy Leary and Bob Wilson. Again I had that "m" next to my name, and I welcomed it because I expected that the other panelists would be talking about their encounters with consciousness-expanding software, brain machines and virtual reality, whereas I've just been sitting home writing books. It was scheduled for Grand Ballroom A, the largest of the conference rooms, and people told me they expected it to be the best attended of any of the panels.

Wilson and Leary were in town primarily to speak at the Libertarian Party convention, which was happening several blocks away at the Marriott, and I wondered how aware they were that they were expected at the science fiction convention. I figured Farmer would show up, since I was told he'd asked to be on the panel. And another last minute addition to the panel at his request was Jim Frenkel, editor and erstwhile publisher, who had long ago worked on *Illuminatus!* and whose Bluejay Books had published two of Wilson's Historical Illuminati Chronicles. But the panel might consist only of me with no weirdness to talk about and Frenkel and Farmer, whose weirdnesses were an unknown quality to me.

So I was relieved to see Bob Wilson standing by the door to Grand Ballroom A. We hugged each other and he told me Leary, who is about 70 years old, had tired himself out the day before and might or might not come.

The room was packed, with people standing in the back. At 10 after 2 Leary still had not shown up. I decided to start the panel and announced that I would introduce each panelist with a superlative. I called Farmer "the best science fiction writer in America" and Frenkel "the bravest editor of all time." As I was about to turn to Wilson a voice from the rear shouted, "Dr. Leary is coming!" and a moment later another voice called, "Dr. Leary is here!"

Leary strode up the center aisle and by the time he had reached his seat everyone was standing, clapping and cheering. I introduced Leary as "the most important and revolutionary figure of the twentieth century," which he took with becoming modesty, and finally Wilson simply as "a genius."

Weirdness, as expounded by the panelists, turned out to be mostly their observations of domestic and international politics. Wilson declared that he was not anybody's idea of a sound, wholesome American. Farmer said, "I am a sound, wholesome American. I never met anybody else who was, so that makes me the standard."

Leary was full of cheerful energy and kept turning to make warm eye contact with the other panelists as he talked. In his view the USSR was saved from a hard-line Communist takeover by Russian youth, inspired in part by the ideas of the counter-culture that are still reverberating around the world. The three young men killed trying to stop armored vehicles menacing the Russian Parliament were hippies, he declared, and one of them, llya Kreshevsky, had spent his life questioning authority.

After the panel Wilson's fans swarmed around him, and he asked me if we couldn't somehow disappear. I didn't feel critical of him for that; once when overwhelmed by too many admirers Jesus himself vanished. We ducked through a back door that led to the empty hall next door. Thence, moving fast, we headed for Stetson's, a bar in the hotel, where we raised and lowered a few pints of Guinness and had a good talk for a couple of hours.

I called home and Mike said that Frank Robinson had left a message for me. I called Frank in his room and we made a date for dinner. This was unexpected good luck; at the last two Worldcons I'd spent more time trying to find Frank than I had talking with him.

I went down to the Dealer's Room and bought a "Hasta la Vista" T-shirt for Michael, but couldn't find a copy of Frank's new novel *The Dark Beyond the Stars*, which I'd hoped to have him autograph for me. One dealer who'd sold all her copies said she wished she had another fifty. I reported this to Frank, and he was gratified but said Tor just hadn't printed enough copies. He said they'd already had to go back for a second printing. A writer doesn't want his book to be sold out, he wants it to be selling out.

Frank and I and two friends of his had dinner in the Swissotel Hotel, a small luxury hotel connected to the Hyatt by underground passageways. Everywhere in the Swissotel, merry folksy Swiss music plays constantly. After an hour or so you start seeing cuckoos.

We had a good couple of hours of talk, among other topics reminiscing about the Chicago pubic wars, when Frank was the *Playboy* Advisor and one of his advisees was his friend, the editor of Gallery, whose office was right across the street.

"Whatever the fuck you want!"

Sunday I sat in the green room with A.J. and Edna Budrys and Bob Silverberg. Another writer at the table talked about his study of French science fiction, which I gather is in bad shape, partly because French publishers are interested only in American SF and partly because the French stuff is so badly written. These factors, it would seem, are mutually reinforcing. It made me very sad to hear that Isaac Asimov is feeling so poorly these days that he isn't writing, which is like hearing that Niagara Falls has dried up.

I had lunch with Jeanne Cavelos, the editor responsible for Dell's science fiction line, which a few years ago was non-existent except for *Illuminatus!* and is now gradually expanding. She said *Illuminatus!* continues to sell briskly – I wonder whether that would make me a "real" SF writer by Pournelle's standards – and they'd like to see Wilson and me work together again. I told her that seemed like a good idea to me, provided the two of us can get our other commitments out of the way.

After lunch I all but ran, being a little late, to the Marriott for yet another panel with Timothy Leary and Wilson and this time Carl Oglesby, one of the founders of Students for a Democratic Society, the most prominent revolutionary organization of the '60s, on "From the '60s to the '90s." I needn't have hurried; when I got there I found the panel hadn't started and Wilson was chuckling because Don Meinshausen, organizer of the event, had been told it couldn't take place unless he produced a paper authorizing it, which he was having trouble locating.

"Don has to come up with a magic piece of paper or we can't have the panel," Wilson said.

"Typical of the Libertarian Party." Meinshausen found the magic paper, and we looped into a huge hall in which, a short time earlier, the Libertarians had nominated their Presidential and Vice-Presidential candidates. The state placards were still up, and workmen were taking everything apart, stacking folding chairs, sliding movable walls into place, shouting at each other over intercoms. In the midst of this, Carl Oglesby talked about his peregrinations in the '60s that had led him from liberal Democratic politics to S.D.S., ending with his conviction that in the '90s the Libertarian Party represented

S.D.S. grown up and, he hoped, more powerful. Wilson, when his turn came, congratulated Oglesby on giving his talk in the midst of something like an Ionesco play, with the set being torn apart even as the actors carried on.

I reminisced about how I'd discovered the counterculture as editor of Cavalier back in the '60s and made Cavalier the only girlie magazine to publish articles by Leary and Wilson and about Oglesby's early S.D.S.

After our initial presentations, Leary jumped up to respond to a hostile-sounding question: "Now that women have been liberated from being women, can they be liberated to be women?" Leary told about a conference he attended in Barcelona where nine languages were spoken. A French Marxist woman asked sarcastically, "Dr. Leary, now that you have liberated us, what should we do?" and he answered, "Whatever the fuck you want!" which had the nine translators in their glass booths looking at each other in dismay.

I'd seen Leary before but never really met him, and appreciated being able to observe him close up. He displays great charm, energy and quick wit, apparently not at all depleted by his experimentation with drugs or his strenuous life.

Back at Chicon, we Libertarian Futurists gathered at 6 p.m. in the assigned room for the awards ceremony. Suddenly a woman in a black evening dress appeared and demanded that we vacate the room at once. She needed it – right now – for the Chesley Awards, the major honors for SF artists.

The conspiracy or curse or whatever it was had struck the LFS again! On the program the Chesley Awards were scheduled for 7:30, but they expected to have a cocktail reception before the ceremony, and they wanted time to set up the bar and stuff before the reception. We told the Chesley lady we only needed 15 minutes and talked her into going away.

Bill Ritch presented the Hall of Fame Award to a representative of F. Paul Wilson for *An Enemy of the State* and I presented the Prometheus Award to Michael Flynn for *The Kingdom of the Blind.* I said that Flynn's novel dealt with a conflict between free will and historical determinism, and in his acceptance he said he was glad to finally learn what the novel was about.

The Chesley lady interrupted these proceedings after only ten minutes, waving her arms and screeching, but one of our guys flew at her, waving his arms and screeching, and drove her out of the room. We finished the ceremony and dispersed as promised. Martin Morse Wooster had been spreading the word that Golden Apans and their friends would meet after the LFS awards to have dinner together. Eleven of us got together, Bill, Carol, Cosmo, Dave, James, Jeff, Marlin, Nancy, Tom, T Rev and me. As often seems to happen with such large groups, we seemed to spend more time hunting for a place that could accommodate us than we did eating. We ended up in the Hot Dog That Ate Chicago, a fast-food joint decorated in a humorous take-off on the style of the '50s.

I finished up the evening sitting in a circle on the carpet on a lower level of the hotel. T Rev told us about his ideas of God, that he is an audience for whom we perform, or perhaps a performance artist himself. A fellow who sounded suspiciously like an Objectivist told me he had no trouble getting himself to do anything his reason told him he should do; he had lost 150 pounds five years ago and was keeping it off without difficulty. I suggested he write a book – *The Ayn Rand Diet.*

The Cuckoo's Nest

The day started with a heartbreaker. Last spring I'd been invited to VolgaCon in Volgograd, USSR; however, the Russian organizers could not pay my plane fare. I wrote back that I would come if it turned out I could afford the transportation. I asked a bunch of questions about what they'd be wanting me to do when I got there. My earnings were poor over the summer, and I let Volgacon's July 15th deadline for informing them on specific travel plans go by. And they didn't respond to my questions. On August 25th I wrote them a letter telling them that very regretfully I wasn't coming. Monday morning, September 2nd, a woman on the Volgacon committee called to find out when I'd be arriving – having naturally enough not yet received my letter – and I had to break the news to her that I wasn't coming. I felt terrible because I'd disappointed the Russian fans and because I'd missed what would have been, especially at this moment in history, a marvelous experience.

That day my panel was "SF and Fantasy on the Live Theatre Stage." The other panelists were Ann Chancellor, Carol Severance, Gretchen Van Dorn, Grant Carrington, and a scholar who knew a lot about the many science fiction plays of the nineteenth century but whose name got away from me. I talked about the two stage productions of *Illuminatus!* Everyone seemed to agree that you can't do science fiction and fantasy special effects convincingly on the stage these days, but should rely on your imagination and ingenuity to come up with exciting gimmicks that suggest special effects. And trust the imagination of the audience to help you.

My last event was a reading from my own stuff, scheduled for 3 p.m., in the Geneva Room, located between two floors in the Swissotel Hotel. Apparently the only access was a flight of iron stairs that ran past a lot of pipes and wheels and things in a space that looked like the innards of a giant steam-driven cuckoo clock. Merry, folksy Swiss music played constantly.

Considering the obscure location, my not being as well known to the con-goers as many other writers, and the timing

– the afternoon of the last day of the convention – I fully expected to read to an empty room. As it turned out about eight people found their way to me, and I considered myself fortunate. I read the scene from *Illuminatus!* in which Otto Waterhouse kills Milo Flanagan and the scene from *Shaman* in which the band rejects White Bear's vision and decides to raise the war whoop.

After that L. Sprague de Camp came to read. Despite the remote location and the late hour, he drew a pretty big crowd, deservedly so. De Camp's story was about time travel and dinosaurs. My love of science fiction began with an interest in dinosaurs.

And with that I bade hasta la vista to Chicon V. We hadn't had to take to the streets to present the LFS awards, and Wilson and Leary had shown up for the High Weirdness panel. I had spent pleasant hours with Bob Wilson and with Frank Robinson in the same day, had enjoyed myself, hadn't worried too much and even – shudder! – had talked to total strangers.

Indeed do many things come to pass, but generally not the things you expect.

G

Larry T. Shaw, An Appreciation

From issue No. 9 of No Governor, Shea's anarchist fanzine, dated November 1987.

I met Larry Shaw at a gathering of the Hydra Club, a science fiction professionals' association, in 1959. I mentioned that I was looking for a magazine editorial job. He said there was an opening where he worked, a place called Magnum Publications, and suggested I apply for it. I did, and got hired to assist Larry with the two automotive hobby magazines he edited. So Larry gave me my start in the magazine business.

Larry was a soft-spoken, shy man who smoked a strong-smelling pipe and liked extra-dry martinis. He never finished college, but he had educated himself better than many a college graduate I've known. He said little unless he was feeling thoroughly comfortable, but behind those thick glasses his mind was always working, often brilliantly.

Larry was the first person to teach me anything substantial about magazine editing. What it came down to, for Larry, was giving the readers their money's worth. This was a pretty radical idea in the publishing industry. Still is. Most of the publishers and many of the editors we knew preferred to treat magazines as a racket, the idea being to separate the suckers from their money with a minimal investment of one's own. Larry's approach, which he practiced as much as his employers would allow him on the various magazines he edited – *Infinity, Custom Rodder, Car Speed and Style, Cars* – meant trying to create the best magazine his resources would permit.

A lot of publishers and editors don't like the magazines they work on. Some don't like magazines, period. Larry believed an editor should like magazines in general and especially his or her own magazine. Editors should also genuinely like the subject matter of their magazines. Larry edited a number of automotive magazines, and he really was interested in cars. He liked cars. Even though he wasn't anything like the Fonzie types who bored and stroked their engines and painted raging flames on their hoods, he could relate to them and respect them.

When I first went to work for him I knew nothing about cars and didn't care about them. By example as much as anything else, Larry taught me to develop an appreciation for the complex and weird-looking machines that filled the pages we edited. I discovered that you can learn to care about a subject you've never thought about before, and I learned how to break through some of the intellectual barriers I'd been hiding behind.

Working together, Larry and I rather rapidly became good friends. We lunched together almost daily at the Mansfield restaurant on 43rd Street between Fifth and Sixth Avenues, where they made good hamburgers and decent drinks. It was a hangout for many people who worked in what we all called the schlock magazine business – the poor man's Algonquin.

Larry also believed that magazines, even schlock magazines, were meant to be read, and that an editor's main job was to fill the magazine with good writing. Good writing, as Larry saw it, should be clear, entertaining, easy to read, grammatically sound, useful and honest.

"I work very hard on transitions," he once told me, a remark typical of his craftsman's approach. A lot of editors worry about leads and endings, but an editor who worries about transitions really cares about his readers. He thought that flashy, chic-looking artwork was secondary in importance to reading matter in magazines, that too much visual dazzlement might even detract from readability.

Honesty was central to his concept of good editing. He hated such common schlock magazine trickery as misleading cover lines, disguising articles that had nothing new to offer with extravagant promises, plugging shoddy products in editorial pages to attract advertising – paying, in general, more attention to the package than to its contents. In line with that he believed a magazine's contributors, writers, artists, photographers, should be paid as much as the publisher could possibly afford, thereby enabling a magazine to get the best available work into its pages. This was another radical idea. Since it's easier to find contributors who will work for next to nothing than it is to get bargain prices out of paper manufacturers, printers or typesetters, most publishers thought last of all about paying contributors.

Larry helped me, not just with my magazine writing, but with my fiction in general. As always, I was writing fiction on the side, and Larry gave me the benefit of his advice and criticism. He lent me a copy of *The Mystery Writer's Handbook.* I still have it. Though it was compiled in the 50s, it's full of wisdom, particularly an article on plot constructing by Lester Dent, one of the great pulp masters, every word of which is pure gold.

Through Larry I met another good friend, who also spent an inordinate amount of time trying to teach me to write better fiction, Algis Budrys – A.J. A.J.'s home was in the wilds of New Jersey and he needed a place to stay to be close to the publishing action in New York. While he was a house guest of the Shaws he wrote his masterpiece, *Rogue Moon*, which is dedicated, in tribute to Larry's devotion to craft, "To Larry Shaw, Journeyman Editor."

Every so often Larry would come out with pithy utterances, which, with becoming lack of modesty, he would refer to as "Shaw's Laws." They were not the Oscar Wilde sort of one-liners, but they would state a useful observation in a clear and memorable way. Probably the noblest of these was, "People are all we have to work with." He said this in defense of anarchism, but the more I think about it the more profound and all-embracing it seems. Another, in reference to fanzines, was, "Short and frequent is better than long and infrequent." I still try to be guided by that one. One time in the early 60s after a rash of short-lived humor magazines, including Hugh Hefner's *Trump,* appeared and then quickly folded, Larry said flatly, "Humor magazines fail." Of course, that was before the *National Lampoon.* Indeed, there might be exceptions to a Shaw's Law, but you ignored it at your peril.

Besides Shaw's Laws, Larry knew all sorts of other important things. For instance, it was he who first pointed out that the Green Hornet is the Lone Ranger's grandnephew.

Larry was the first person I ever met who unabashedly called himself an anarchist. This came as a surprise, because a gentle, rational person like himself didn't fit the bomb-throwing madman stereotype at all. His anarchism grew out of his trust in people and his belief that most of the harm done by institutions came about when people were unwilling to trust one another.

He introduced me to other gentle, rational anarchists. It was from Larry that I learned about the Industrial Workers of the World. He was an I.W.W. member. He didn't convert me, or even try very hard, but he prepared the ground for my adopting anarchism some years later. Another mental barrier breached. Again, by example as much as by argument.

Larry was a quintessential science fiction fan. He had come to New York City from Schenectady in the 1940s and had been a member of that legendary science fiction fan club, the Futurians. He was editor of *Infinity*, a respected magazine that flourished and perished along with the SF boom of the late 50s. He was always working on one fanzine or another.

Larry and his wife Noreen were among the founders of the Fanoclasts, and with their encouragement I boldly went deeper into fannish realms than I'd ever gone before. He introduced me to the fascinating people who were active in New York fandom in the 60s and got me to read fanzines from the stacks he kept on his coffee table. He even inspired me to start a publication of my own, a mimeographed literary magazine called *The Scene*, ancestral to the journal you hold in your hands.

I spent a lot of time visiting with Larry and Noreen in their homes in and around New York City on the Lower East Side, on Staten Island, then Westchester, then Long Island. I watched their family grow with the birth of Mike and then Steve.

Our careers took us out of New York to different destinations, me moving first to Los Angeles, then to Chicago and the Shaws moving first to Chicago, then to Los Angeles.

Neither one of us was all that great a letter writer, and when I heard from the Shaws it was most often a birthday card from Noreen. Sometimes even a Saint Patrick's Day card. Then in 1984 I got a letter from Noreen telling me that Larry had cancer of the throat. I started writing longer letters, more frequently. I thought of writing to tell Larry what an influence he'd been on me – something like what I'm writing here – but I felt such a letter might read too much like a farewell to a dying friend and be depressing or discouraging to him. Anyway, I was glad that Harlan Ellison and Robert Silverberg arranged for Larry to hear at the 1984 Worldcon in Los Angeles how much people appreciated his contributions to science fiction.

In April, 1985 Noreen called to tell me that Larry had died. Something of him lives on in the many people whose minds and lives he touched.

And I've thought many times since then how important it is never to miss a chance to tell people what they mean to you.

Ayn Rand Is Still At Work

As it did for many thousands of people, reading Ayn Rand's *The Fountainhead* in my teens programmed me in ways I still don't fully understand. I read *The Fountainhead* five times during my college years and several more times after that. Rand's software seems not to have been fully compatible with my operating system, though, and I never succumbed totally to her influence.

I did for a time think that *The Fountainhead* held more truth about politics, creativity, economics, esthetics and philosophy than anything else I had ever read. And I fell in love for several months with a young woman, at least in part because she reminded me of Dominique Francon.

But I also found much to admire in Gail Wynand and even in Ellsworth Toohey, which was surely not the author's intention.

One of the many interesting things I learned from *The Passion of Ayn Rand* by Barbara Branden (Doubleday, 442 pages, $19.95) was that the character of Ellsworth Toohey was largely modeled after Harold Laski, the influential British Socialist theoretician, whom Rand saw lecture at the New School for Social Research in the late 1930s.

I eagerly read *Atlas Shrugged* soon after it came out, and though its storytelling qualities held me, I was somewhat disappointed in it. It seemed to me longer than it needed to be and too pat a demonstration of Ayn Rand's philosophy, and so I found it less enthralling as a piece of fiction than *The Fountainhead*. There were, for instance, no interesting villains in it. All the bad guys in *Atlas Shrugged* were wimps or nonentities. I suspect that Rand decided that from a propaganda standpoint she had made a mistake in creating such fascinating characters as Toohey and Wynand as examples of wickedness, and she carefully avoided it in *Atlas*.

This may have been better propaganda, but surely it is unsound political reasoning. One can imagine the masses succumbing to the impressive demagoguery of a Toohey, but no matter how low one's opinion of the American public, it is difficult to believe it would grant power to ciphers like Wesley Mouch.

I did find *Atlas* full of good lines and good ideas, though, and I continued to take an interest in Ayn Rand. I fully agreed with her devotion to individual freedom and her belief that reason is the most reliable guide to understanding our lives and the world and to make personal decisions. I eventually came to agree with her materialism and her rejection of organized religion.

But from these premises I found myself coming to conclusions that often differed greatly from Rand's. For example, whereas she supported people like Goldwater, Nixon and Ford, I moved steadily leftward from liberalism to democratic socialism to anarchism. So it was from a distance I followed the growth of the organized Objectivist movement and the steady spread of Rand's influence throughout the '60s. I wondered who this Nathaniel Branden was, with a name too like an Ayn Rand hero's to be real. I wondered if she'd had this young spokesman of hers manufactured to her specifications in some Bavarian laboratory.

As an editor at *Playboy* (from 1967 to 1977) I was aware of, and mostly approved, Rand's extensive influence on Hugh Hefner's thinking. One installment of the "*Playboy* Philosophy" could almost have been written by Rand. But I felt that swallowing the Objectivist line whole, as some did, was bound to have a pernicious effect.

I read much of what Rand published after *Atlas Shrugged*, and I found myself accepting some of her ideas and rejecting others but always very interested in what she had to say. Because of the initial impact on me of *The Fountainhead,* she was never a person I could neglect. A few months after she died I took great pleasure in reading, and writing about, her posthumously published *Philosophy: Who Needs It.*

• • •

The attraction was still strong enough to make me buy and read Barbara Branden's *The Passion of Ayn Rand*. I got almost as much enjoyment and intellectual stimulation from reading it as I would have from a new Ayn Rand novel.

Part of the fascination in reading and thinking about Ayn Rand, I must admit, lies in asking oneself where and why someone who was right about so many things went wrong. What can be learned from her mistakes?

It is ironic that the woman who asserted that the purpose of life is individual happiness should herself have had, so much of the time, an unhappy life. Not that she had more than her share of unhappiness, really, though her misery sometimes took rather dramatic forms. The irony lies in the fact that her philosophy, which was supposed to guide people to happiness, served her and others who wholeheartedly adopted it so poorly.

Barbara Branden, erstwhile wife to Nathaniel, tells of one intelligent and talented young woman, accepted into Rand's inner circle, who was subjected to a ruthless psychological cross-examination by Nathaniel Branden with Rand looking on and applauding. This young woman later wrote, "I have not been this unhappy since I was a kid, when I used to look out the window and calm down by watching the stars. But then I had the promise of a brilliant, beautiful future . . . I'm afraid to care about anything, because I'm afraid I'll get all mixed up again . . . Yet I will always remember the day I met Ayn as one of the happiest days of my life." And perhaps the last happy day. As Branden tells it, no one who became deeply involved with Objectivism obtained the freedom and joy that Rand's ideology promised when first glimpsed in the novels.

Rand could think and write about happiness in the abstract and portray it memorably in fiction, but she does not seem to have been capable of experiencing much concrete enjoyment. Even when she had the most reason to be happy in her own achievement – surely the very essence of being a Rand hero – she had a way of falling into a funk.

Writing itself was an ordeal for Rand, although it was at the same time the whole meaning of her life. One of the most rewarding aspects of *The Passion of Ayn Rand* is the wealth of information it gives about Rand's working methods as a novelist, including actual glimpses of the thought processes that went into the creation of her most memorable characters and scenes. Here, as in other aspects of Rand's life, her philosophical outlook seems to have made the work of writing much more painful for her than it might otherwise have been.

Many writers allow their stories to develop spontaneously; writers often report that when their work is going well the characters seem to come to life, and the writer merely reports their doings. Writers often make their literary decisions by a non-analytical process in which years of experience and practice come together in what might appear to be a snap judgment.

Rand had to work out every detail of her novels consciously and in advance of the actual writing. Branden writes, "To work primarily by 'feel,' by inspiration, was abhorrent to her; as in every area of her life, she had to know what she intended, she had to remain in conscious control, the work had to be an intellectual, not an emotional process."

Rand wrote two lesser novels and two major ones and largely exhausted her creative energies in their production. Writing those novels took so much out of her because she was fighting herself every step of the way. Branden writes, "She was rarely solely creator, she was editor as well, during the very act of creation, often devising each paragraph, each sentence, each phrase, sometimes each word, by conscious, rational calculation." The tension between her creative impulses and her analytical faculty must have been enormous, something like the tension along the fault line that produces a major earthquake.

This is not to suggest that the method of other writers was "right" and Rand's was "wrong." It just shows that the stress Rand's philosophy put on conscious reasoning required her to work somewhat against the grain of the creative process as usually experienced. And from Branden's account Rand found writing an utterly draining process: "Sometimes she would come out of her study at midnight after fifteen uninterrupted hours at work, her body aching from strain, looking frighteningly exhausted – having written that whole day and evening perhaps a page, perhaps only a paragraph."

Surprisingly enough, the part of *Atlas Shrugged* that was hardest for her to write was the part most frequently criticized as an instance of the author's self-indulgence – John Galt's 60-page radio speech. In this speech Rand intended to sum up her entire philosophy. One might think that such a writing job would be a pleasure and a breeze, an interlude of unalloyed self-expression (it would be for me), but it took Rand two whole years to write that speech. She described it as two years of "pure hell."

The great difficulty for her, it seems, was getting the philosophy right and at the same time casting it in the form of "a rousing speech." According to Branden, "Rand suffered both physical and mental agonies in her struggle." Frequently Rand's husband, Frank O'Connell, "would find her slumped over her desk as if she were unable to rise again; she would emerge from her study with new deep lines on her brow and her body sagging with weariness."

After *Atlas Shrugged* was finished, published with her insistence without editorial changes, and became a huge best seller, she became deeply depressed and stayed that way for two years. That the success of her writing did not allow her to feel the satisfaction she deserved was doubtless a symptom of unresolved, unrecognized emotional conflicts. These same conflicts caused her philosophy to develop as it did, and her philosophy in turn made her psychological problems even more insoluble.

On the philosophical level she seems to have arrived at her first principles quite early and spent the rest of her life drawing further inferences from them, without ever seeing the need to change them. Such consistency does make for a certain kind of intellectual strength. Conservatives like William Buckley, who believe that all the major truths were discovered long ago, have it too. But it is the strength of a coral reef, largely composed of hardened materials no longer living, rather than of a mobile, adaptable, evolving organism. Those rigid principles made it terribly difficult for Rand to make friends and made it nearly impossible for her to keep those she did make.

In the 1970s Rand asked a friend, "Do you know what it's like to have no one to look up to – always to look down?" With very little effort one can think of dozens of people alive in the 1970s (the reader is invited to make his or her own list) who would have been Ayn Rand's intellectual equals or superiors. She might have associated with many whose intelligence and accomplishments she could have admired, and who would have treated her with equal respect, whose differences of opinion could have challenged and stimulated her. But she was incapable of forming a close friendship with anyone who disagreed with her, even on minor issues.

Rand seems to have felt that people were intelligent to the extent that they agreed with her – up to a point. That point would be reached when she recognized that they were merely repeating her ideas. As the originator of these ideas, it would follow, she herself must be the smartest person of all, from which position she could only look down on the rest of the world.

If disagreements developed on first meeting someone, she could not form a friendship with that person. Robert Anton Wilson, my friend and co-author of *Illuminatus!,* has described to me being invited into Rand's home during the '60s, after Rand heard him say some complimentary things about her writing on the Long John radio talk show in New York. Wilson's wife, Arlen, was shown to a chair in a distant corner of Rand's apartment. Rand's passive husband, Frank O'Connor, dozed in another chair. Wilson was seated facing a semicircle of Objectivist heavies, Rand in the middle, and subjected to an inquisition about his philosophical, political, economic and scientific views. Eyeball to eyeball, Wilson and Rand saw eye to eye on so few issues that he was not invited back.

Nothing so infuriated her as the suggestion that she had made any mistakes. I can't remember a single instance in Branden's book in which Rand admits to having made an intellectual error. She would frequently declare herself wrong about people; she was constantly breaking with friends who had the temerity to differ with her. She would then claim that her former high opinion of them had been incorrect, but she would often imply that this was more because they had deceived her than that she had made an error.

Her closest friends in her mature years were, inevitably, not peers, but her two most enthusiastic young disciples, Barbara and Nathaniel Branden. Nathaniel was so enthusiastic that he changed his name from Blumenthal to Branden, the latter being derived from "ben Rand," which means "son of Rand" in Hebrew.

Nathaniel was the only person Rand accepted as an intellectual equal. Because they were the people closest to her, the explosive breakup of Ayn Rand and the Brandens was of far greater significance for Objectivism than the usual casting out of heretics that occurred regularly in Rand's circle. The Brandens were her chief apostles, the very first Ayn Rand activists. It was they who created the primary means, other than Rand's own novels, for the propagation of Objectivism: *The Objectivist Newsletter* and the Nathaniel Branden Institute. Together with Rand herself, they were the chief exemplars of the Objectivist lifestyle.

But these three key figures of the Objectivist movement acted in such a totally non-exemplary fashion as to raise fundamental doubt about the validity of Objectivism. If Rand's philosophy didn't work for these people, didn't prevent them from making a mess of their lives and didn't extricate them from the mess as it developed, for whom could it work?

The five-sided relationship formed by Rand, the Brandens, the devastated Frank O'Connor, and Patrecia Gullison, who later married Nathaniel, turned into a disaster not merely because of what the participants did, but because of their attitudes toward what they did. And, of course, because of the attitude of others in the Objectivist movement as bits of the story leaked out.

Had Objectivism been more the rationalistic celebration of individual happiness it was proclaimed to be, the Rand-Branden affair might have shaken it, but need not have destroyed it. Rand had the intellectual and moral courage to see that she needed a loving sexual relationship with Nathaniel Branden to enrich and complete her life, and to ask for it. Frank O'Connor acquiesced in this, but no one seems to know how he felt about it. Barbara Branden tells us she agreed also, because, reasoning as an Objectivist, she told herself she should accept this as the union of two superior beings, like Roark and Dominique or Galt and Dagny. In her heart she was screaming out against it, but as an Objectivist she had learned to pay no attention to her heart.

In other circumstances it might have been possible for Barbara and Frank to have become emotionally, as well as intellectually, reconciled to the affair. But this would have required their feelings be taken into account, taken seriously, dealt with compassionately, not suppressed.

Another attitude that made the situation seem worse was Barbara's feeling, and later Nathaniel's, that there was something fundamentally wrong with a younger man's having an affair with an older woman. Branden himself, in an essay defending himself after the affair became public, ended by urging the impossibility of a man having a "romantic relationship" with a woman 25 years his senior. Their affair began in 1954 when Rand was 49 and Branden 24. If a 49-year-old male novelist started a "romantic relationship" (to use this favorite Randian term) with a 24-year-old female admirer, the shock value would be far from equivalent.

When Nathaniel's feelings for Rand declined and he began an affair with another woman, he was unable to tell Rand what was happening. In part, this was because he knew she would never accept his preference for a woman she considered her intellectual inferior. Eventually, Barbara felt forced to break the news to Rand herself. In her jealous rage she broke with Nathaniel, and this came to destroy the movement she and he had founded together.

Had all of those people been able to recognize their attachment to the Judeo-Christian ethic of monogamy and to look at that ethic with real objectivity, they might have been able to accept one another's actions and feelings. And then, had knowledge of their affairs come out into the open, they might have been able to say, "Yes, we have done these things. We are entitled to seek happiness, and that includes sexual fulfillment, in this imperfect world, in this short life. We have tried very hard not to hurt one another."

One might speculate that had things come into the open in that way, Objectivism, instead of falling apart, might have found itself marching in step with the sexual revolution of the '60s and '70s, and its strength might have grown tenfold.

But it was not to happen, because the creator of Objectivism was unable to deal rationally with sexual jealousy. And because there was no place for kindness in the Objectivist lifestyle, but plenty of room for hate.

Of course, it is unfair to judge Rand and the Brandens harshly because they weren't as enlightened as one thinks they should have been. Hardly anybody is. One judges them only insofar as they asked to be judged. They set themselves up as models, established rigorous standards, and judged others by them. They made others feel ashamed of having human failings. That is why it is important to know that they had serious failings of their own.

• • •

Branden does a marvelous job, without stinting her admiration or her compassion, of showing how the experiences and the personality of the philosopher herself led to the fundamental weaknesses in Ayn Rand's philosophy.

Doctrines that take moral positions frequently become very powerful and influential. Probably the greatest single reason for Rand's popularity was that she made a convincing case for selfish, egotistical behavior being morally good. She may have liberated as many people from guilt about selfish feelings and acts as Alfred Kinsey did from guilt about sexual feelings and acts.

Just as *Playboy* achieved its popularity by offering a moral validation for sex outside of marriage, so Rand won her following by offering a moral validation for the pursuit of one's self-interest. In both cases, people had been made to feel guilty by a standard that required them to deny their own natures.

By giving people a rationale for freeing themselves from these guilt feelings, both Rand and Hefner performed a great service. But they, or their apostles, also caused more suffering when their respective revolutions became compulsory. Hefner's philosophy was sometimes taken to mean that anybody who is not engaging in plentiful sexual activity outside of marriage must be a pitiful neurotic. Rand and her followers were not content to make a case for selfishness; they insisted as well that all altruistically motivated human behavior was evil.

Rand seemed to see evil in the mere fact of people joining together for any purpose. Roark, in *The Fountainhead*, declares that no group, no committee, will ever give him a commission to build a building; add one human being to another, and the judgment of the two together is likely to be inferior to that of either separately. And yet, with amazing irony, *The Fountainhead* ends with Roark's great act of self-assertion – dynamiting Cortlandt Homes – being validated by the collective decision of a jury. And, in writing the novel that most fully expresses her philosophy, *Atlas Shrugged*, Rand has her heroes establish their rightful place in the world by means of the quintessential collective weapon of the labor movement – the strike.

It may be that, having suffered under a Marxist government until she was 21, Ayn Rand's fantasy was to become an anti-Marx, to develop a philosophy that would destroy the Marxism that made her youth so miserable. This would mean, of course, that hers must be a philosophy armed. It must be designed to destroy the ideas of those who contradict it and to purge impure influences and heresies from the minds of its supporters.

It is credible that Objectivism might be a serious antagonist for Marxism. Objectivism is neither good science nor good philosophy, but neither is Marxism. But, as with all antagonisms, the harder one fights, the more one comes to resemble one's enemy. I get the feeling that while explicitly Rand was a thoroughgoing libertarian, on an unconscious and emotional level she was carrying on a flirtation with a totalitarianism that ultimately proved deadly to the achievement of her purposes.

Like many revolutions – again, like the revolutions inspired by Marx – Objectivism threw open the doors of one prison, only to lead its followers into a deeper dungeon.

An ideology that insists that there is only one right answer to every question is inevitably led to an authoritarian stance. No matter how much it encourages individual thought, in the end it will condemn any thinking that does not arrive at the conclusion it approves. Objectivism treated its disciples as Rand treated her friends; they were expected to agree in every tiniest degree and particular or be cast out.

Another feature of Objectivism that pushed it in the direction of authoritarianism was its ferocious moralism. More and more, as the movement developed a head of steam, those who differed with Ayn Rand were seen, not just as mistaken, but as evil. This applied not only to religious leaders, Left-wing politicians, and modern artists, but also to anybody within the movement who departed in any way from Ayn Rand's views. Having established that her own opinions were not only right but good and that all alternative opinions were not only incorrect but evil, Rand became as assured of her infallibility as any guru, ayatollah or pope.

Rand's opinion of her philosophical heft was so exalted that she declared Aristotle was the only philosopher who had anything to teach her. She was this century's best-known Aristotelian philosopher (Mortimer Adler running a close second). Her logic was strictly of the either/or variety. A thing was either A or not A. Never partly A and partly not A. "Both/and" was anathema to Ayn Rand. She seems never to have heard of – or to have rejected – the non-Aristotelian logic of Alfred Korzybski's General Semantics. She seems, like many another Eurocentric cultural chauvinist, to be unaware of the philosophies arising from the religions of Asia.

Her choice of Aristotle as the greatest philosopher of all time is significant because Aristotle's philosophy formed the basis for another great totalitarian system – medieval Scholastic philosophy. Like Objectivism, Scholasticism was a philosophy designed to attack and defend – to defend the doctrines of the Catholic church and to demolish all points of view it identified as error. The Schoolmen devoted their careers to disputation, sometimes with the pen, sometimes face to face in lecture halls.

Like Objectivism, Scholasticism tended to be a philosophy built in a vacuum. Neither philosophy was very interested in empiricism, in firsthand experience, in the gathering of facts, in experiment. The creators of both philosophies worked in cloistered surroundings deducing their truths from axiomatic first principles. They considered themselves to have established the truth if they were able to beat opponents in debate.

Like the Scholastics, Rand declared reason to be humanity's highest natural faculty. The Scholastics made faith, supernaturally conferred by divine grace, superior to reason. For Rand reason alone was supreme. For Rand, this meant that one could and should act strictly in accordance with reason at all times. She seemed at times to believe that reason was mankind's only faculty. Emotion was never to be admitted as a guide to conduct. Rand and her followers were forever tormenting themselves for not being as rational as they thought they should be. Which is a very irrational attitude.

To see the error in rationalism as Objectivism taught it is not necessarily to place a lower value on reason. It is reasonable to recognize the limitations of reason. Rand's major mistakes were not caused by trying to be reasonable, but rather by not being reasonable enough to see that reason isn't everything. It is unreasonable, for example, to despise emotion and to refuse to take one's feelings into account in making decisions. And emotion so treated exacts vengeance by exerting an influence on decisions that the would-be rationalist is unaware of and therefore powerless to defend against.

For example, Rand convinced herself that her refusal to give up her two-pack-a-day smoking in the face of her doctor's warnings was perfectly rational, because "statistics aren't proof." Before she would quit smoking, she told the doctor, "You have to give me a rational explanation."

Eventually she encountered the ultimate empirical argument – lung cancer. She bravely endured the surgery and the subsequent pain, but was unable to come to terms with what had happened to her. According to Barbara Branden, Rand had a tendency to believe that people contracted cancer and other serious illnesses as a result of "bad premises." Since she had no "bad premises," this should not have happened to her. Furthermore, although she had frequently declared to her followers and students that the evidence for smoking being dangerous was "unscientific and irrational," she now refused to publicly announce that she had developed lung cancer or even that she had stopped smoking.

Cigarettes were remarkably important to Rand as props and symbols. One thinks of scene after scene in her novels in which a style of smoking is used to characterize someone or a cigarette serves to intensify drama. Cigarettes with the dollar sign stamped on them keep turning up in *Atlas Shrugged.* One of Dagny Taggart's important character tags was her cigarette holder. Cigarettes smoked in a long black holder were to Rand what a corncob pipe was to Douglas MacArthur. Another irony: A cigarette holder was also a major prop for Franklin D. Roosevelt, whose policies Rand loathed.

Many students of Objectivism made a point of smoking with the panache of Rand's heroes and heroines, and many of them were influenced by her rejection of the medical warnings against smoking. She never shared with them the full truth of what she learned about smoking, just as she never shared with them the full truth of her happiness and unhappiness in sex and love. To a great extent Objectivism was a movement built on illusions.

Branden is very moving as she describes the magic effects on those who were the most drawn to Rand's philosophy, with its authoritarianism masked as individualism:

"Those who accepted the package were on their way to becoming true believers, growing self-alienated and alienated from others, intellectually rigid, guilty over their failures, quick to judge and accuse others. It was the path that had been followed by those of us in the circle they were expected to emulate, as they moved from the ecstasy of learning their own powers and the power of reason – to the agony of grasping their supposed failures and flaws. And psychological problems and inadequacies – and then back to the ecstasy – and then back again in the agony, in a never-ending cycle of pleasure and pain, until at the end of the path pain became the dominant emotion."

It was "those of us in the circle they were expected to emulate," especially the Brandens and Rand herself, who were hurt most by the paradoxes of Objectivism. The inner circle may have deceived their followers by posing as perfect people, but Objectivism was not a movement in which the leaders flourished at the expense of the followers. The leaders suffered most of all.

It has become a popular pastime to label any unusual movement or organization as a "cult," thereby implying that its members are the sort of people who try to swindle gullible passersby in airports, believe that the Queen of England is a dope dealer, and are equally ready to marry a total stranger or drink cyanide at their leader's command. Is it fair to call Objectivism a cult?

Barbara Branden argues that Objectivism does not deserve to be called a cult because, in spite of Ayn Rand's authoritarian character, most of those who participated in the Objectivist movement were sincerely dedicated to individualism and reason. After the collapse of the movement, she says, its members for the most part remained individualists and rationalists and did not seek other gurus to tell them what to think and do.

If, however, a cult is an organization that coalesces around a quasi-deified leader and prescribes every detail of its members' lives – from their choices of lovers or spouses to how they should vote, what books they should read, what music they should prefer, and what kind of painting they should appreciate – then Objectivism was, when it fell apart, well on its way to becoming a cult. Its members were rationalists whose reasoning was condemned if it did not lead to the correct conclusions, individuals whose deviations were punished with ostracism.

It is a blessing that the organized Objectivist movement collapsed when it did. Many impressionable young people were probably saved from a great deal of suffering.

• • •

Happily, no one has to accept the whole Randian system to derive inspiration or enlightenment from the works of Ayn Rand. One can reject what is faulty – the authoritarianism, the dogmatism, the one-best-wayism, the very insistence that if you agree with part you must agree with all.

What is left is an assemblage of valuable ideas: That humanity is not depraved and sinful by nature, but a species whose capacity to do good is as infinite as its capacity to imagine good. That reality is not some sort of illusory mush, but facts that can be discovered and shared and relied upon. That we can trust our reason to help us build on what we know already and so guide us to new knowledge. That the wellspring of creativity is individual freedom of choice. That the arts should induce a feeling of love of life in us. That novels should tell good stories. That it is always wrong to initiate the use of force against another person. That the only effective way to change a society is, not through violence, but through influencing the way people think. That we should respect ourselves always and refuse to listen to any preacher or teacher who tries to humiliate us. That we can only love others to the extent that we wholeheartedly love ourselves.

The works of Ayn Rand are a cornucopia of ideas that add to the sum of human happiness, expressed in language that is powerful, memorable, exact and convincing.

In an epilogue to *The Passion of Ayn Rand*, Barbara Branden lists the accomplishments of a multitude of people inspired in one way or another by Ayn Rand's work. Some of this influence found its way into the Reagan administration, where it took the form of advocacy of more freedom in the marketplace, lower taxes, and less government regulations of business. But also, one can hope, those influenced by Rand may have formed a center of opposition within the administration to the religious Right and its crusade against personal freedom.

Rand's ideas were fundamental to the creation of the Libertarian Party and drew many people to the small "l" libertarian movement. Her influence made itself felt as well among anarchists, as distinguished from libertarians, though she herself denounced anarchists.

Illuminatus! is full of large and small tributes to Ayn Rand because Robert Anton Wilson and I so much admired and enjoyed her work. Some of the tributes were satirical, such as the plot summary of a novel called *Telemachus Sneezed*, and Maviss' complaint that she rarely encounters a man "who meets the requirements of my belief system." But some items intentionally acknowledge indebtedness, such as the resemblance of Hagbard Celine to Ragnar Danneskjold of *Atlas Shrugged* and the assertion in *Illuminatus!* that creative freedom is the fountainhead of all human values. I feel honored that *Illuminatus!* has joined *Atlas Shrugged* in the Libertarian Futurist Society's Hall of Fame.

Ayn Rand is still at work in some level in my own mind as a philosophical and literary influence. I try to write novels that resemble those I have enjoyed reading, and for many years *The*

Fountainhead was near the top of my list of all-time favorites. I'm sure that has left its permanent stamp on my work.

Rand's effort to build an all-embracing philosophical system and an organization of true believers may have collapsed like a structure by some visionary architect whose ambition exceeded his technical skill. But there are treasures in the ruins. We are left with the body of Ayn Rand's writings and ideas to experience directly, without the interference of a movement, and to sift through for ourselves, selecting what in our judgment is useful to the building of our personal philosophies of life. And surely in doing that we are being true to what was soundest in Ayn Rand herself.

Toward the end of *The Passion of Ayn Rand,* Barbara Branden raises a very important question that applies not only to Ayn Rand but to many of the people whose achievements we admire:

"And yet, when one looks at the life of Ayn Rand, one must wonder if the dogmatic absolutism of her certainty, the binding conviction of her own rectitude and special place in the world, the callousness of her intolerance for opinions that were not hers, the unwavering assurance that she was alone to know the truth and that others must seek it from her – the eyes that looked neither to the left nor to the right – the savage innocence of her personality – was not the fuel required for the height of achievement she attained. Just as when one looks at history's great achievers one often encounters the desperate loneliness and alienation which is perhaps the emotional price paid by men and women who see farther than their brothers, so one also encounters these qualities of Ayn Rand."

I can't help but feel that if Ayn Rand had ever been able to recognize that she had such serious faults, she would have struggled to overcome them. We all have abilities and we all have flaws, and when we make good use of our abilities it is probably in spite of, and not because of, our flaws. To know Rand as a woman whose personality was tragically warped is to admire her more, seeing what she had to overcome to accomplish as much as she did.

And yet, Barbara Branden's question remains, for each person who cares about Ayn Rand to answer individually.

Judged by her own standard – that a person must be perfectly rational at all times – Ayn Rand was a failure. But judged by any fully rational standard – one that takes the irrational and nonrational into account – her life and work add up to a superb achievement.

Ǥ

Abolish Obscenity Laws

"The fundamental freedoms of speech and press have contributed greatly to the development of our free society and are indispensable to its continued growth. Ceaseless vigilance is the watchword to prevent their erosion by Congress or by the States." This well states the widely-held view that freedom of expression is the single value most vital to this free democratic society. Ironically, the statement comes from Justice William J. Brennan's opinion in Roth v. United States, upholding the right of federal and state governments to exercise censorship in the area of so-called obscenity.

Roth, decided in 1957, is the Supreme Court's Original Sin. It is the fork in the road at which the Court had to choose between rational treatment of erotic literature and giving in to the power of blind bigotry. The Court chose the irrational course. It chose to fly in the face of simple English words: it stated that speech that is obscene is not speech and that the First Amendment's provision that Congress shall make "no law" limiting freedom of speech means that Congress can make "some law" limiting freedom of speech. Only the most powerful pressures, doubtless personal and internal as well as political and social, could make learned men claim that words mean the opposite of what they do mean, in order to defend an irrational conclusion. And the pressures connected with sex in this country have always been among the strongest, the taboos the most inviolable.

I believe that the free exchange of communications should be unrestricted unless there is evidence that a particular communication will cause immediate, tangible injury to an individual or society. I am a relative absolutist on the First Amendment. I accept the need for military censorship in wartime, for regulation of advertising, for libel laws. But these are instances where there is no doubt, no question about the injury that will be done. I am absolute in my conviction that unless clearcut, tangible harm can be proven, there is no justification for limitations on freedom of expression.

When it comes to material dealing with sex, the government, courts and a powerful segment of the populace take a different position. Sexual materials don't ruin anyone's reputation; they don't cheat people out of money; they don't cost lives on a battlefield. But sexual materials are condemned without a trial. They are condemned even though there is not one shred of scientific evidence that they cause any harm.

There is no evidence of a cause-and-effect relationship between erotic materials and behavior seen as socially disruptive. Frequently the behavior judged antisocial is merely something pro-censorship people see as sinful, such as masturbation or non-marital intercourse.

Another alleged reason for suppressing erotic materials is the belief that it is proper and necessary for the law to uphold certain standards of what is called public morality. Apparently upholding public morality means that the law should take a stand against sin, even when it is not possible or desirable to enforce the law effectively, even when the behavior in question is harmless or trivial, and even when a large sector of the populace does not consider the activity a sin. According to one widely-held religious tradition, permitting oneself to be sexually aroused by viewing erotica is a serious sin. According to this same tradition, most of the conduct portrayed in erotic films, magazines and books is itself sinful. What censorship boils down to, then, is an effort to impose this morality, religious rather than political or scientific in origin, on our reading and viewing. Obviously, this is a violation of the principle of separation of church and state.

It is true that, in some sense, all laws are based on some moral or ethical values. But when we are trying to create a free, yet unified, society out of people adhering to many different beliefs, it is necessary for laws to be based on practical considerations that can be factually demonstrated. We know that murder and stealing injure people and threaten our social and economic order. We know that sexual and racial discrimination injure individuals and deprive society of human resources. Laws dealing with these matters have some basis in pragmatic social utility. The fact that we may consider such laws to be also morally worthwhile should be secondary and subject to a great deal of disagreement. Hundreds of years of bloody religious wars and persecutions should have taught us the unwisdom of trying to establish a state religion or an official moral code.

The narrow moralism underlying censorship was revealed in a courtroom scene made by a Nashville district attorney in the case of a bookstore owner charged with selling obscenity. A defense witness, a married librarian, testified that she did not believe an erotic magazine was in violation of community standards. The prosecutor asked the lady at what age she had begun sexual intercourse and whether she had practiced oral sex. In response to the defense objections to this line of questioning, he declared:

"She has testified that this filthy thing right here is community standards in this community. She has testified that her understanding of community standards is based on her personal experience. I want to know what she has experienced.

I want to know if she is a prostitute. I want to know if she has experienced oral sex."

Doubtless there are those for whom a witness' admission that she engaged in oral sex, even in the sanctity of the marriage bed, would be enough to discredit her. She made no such admission, but sadly the prosecution won the case.

Each group of believers or unbelievers has every right to adhere to moral rules of their own choosing. People even have every right to abstain from oral sex, as long as they do so in private, have the consent of their partners and do not injure others.

But the only guarantee that each of us will be free to follow morality of our choice is for the practitioners of all moral codes to be equally free. And this, in turn, requires that the law attempt as far as possible to be morally neutral. A religious organization has every right to condemn oral sex as a perversion and a sin, but for the law to condemn oral sex – or any other harmless sexual activity – is a perversion of justice.

I'm confident that time and history are on the side of freedom in this controversy, and I expect obscenity laws will be abolished when enough of us realize that there is no rational or factual basis for them.

(A portion of the speech delivered to the Individual Rights and Responsibilities Section at the American Bar Association meeting in Chicago. Shea at the time was a senior editor of Playboy.)

Ɠ

From Catholicism to Zen

The Association for Consciousness Exploration, based in the Cleveland, Ohio, area, was founded in 1983, provided programming that explored "magic, mind-sciences, alternative lifestyles, comparative religion/spirituality, entertainment, holistic healing, and related subjects." It brought in speakers such as Robert Shea, Robert Anton Wilson and Timothy Leary.

One of the group's leaders was Jeff Rosenbaum, who died in 2014. According to another ACE leader, Joseph Rothenberg, Rosenbaum introduced Robert Shea to his third wife, author and scholar Patricia Monaghan, at an ACE event.

Rosenbaum also recorded, edited, preserved and distributed an audio recording, "A Meeting With Robert Shea," which was recorded in 1992. Below is an excerpt from that recording. It is included here with Rothenberg's permission.

Robert Anton Wilson and Robert Shea were both former Catholics who left the faith, but while Wilson left the church at an early age, Shea was an adult when he became an ex-Catholic. Here, he describes how he left the church and acquired a strong interest in Zen Buddhism.

[This chapter is a transcription from an audio file, and so may have some odd grammar in places that were part of natural speech patterns. – Ed.]

I began reading works by Alan Watts, Aldous Huxley, and Eugen Harigel, among others. At that time, there weren't many resources available, but I was drawn to these ideas. Despite my attraction to them, I struggled to understand how to apply these concepts in my life. This marked the beginning of a long process of exploration and understanding. I was also navigating my identity as a practicing Orthodox Catholic, which complicated my relationship with Buddhism.

When I fully commit to a belief system, I tend to embrace it wholeheartedly. At that time, my Catholic faith was my primary belief, making it difficult to reconcile with Buddhist teachings. For me, Buddhism had to remain an academic pursuit rather than a spiritual one. Unlike some of my peers, such as Thomas Merton and Dom Aylward-Graham, who found ways to integrate these philosophies, I felt a conflict that prevented me from doing the same.

One of the appealing aspects of Zen Buddhism is its adaptability. It is undogmatic and allows for the coexistence of various philosophical beliefs. However, this raises questions about the value of attachment to other dogmas or moral codes. What attracted me to Zen was the emphasis on action and doing rather than overthinking. It encourages one to act without the burden of self-criticism, which is particularly liberating for those of us who tend to overanalyze our thoughts and actions.

I mean, I'm the kind of guy, if somebody comes in and robs my apartment, I think, now, I wonder why he did that. I wonder what his problem was, that he needed money, that he had to take all my stuff. And I always have this problem of psyching myself up to get mad and do something about it. So naturally, the result is that I admire people who are people of immediate and decisive action, people like the samurai. When I read about the samurai, and so many of the samurai when Zen came to Japan, it's very hard to reconcile their practices with the teachings of nonviolence and ahimsa, which I think was the original word, harmlessness. It seems contradictory that such a philosophy could be the favorite religion for so many of the Japanese samurai, except that conceivably it was a matter of a code. You know, you don't go around chopping just anybody's head off, but if you're really a good warrior, you restrict yourself to practicing and competing with other warriors.

One of my favorite movies is, have you all seen the *Samurai Trilogy*? It stars Toshiro Mifune as probably the greatest Japanese swordsman, a man named Miyamoto Musashi. Musashi was fascinating because he was a sort of Leonardo da Vinci of samurai. He wrote poetry, he wrote philosophy, he was a sculptor, he was a painter, and he was also head and shoulders above any other samurai of his time. This was a time after the Tokugawa took over in Japan and the samurai no longer really had much of a function because the entire country had been pacified by the Tokugawa shogunate. That was the period when Japan was isolated from about 1600 down to the 1850s when the United States acted out its karma, having by that time destroyed the Indians. It was our turn, and it was our karmic destiny to open up Japan, to encourage Japan to come out into the world and participate in the 19th and 20th century world. We're still paying the price for that.

So anyway, Musashi was so good that there's one scene where he's in an inn and he's eating rice, and there are flies in the rice or there are flies flying around the rice. These low-life types are creeping up on him because they don't know who he is, but they figure they're going to beat him up and take his money. He's sitting there with chopsticks eating the rice, and then these flies start bothering him. So he starts plucking the flies right out of the air with the chopsticks.

And all those people who were going to attack him creep away again. But I guess the reason why I mention this is that throughout the three movies, there is another layer to the story. While he is kind of establishing his reputation as the greatest swordsman in Japan, he is taught by a monk. He learns everything from this monk, not in terms of fighting techniques, but his whole philosophy comes from him. The monk starts his teaching by trapping Musashi and hauling him up with a rope around his waist, leaving him dangling there for a couple of days until he finally promises to listen.

At this point, Musashi is kind of a wild man, and the monk tames him, saying that if he listens to what he has to say, then he will be fed and let down. This other fellow, Sasaki, is introduced as a rival, but we don't know yet if he is the greatest swordsman of all time. Samurai simply wandered around the country competing with one another because there wasn't anything else for them to do. By the third movie, Musashi and Sasaki finally meet, and you can watch all three movies in one night, as each one is about 90 minutes long.

The first movie covers Musashi's early life, while the second one depicts the middle stages when he builds his reputation. In the third movie, he and his rival meet on an island under the sponsorship of a local daimyo. They fight, and the fight lasts about 10 seconds. Sasaki is standing there smiling when it's all over, but then he just keels over because something happened so fast that you can't even see it. Musashi has defeated him, and he gets into a boat rowed by a philosophical old boatman.

Toshiro Mifune is such a wonderful actor, and in this scene, he is sitting in the boat weeping, sobbing uncontrollably because he has killed this other guy. There is some kind of connection between the teachings of Buddhism and the actions of the samurai. Not only does Zen teach the idea of not allowing thought to get in the way of action, but the samurai somehow managed to reconcile the fact that they went around killing people with their Buddhism, and it somehow worked together.

So the thing that attracted me was a kind of philosophical break with the Catholic Church that I started to experience by the 60s. I don't know if any of you remember my senior Fulton J. Sheen. Oh yeah, I saw him and Bela Lugosi at the same time. That's right, that's right. Monsignor Sheen had certain signs about him, one being that his eyebrows grew straight across. My mother used to put him on religiously every Sunday night, and I remember this was on the radio. By the time he became Bishop Sheen, he was a star of religious TV and an early televangelist.

To his great credit, before his death, he was a very outspoken opponent of the Vietnam War. Generally, he tended to be a pretty orthodox guy, and if I'm going to talk about him, I should mention how he became a major anti-war figure. One of the things he said that really stuck with me was that no Catholic has ever left the Catholic Church because of philosophical differences. It's always because they can't live up to the moral code of the church, particularly in the area of sex.

I don't know if he explicitly mentioned sex on the radio, but he talked about divorce and the fact that Catholics can't remarry if they get a divorce, as well as issues like birth control. This resonated with me because I left the Catholic Church for the same reason: I could no longer live up to its moral code. I thought he was right, but he believed there was something reprehensible about that. His point was that it shows you're a person of poor character and a bad person, which is why you leave the church, not because you've reasoned your way out of it.

I started off with reasoning that a lot of the things I was doing were in conflict with the church's teachings. I had married, and my marriage ended in divorce; it was a regular Catholic marriage and everything else, but it lasted just a very short time and was a big mistake for both of us. I thought then that if I wanted to stay a good Catholic, I would have to spend the rest of my life celibate. Up to that point, I hadn't really been celibate.

But I thought, well anyway, I'm not going to be able to get married again or if I do get married, it's not going to be the real thing. I mean God really isn't going to approve of it. So I thought that's crazy. It doesn't make any sense at all. And then I was fortunate enough to meet a woman with whom I began an affair shortly after my marriage broke up and I thought gee, this is all according to the church. This is wrong. This is bad. This poor woman here is an adulteress and I'm dragging her into this whole thing. So I thought well that's crazy too. What we're doing is very good. I cannot feel bad about this. I cannot feel guilty. I can't feel wrong about it. Oh and of course we were practicing birth control. I mean this lady and I were practicing birth control so we had the additional sins. So I began, well is that, oh should I be siring children here in this convoluted situation?

So that basically is where that led to my breaking with the church. And one of the things that I found myself turning to at that point was turning back to my old interest in Buddhism and starting to read about it again and starting to in fact, and that was what I'm talking about now. This was 1965-66 which was really the beginning of the era, the decade that we call the 60s. The 60s didn't begin in 1960. Well some of the threads began there but it really kind of got going around 1966 I would say.

And one of the big things was that Zen people started popping up all over the place. I didn't actually get the opportunity to meet and work with any Zen teachers then but the literature expanded tremendously and Alan Watts was writing a lot of stuff at that time and it was very influential articles and books and so on.

And I have to say, Zen, orthodox Zen people have a tendency to put down Alan Watts which I think is very unfortunate. I think that they do it on the grounds, you know, people say, well he never really had a satori, you know. I think that in his own way he was, I met him a couple of times so I'm not talking just from, I'm not talking just from what I think about him based on his books.

I think that he was, I think that he was in his way a very illuminated person and that he certainly was able to take very, very difficult ideas, philosophical ideas that are very, very difficult for people trained in Western thinking to understand and make them understandable and sometimes only momentarily. I mean you would read a book by Alan Watts and for about an hour afterwards you would go around thinking you finally got it, you know. And then it would kind of fade out again and sometimes even if you re-read the book it wouldn't be enough. But anyway, it kind of gave you the idea that there was something else out there that was another way of looking at things and I really think, I think I keep all of his books on my shelf now and I refer to them from time to time.

I really think that he's still one of the best teachers in this area, one of the best writers in this area that I know of. Yes? Actually there is no Zen orthodoxy. We don't have a Pope so nobody can declare who's orthodox and who isn't.

Ǥ

Anarchism and Crime

By Robert Anton Wilson and Robert Shea

Because anarchists aim at the abolition of government, the first question they are usually asked is, "What about murderers, thieves, rapists? The government protects us from them. Would you just let them run wild?"

The answer, first of all, is that government does not protect us. Its claims are a total imposture, like the fraud of a primitive shaman who claims to bring rain and warns everybody, "If you abolish me, it will never rain again." Thus, *the major crimes are all legal*; the thieves who have stolen the land and the natural resources from under our feet operate with a government franchise. These huge banks, corporations and land monopolies finance both political parties, train the corporation lawyers who become Congressmen or Presidents, and can never be successfully resisted in the courts because they own the judges, too.

Second, the next level of crime, the so-called Syndicate or Mafia, is also in cahoots with big government and big business, and only token arrests and light sentences are ever imposed on "gangland leaders" – usually rebels who have become unpopular with the higher-level mobsters. In every big city, the links between the mayor's office and the Mob are well-known and often "exposed" in the press, but no reforms are permanent and never can be under this system. The links between the national Mob and the national government are less well publicized, but books like *The Politics of Opium in Southeast Asia*, the recent *Harpers* magazine issue on the CIA and heroin, etc., show that the heroin syndicate could not operate without high-level Federal protection.

Finally, the small-time free-lance criminal – the rapist and sneak thief – can be arrested and prosecuted in this system; but is he, usually? In New York, in 1972, there were 300,000 burglaries but only 20,000 arrests for burglary. The police are too busy protecting the high-level criminals – as we will explain – to have the manpower to really battle the small independents.

Do you deny this? Well, of course, you have been trained by the State-run schools and the mass media to deny it, do you believe your own denial? How safe do you feel in a large American city, especially after dark? Do you honestly think the government can and will protect you?

IS MORE LAW THE ANSWER?

Many admit that they are frightened and appalled by modern American life, but they think the answer is more laws, tougher laws, an evolution toward the total Police State.

This is, of course, the natural direction of government. The more honest (and misguided) a politician happens to be, the more laws he will write – to prove to himself that he is "working" for the people. Obviously, every time the legislature meets, the honest politicians will introduce more laws, to show how hard they're working. Eventually, nothing will remain that is not covered by some law or other. Everything not compulsory will be forbidden, and everything not forbidden will be compulsory.

Stop and ask yourself if you really want that kind of Nazi-, or Communist-style tyranny.

Now, even if we (or most of us) do want it – to be protected from criminals – and even if we escalate our progress and pass a billion new laws a year, arriving at Total Law in say five or ten years, what then? How will such a system be enforced? Kinsey estimated that to enforce our sex laws alone, 95 percent of the population would have to become either police or jail-guards – except that they would all be in jail themselves. This is already impossible, but suppose we tried to enforce the anti-drug and anti-gambling laws, also? We would all spend our lives in Federal prisons, spending part of the day guarding others and part of the day being guarded by them.

This is absurd, but within the framework of government and law, how can we stop short of such a total prison-society?

And remember: each step in this direction – each new law, and each new bureaucracy to enforce the new laws – raises your tax burden. Already, you are working from January 1 to May 23 for the Federal government, to pay your IRS bill for the year. For a few months thereafter, you are working to pay nuisance taxes, state taxes, and various other concealed taxes on every item you buy, every movie you see, every drink you take. Already, it would probably be cheaper to just let yourself be robbed every week by a casual sneak-thief. Government may be more genteel than a mugger (occasionally) but it usually ends up taking more of one's money.

THE FUNCTION OF LAW

There are three kinds of laws on the books today, and to understand them is to understand the State.

The first kind of law declares the State's power over you. It says: we may rob you of this much per year (taxation), we may enslave you for this period of time (the draft), we may do this and that and the other thing to you, and you cannot resist because we are your Masters. This is the earliest kind of law and was originally imposed on conquered people by conquerors. No attempt to justify it has ever been convincing to anyone bold enough to question it in the first place. It is based on mere Force; its only argument is the gun.

The second kind of law is coercive morality. This makes the State into an armed clergyman. It says you can enjoy yourself this way, but not that way; you can smoke this, but not that; you can drink this, but not that. Thou Shalt Not Play Parchesi On The Night of the Full Moon. Thou shalt not gamble on Sunday. Thou shalt not make love to your wife the way you and she both like, but the way the legislators like. Four million arrests a year, and an incredible expenditure of time and manpower and money, go into enforcing these laws.

These are the laws that establish crimes without victims. These are the laws that everybody occasionally violates and some people violate constantly. Their only justification, as with the first type of laws, is sheer brute force. That is, without force, a man who believed in, say, the Seventh Day Adventist vegetarian diet would still obey that diet's rules; with force, the Adventists, if they get into government, can make all of us obey it. The day is not distant when pot-smokers will take over, and if they are vengeful, anti-booze laws will come back on the books. This stupid bullying can go on forever, each group getting its turn to impose its own prejudices on others. Anarchists say: stop it now, get off your neighbor's back, get him off your back, and let everybody enjoy his or her own lifestyle.

Finally, there is the third class of laws – the class that every decent person wishes society would live by. No killing. No stealing. No rape. No fraud. Anarchists, just like you, would like to see these laws really functioning. We just don't believe that government can do that job. We think government is, always has been, and always will be preoccupied with the first two kinds of law. Read on and we will explain this.

THE NATURE OF GOVERNMENT

Government was instituted to guarantee that property would remain stolen. The chief function of every cop, every judge, every bureaucrat is to see that property remains stolen.

The first kings were conquerors. They stole the land by shot and shell, period. Then, they settled down to rob the survivors at a certain rate per year, called taxation. Next, they divided up the land among their relatives or officers in the army, who all became lords-of-the-land, landlords, and were empowered to rob the citizens at a certain other rate per year, called rent. When science and industry appeared, other satraps and sycophants of the royal families received charters to monopolize the resources and means of production, and to rob at a certain rate per year, called capital interest or profit. When banks were formed to circulate the medium of exchange (money), other charters were handed out to others in the bandit-gang, who became bank directors with a license to rob at another rate per year, called money interest or economic interest.

It soon became evident that those not in the gang, the majority of the population, were inclined to rob back as much as they could. The Robin Hood hero appears in all societies at this point, and most of us still admire him, although shamefacedly, since the schools and mass media tell us not to. (Still, who doesn't heroize Jesse James or John Dillinger a little?)

Anarchists say that the first crime was the crime of the

conquerors/governors, who seized a whole land, cut it up among themselves, and proceeded to rob all of us forever by taxation, rent, corporative profit, money interest, and various sub-classes of the same basic fraud. Anarchists say that the Earth belongs to its inhabitants, not to this small "owning" and "governing" class of less than 1 percent of the population.

Anarchists say that the way to stop crime is to stop the primordial crime, the State, and administer the land through voluntary associations (syndicates) of all the people.

Anarchists say that if people could work for themselves – if they received the full product of their labor through a syndicate of fellow-workers – almost all motivation for crime would disappear. If you didn't have to pay taxes and rent, starting tomorrow, your purchasing power would be more than doubled. If other forms of exploitation and robbery, through the financial-interest system, were also abolished, your purchasing power would more than quadruple. How much envy, how much worry about money, how much irrational fear, ulcers, nightmares, headaches and other motivations to cheat a little or steal a little would survive after this simple economic justice was achieved?

THE OTHER CRIMINALS

"But, but – how about the violent criminal types? How about the thrill-killers, the nuts, the psychopaths or sociopaths or sadists? How about those who simply enjoy being evil and destructive?"

We are not evading that question. It is absolutely necessary, however, to put it in perspective by explaining the Major Economic Crime of capitalist government (and feudal and other governments) and how other, lesser crimes mostly derive from that primordial injustice.

Now, after economic justice is achieved and voluntary associations of all sorts (labor unions, credit unions, consumer-owned co-ops, people-owned insurance companies, rural communes, tribes, any type of free human grouping) have taken over the functions of government, some persons, due to sickness or perversity or one damn thing or another, will still make trouble. Rape. Pilfering. Attempts to defraud. How will anarchists deal with these remaining no-goodniks?

EDUCATION AND THE FAMILY

The first step in solving any social problem, like any medical problem, is prevention. Other remedies are necessary only when prevention fails.

Anarchists claim that the violent-nut-type of human being is produced by our current methods of child-rearing. This claim is hardly radical or extreme: every psychiatrist, every sociologist, every anthropologist, in one way or another, admits that this grave charge is true. We would not have so many rapists and other violent nuisances if our society were not, in some way, training them from birth onward to behave like that. For instance, Sweden has only a few rapes per year; the United States has one every seven minutes. One rape every seven minutes is not natural male behavior (whatever Womens Lib may say); it is a function of the sexual misery in this society.

Anarchists believe that the repressive, authoritarian, coercive, brutal and degrading practices currently used in the family and the school are only necessary to condition the young human to live in a government-run society. Children must be beaten or otherwise terrorized and bullied in the home and the school in order that they may "adjust" to the terror and brutality of government as they mature. In short, a State-run society must be repressive because repression is the essence of the State.

Libertarian, free-form families and schools – the open family, the Summerhill school, the free association of men, women and children without authoritarian control – will not produce the deformed, mentally twisted, violent and "mean" and "crazy" types so common in our authoritarian society. So anarchists aim, first of all, to prevent violent criminals by changing the child-rearing methods that produce them.

THE DEMONIAC OR MONSTER

There still remains the inexplicable criminal – the guy who enjoys harming others for reasons nobody today can understand. The superstitious say he is possessed by demons; the naturalists imply that maybe he has bad genes or is a throwback to an earlier stage of evolution. Whatever the explanation, he will appear, presumably, in anarchist societies, as he has appeared in all other societies, even after economic injustice and mind-warping education are abolished.

Human-centered societies (as distinguished from governmental or property-centered societies) have been dealing with this problem for thousands of years. Tribes, clans, bands, free communes, have existed outside, before and alongside the States which get all the attention from historians. Anthropologists have investigated these free human groupings and have found a variety of methods of dealing with "demoniacs," many of them as good or better than the State's traditional jails, tortures or executions.

Ostracism should not be underestimated. One critic of anarchism, George Orwell, actually complained that ostracism was so cruel that most people would rather fall afoul of government and go to jail than be the sole ostracized person in an anarchist community.

Exile, widely used by governments before jail became

popular, is also effective. At least, it solves the problem for the community that uses it (while, alas, passing the problem on to the unlucky community that next gets the offensive nut.)

The Quakers have widely practiced a form of moral forgiveness which sounds impractical to most of us, but which is murderously effective. Bertrand Russell was so impressed with this that he suggested it as a fit punishment for Stalin. Until you have seen a group of Quakers reciting somebody's sins in public, weeping over them loudly, and then forgiving and praying for the culprit, you can't imagine how much psychological impulse-to-change this generates.

Many anarchists believe the private defense groups are legitimate; some even are willing to allow such groups to use traditional Vigilante methods. Clarence Lee Schwartz, an American anarchist who observed this system first-hand in the Old West, thought it both more humane and more effective at peace-keeping than the government law system back East. Other anarchists fear this as the possible source of a new State.

Most anarchists believe that criminals should not be caged under any circumstances, due to the overwhelming evidence that every prisoner comes out of a cage worse than he goes into it. Others believe, however, that punishment in a form of indemnification is compatible with libertarian ideas and should be rigorously enforced by anarchist syndicates. Under the indemnity system, every criminal must pay in cash or work or some needed good to compensate his victims (or their survivors). This certainly does the victims more good than having the criminal put in a cage and fed at community expense, to say the least of it; and is probably just as discouraging or more discouraging to every nut with even the remnant of an ability to foresee the probable results of his actions.

Finally, we must mention miscellaneous solutions. Just

as crime in an economically just and free community will be freaky and sporadic (rather than the steady hour-after-hour terror that it is in this mad, unequal and unfree society), the remedies will also be individualized and peculiar to each situation. In some cases, undoubtedly, an anarchist community will decide the "criminal" was right and the community was wrong; for this reason, anarchists do not believe in unalterable laws, but only in general policies.

The acme of anarchist theory is the principle of non-invasiveness or non-coercion – Mind Your Own Business – and those found to be violating this will be given, usually, some method of compensating those whose lives they have damaged. If they refuse, methods like the boycott-ostracism-exile or general cold shoulder need not always be deliberately organized against them. The good sense, the social bonds, and the sense of humor of the organic community will find some way to make known that human tolerance, even under anarchy, is not infinite. In the Old West, men booted through town with a skunk tied around their necks, and then shoved onto the highway, often became valuable, co-operative and productive citizens in the next town, after some time to figure the likelihood of a repetition of that public amusement if they were to try similar modes of behavior again.

Ǥ

Kids in Pornography

From *Playboy* magazine, August 1977.

By now, there can scarcely be a man or woman – or child – in this country who is unaware that young children are being used as performers in pornography. Early this year [1977] Dr. Judianne Densen-Gerber, a New York psychiatrist, began traveling from city to city, holding press conferences and displaying her collection of child pornography. In May, *Sixty Minutes* did a segment on child porn, the *Chicago Tribune* launched a series of front page articles with such headlines as "CHILD PORNOGRAPHY – SICKNESS FOR SALE," the FBI announced its own investigation and promised indictments in New York and California, hearings were scheduled by House and Senate subcommittees and, in Illinois, separate investigations were launched at state, county and municipal levels. There were raids on bookstores and theaters in New York, Chicago and San Francisco. Kiddie porn had arrived as a national scandal.

The resultant uproar has raised questions that divide even experienced obscenity defense lawyers. Some, like Charles Rembar, who defended *Fanny Hill* and *Lady Chatterley's Lover*, think sellers of child porn could constitutionally be prosecuted. Other civil libertarians say that everything published should be protected by the First Amendment. Some attorneys who have fought censorship for years are wondering whether or not a lawyer can properly refuse to take child porn cases. Everyone agrees that the sexual abuse of minors can and should be prosecuted. The problem is that the traffic in the resulting pornography encourages child abuse by making it profitable. And police claim they find it difficult to identify the actual producers or to trace down the abused children – let alone to get them to testify and have that testimony accepted in court. The obvious course is to shut down the market.

The emotions stirred up over the sexual abuse of children are easily channeled into an attack on all kinds of sexually explicit material. For example, in Chicago at the height of the press outcry, 34 adult bookstores were closed under those old police standbys, alleged building-code and licensing violations, without regard to whether or not the shops sold anything dealing with children. It is possible that this scatter-gun pattern of enforcement will be repeated all over the country.

The current furor has also increased bigotry against homosexuals. Columnist Irv Kupcinet reports, "Anita Bryant's battle in Florida to rescind an ordinance prohibiting discrimination against homosexuals is getting a tremendous boost from the current headlines linking sexual perverts with child pornography. She's making the most of the stories in the bitter campaign being waged down there."

State legislatures all over the country are rushing to enact new anti-porn laws. As attorney Elmer Gertz, a veteran of many censorship cases observes, "Legislators and law enforcement officials tend to think in terms of new legislation instead of looking at the books to see what is already there. The attitude is: To hell with the old law – let's go with a new one. There's no publicity mileage in using the laws that exist." But many of the hastily passed laws may lead to prosecutions not just for child pornography but for any material law enforcement agents deem obscene. Will we see bookstore owners going to jail for selling *Show Me*, the sex education book depicting nude children, or even for stocking a classic such as *Lolita*?

Until child pornography became a national cause célèbre, the issues in the debate over pornography and censorship were fairly clear. There is no evidence that most types of pornography hurt anyone, either the ultimate consumer or those who participate in making it. The production of child pornography, though, is a special case: It is not a victimless crime. Those who seduce or coerce children into performing sexual acts to make pornography are unquestionably guilty of criminal child abuse – and should be prosecuted for it. Child abuse statutes are already on the books. The danger in the current outcry is that the public's fury in seeing children sexually exploited will be siphoned off to fuel a crusade for censorship in general. Protecting children is important, but so is protecting freedom of expression. How to balance the claims for each of these social needs is a difficult problem. It will not be wisely resolved in a tornado of hysteria whipped up by journalistic hyperbole and political publicity stunts.

Some Ways to Ease Depression

This is a collection of ideas about dealing with depression that I have gathered from personal experience, from discussions with others and from reading. Not all of them may be useful to anyone else, but if even one or two are worth passing on, that will make this compilation worthwhile.

The feeling of being depressed is like a headache or a bad cold. If you can put up with it for a while, it will eventually go away. It is not caused by the real situation in which you find yourself.

It is not the same as grief, which is a natural response to a painful situation. The thing that marks depression is a feeling of helplessness, hopelessness and worthlessness that is not warranted by the facts of the case and that discourages you from doing anything constructive. Depression is a form of self-hatred, grief is not. It is possible for people to live with grief, but depression is so painful it seems almost unendurable. That is why it is important to remember that it will go away after a while.

Depression bears no relation to the facts of our lives. People who are not depression-prone can endure the worst blows of life without succumbing to depression. People who are depression-prone can get depressed about trivial things, or about nothing at all. Depression is never necessary or justified. Since this is so, it is possible to ease depression or even get rid of it altogether.

Why are some people depression-prone? According to some psychologists, to the extent that things are done for us in childhood, we are predisposed to depression. Depression involves a feeling of helplessness, a feeling of not being able to do anything about a problem. Thus, people who did not learn to do things for themselves in childhood are more likely to get depressed. You can help children to grow up not depression-prone by encouraging them to develop self-sufficiency.

Being depression-prone is primarily a matter of attitude. Attitudes that encourage depression are: 1) Belief in one's helplessness. Nothing I do will improve the situation. 2) Belief that the cause of the traumatic event is in oneself. This bad thing happened to me because of the way I am, or because of something I did. 3) Belief that the cause is stable. It will never change. It is not a temporary condition but a permanent one. 4) Belief that the failure is due to a global, rather than a specific cause. Not, "I had a bad day or a momentary lapse," but, "I am a totally stupid and incompetent person."

These attitudes that promote depression suggest certain strategies for dealing with it. 1) Change the helplessness. Do something constructive about the problem. 2) Change values. Attach less importance to the event, whatever happened that's making you feel depressed. 3) Change your attitude toward the cause of your failures. Recognize that the cause of the trouble is not in yourself, or that the condition is temporary, or that it is caused by one specific lapse, not a state of general failing. 4) Change the environment. For example, if conditions on your job are depressing you, quit and get a new job.

It is possible to change attitudes and feelings, but it is not easy. Feelings cannot be suppressed or changed by a command of the will. In effect, you have to do a job of persuasion on yourself, which takes time and patience. A key element in this persuasion process is repetition. Repeatedly call to mind the attitudes you want, attitudes that combat depression. These attitudes can be put in the form of simple statements, such as, "This condition is only temporary," which you can repeat to yourself at intervals. At first you may feel no conviction about these statements, but with time they will sink in and become part of your emotional structure. The longer we hold ideas, the more emotional intensity they acquire.

Practice re-evaluating whatever it is that seems to be causing depression. Contradict, in your thinking, depressing versions of the facts with evaluations that are more optimistic or realistic. Emotions have a tendency to follow the lead of the intellect. If you think a thing is so, pretty soon you will start to feel that it is so.

It may be useful to write down your positive evaluations of the situation. They will make more of an impression on you. Collect them somewhere – maybe in a notebook – and read them over from time to time.

If you're having trouble sleeping because of depressing thoughts, don't stay awake for hours and hours. Get up and do something.

When you feel depressed, don't mope around or lie around. Find some work or some absorbing activity as quickly as possible.

Don't turn to drugs, especially psychoactive drugs like alcohol or marijuana, as a cure for depression. You can't do anything useful about your problem, whatever it is, while intoxicated. Marijuana often intensifies negative emotions. And after intoxication there is a letdown that intensifies the depression and makes it worse – for example, the hangover after drinking heavily. The post-drug depression is generally so bad that the temporary relief you get by using drugs isn't worth it. Drug use to combat depression is self-defeating.

There are substitutes for drugs that will also take your mind off your troubles and are beneficial. One is work. Work can function like a drug. The advantage of turning to work is that it does not deplete you physically and mentally, that you accomplish things, and accomplishing things makes you feel good and thereby relieves the depressed feelings. This doesn't have to be a job you're paid for. There are always many jobs to be tackled – hard work around the house, papers to be organized, books, magazines and newspaper articles you've been saving to read, community or political work, arts and crafts. Work until you are tired out, or until the black mood passes.

The point of life is the present, not the future. The only reason we set goals for the future is to enrich the present by giving it more meaning. Therefore, it is not necessary for us to achieve our future goals, and not necessary to get depressed because some goal seems impossible.

Learn to rate yourself on the effort you make to solve a problem, rather than on whether the efforts succeed or fail. You often can't control the results of your efforts, but you usually can control the amount of effort you make or the number of times you try. For example, in these times of heavy unemployment, job hunters should rate themselves on the number of companies they contact, rather than how fast they actually get the job.

It is more intelligent to find your happiness in the pursuit of values than their attainment. Quite possibly the happiest people are those who set themselves unattainable goals.

Some people get depressed when it seems as if they will never achieve something they want. Others get their greatest pleasure in life from trying to do the impossible. This shows again that depression is a matter of attitude. The same set of facts will depress one person and galvanize another.

Accept the conditions of your life as they are. Try to feel that everything is as it should be. This includes your personal habits. If you feel you should struggle with yourself, struggle against one problem at a time. If there are things about yourself that you can't simply accept, like suicidal eating habits, you can at least accept the fact that it is going to take a long, patient struggle to change them.

Make more time for social life and for love and sex, even when it interferes with work. Closeness with others is a great antidote for depression.

If you are depressed about not being able to do as well as you'd like for your loved ones, remember that what they need from you first of all is good cheer, rather than any material accomplishment.

The attitude with which you approach your problems is ultimately much more important than the nuts-and-bolts tactics of how you go about solving them.

When those near and dear to you are hurting, for example when they are depressed, concentrate on giving them affirmative attitudes to work with rather than advising them on the specifics of how to solve their problems. Even if your affirmative statements meet skepticism or resistance, keep them up. Repetition counts for a lot.

The root of depression is a moralistic evaluation of yourself and your situation. People get depressed when they blame themselves for the bad things that are happening to them. They say, these bad things are happening to me because I am fundamentally a bad person. I am to blame for all the evils that befall me. Practice reminding yourself that pain in life is everyone's lot whether they be sinner or saint, and that in any case you are a fine, wonderful, lovable person in all sorts of ways.

Think of the things you like about yourself. Write them down, and improve on the list as you can. During periods of depression read this list over thoughtfully once an hour or so.

Heavy physical exercise frequently drives out depression.

The way to handle negative emotions is not to try to reject, hide or drive them away, but to learn from them. We should trust our feelings enough to understand that they may be trying to tell us something, and instead of fighting against them, we should find out what they are trying to tell us. For example, if you're bored with your job, don't just grit your teeth and endure that feeling. Try to figure out what about your job is boring, and try to correct that condition.

If you suffer from stage fright, what can you learn from your stage fright?

When you find yourself worrying about something, state in a few sentences in your mind the precise and rational and usually comforting truth about the matter. Do not allow wildly exaggerated thoughts – such as we're all prone to think in times of stress – to take control of your mind. Example: "Nobody will hire me." Answer: "Somebody will, eventually. And probably in the next ten weeks."

You are the one who inflicts negative emotions on yourself. You have decided to be depressed. This does not mean you should blame yourself for feeling depressed. It does mean that you should look within for the cause of depression. It means that you can relieve yourself of your depression by changing your attitude, rather than by changing the conditions around you. (Although changing conditions should not be ruled out as a positive step.) But just because you are the one who inflicts negative emotions on yourself, it doesn't mean that you can halt the process by an effort of will. First, you have to take responsibility for your guilt, anxiety or depression. Responsibility does not mean blame or self-hatred. It is simply a neutral recognition of the fact that the key to the problem is somewhere in your psyche. Then you have to discover the attitude, the principle of personal philosophy, that is at the root of the feeling. Then you have to change this moralistic evaluation to a more reasonable one.

It helps to keep restating the reasonable attitude in your mind, even if it doesn't take hold emotionally at once.

Any time you have a problem, remember that it is having the right attitude, first of all, that counts. How the problem is solved – or even whether it is solved at all – is secondary.

For example, we give meaning to our sufferings by the way we respond to them. If we meet them with grace and courage, rather than whining or complaining or falling apart, we triumph over them. This is what it means to live well – it means to live with the right attitude.

Mystical enlightenment means having a right attitude about all things. Generally speaking, the right attitude is one of good cheer and optimism and continued interest in making an effort, rather than one of bitterness or anesthesia. This applies both to the conditions of our lives and to the way we live. The right attitude toward our so-called vices is not blaming yourself or feeling guilty or depressed about past slips or even current slips, but being cheerful about the struggle, not giving up, being satisfied with one day's effort at a time, not struggling in a spirit of masochism, self-contempt or pessimism. Cultivating the right attitude is the primary step to take when you recognize a problem and even before you start looking for a solution.

Never let a bad moment or a succession of bad moments let you down. Always try to see the whole trend as onward or upward. And always remember that the whole point is to work, to be active, to use energy, not to be concerned about rewards or results, success or failure.

The immature find fulfillment in being taken care of, the mature find it in bearing fruit.

Do not let yourself be depressed by the apparent meaninglessness of life and its misfortunes. Meaning was invented by human beings. We give meaning to unfortunate events by responding nobly and heroically to them. Continuing to live, love and work in spite of tragedy or hardship is one most important kind of heroic response.

Doing Anarchism Yourself

Deciding to call oneself an anarchist is usually the end of a long process of eliminating other philosophies and the beginning of another long process of learning what anarchism really is all about. One new thing that has to be learned and is rarely fully appreciated is the role of the individual in anarchism. It's easier to give lip service to an abstract ideal of individualism than it is to act as if you actually believe that no one and no group and no principle is more important than you, yourself. Or more important than any other particular person. By this belief you commit yourself to no longer passing the buck to others. You declare your preference for a way of life in which you make all decisions and take all responsibility and expect to rely on your own thinking and your own efforts. This is a difficult ideal.

The anarchist movement in this country is very small and has difficulty making itself heard. This is due, not so much to any inherent implausibility in anarchist ideas, but rather to the problem that once people accept the ideas there seems to be no clear-cut direction to take. Groups come together and drift apart; publications appear and vanish; actions and demonstrations are staged and forgotten. Meanwhile, governments and state-supported economic systems seem to grow stronger. Sometimes it seems hopeless.

Here and there much is accomplished, often by one person

or three or six. One group in one place will get its energies together and be printing and distributing literature, organizing, picketing, demonstrating, finding imaginative ways of getting the message across, setting an example for the rest of the movement. But in many places another picture is typical: Nobody knows what to do. Meetings are boring and seem purposeless. If new people come into the group they soon drop out for lack of promising projects to work on. Constructive suggestions or good ideas die on the vine because objections are raised or because no one follows through. It seems impossible to raise money. The group is divided by personality clashes. Publications die after an issue or two. The temptation is great to chuck it all and go to work for some local reform candidate or join some local Marxist group, just to have a feeling of accomplishing something.

Of course, the desire to accomplish something is itself a product of authoritarian thinking. Authoritarians are always measuring themselves by their numbers and the size of their accomplishments. During the first couple of million years of our species' existence, on this planet we didn't accomplish much. Life for hunting and gathering people would seem relatively monotonous to a modern person. The really heavy demands for accomplishment must have originated with the domestication of man, with the invention of the state, when work and production quotas were set by priests and kings and taxes were imposed. The hunting and gathering life would probably have been much more congenial to anarchists. The accomplishments of individuals acting on their own or in small groups need to be measured by different standards than those of disciplined mass organizations.

At the same time, it would be good if we could achieve more than we are doing now and if we could feel better about what we do achieve. Not for the sake of assuaging guilt, not to feel that we're as good as various political movements, but simply to keep anarchism itself alive. Our main task today, as I see it, is not saving the world, but the humbler goal of keeping anarchism going, so that those who think as we do will be more numerous and more influential in the next generation than they are in this. If the race can manage to survive without our help for a generation or two more, there may come a time when we actually will have the strength to halt the doomward march of civilization and turn it around.

The sense of futility that afflicts some anarchists is due, I think, to each person's expecting others to come up with ideas, to waiting for someone else to make the first move, to seeking group approval before launching a project, to expecting others to take some of the responsibility and help with some of the work, to limiting one's own role in the group to the performance of some specialized function. In some people, this excessive reliance on others extends even to an unwillingness to define for oneself the aims and strategy of the movement. The result of this dependency is that nothing gets done unless some obvious project or fortuitous opportunity for action galvanizes everybody at once. Otherwise people blame one another for the group's failure to act constructively and eventually drift apart. Some turn to authoritarian movements of the left and right because that's where the action seems to be; others go into more conventional politics; still others subside into quietism. Or leaders may arise in the group and take charge. This can help for a while, especially if the leader is tactful and the group understands the practical need for temporary leadership. But in an anarchist group sooner or later a faction is likely to arise that will reject the leader just because the mere exercise of leadership, no matter how informal and non-coercive, is thought to be inimical to anarchism. In any event the emergence of a leader can be disruptive and, while postponing disintegration for a time, will lead to it in the long run. And the breakup of the group, unfortunately, often means the abandonment of anarchism by the members of the group as a philosophy that doesn't work. I think the real reason for these developments is not that anarchism doesn't work, but that it often isn't fully thought through and applied. What's needed are distinctly anarchist ways of getting things done.

There is an authoritarian pattern of group action that is pretty much universal regardless of the group's purpose, or political-economic philosophy. Primary is the assumption that the group needs a leader and that very few people are capable of leadership. The responsibility for setting aims, coming up with ideas for action and assigning tasks then belongs to the leader. Followers do not expect themselves to work as hard as the leaders, or to have ideas or display initiative. Among authoritarians the division of labor produces the impression that most work is unpleasant and undesirable, resulting in a demand that the drudgery be distributed equally among members of the drudging class. Everyone is expected to contribute an equal amount of labor to the group's well-being; there are to be no slackers. One of the tasks of the leader is to keep everybody busy, get everybody to obey orders. At some point in humanity's past it became customary to use force to control people. This was the origin of the state. As Jacques Ellul puts it in *The Political Illusion*, "To say that the state should not employ force is simply to say that there should be no state."

In authoritarian thinking there is an invisible line which people cross when they become members of the group. They have in their own minds, and in the minds of other members, surrendered a certain amount of personal sovereignty. The welfare of the group becomes more important than individual self-interest. It is this sacrifice of autonomy that supposedly gives leaders the right to discipline and punish.

Democratic organizations don't differ from this pattern, and such groups are also authoritarian. Although decisions are made and leaders appointed by vote, the leader-follower structure is the same, as is the claim of the supremacy of the group's will over the individual will. Once a decision is made by vote all members are expected to support it whether or not they agree with it. As has often been said, democracy does not do away with tyrants, it merely makes the majority a tyrant.

What happens when people reject authoritarianism? What they are rejecting, essentially, is the use of force to coerce the unwilling. This is the essence of government. In order to justify its use of force, government claims that the welfare of society has a higher moral claim than the individual will. To reject that claim means that you rate individual autonomy as the higher value and hold that a group or its leaders are never justified in forcing a recalcitrant member into line. (Of course, it is possible to take the position that the group's welfare is more important than the individual's welfare but that the group has no right to coerce the individual. But I can't see on what basis the group could be so limited.)

Anti-authoritarian groups generally have no constitutions, no leaders, no formal procedures for reaching decisions. They are usually open to all comers and neither officially induct nor expel members. So membership and its obligations tend to be self-defined, or at least a matter for debate. The clear line which distinguishes authoritarian group members from non-members is missing. In many cases, however, these groups, though they have rid themselves of the trappings of authoritarianism, have retained authoritarian habits of thinking. Also, they have jettisoned authoritarian methods of getting things done, but they have not developed anarchist ways of doing things. For example, the idea that there are few qualified leaders and many followers often induces people to wait unconsciously for a leader, to expect strength and guidance from an external source, even though they had explicitly rejected the principle of leadership. Then there are those who spend all their time denouncing anyone else's initiative as an attempt to lead. Still other people are inhibited from showing initiative, fearing that they harbor within themselves impulses toward leadership.

Anarchists also carry authoritarian notions of the division of labor into their groups. This mainly takes the form of those who are productive resenting the non-contribution of less active members. One person may be working 16 hours a day while ten people who claim to be part of the group appear to do nothing. Since discipline is considered un-anarchistic, the usual way of coping with this imbalance is to harangue the less productive members, warning of dire consequences if everybody doesn't get behind the program. Haranguing, unlike coercion, is consistent with anarchist principles. Sometimes, if the energetic members get fed up with the invincible apathy of the others they may quit and let the group founder. Rarely do the hard workers expect gratitude, but the unfair criticism they are sometimes subjected to – charges of trying to be leaders, gurus or superstars – can sometimes be the last straw. Too often, instead of manifesting Kropotkin's ideal of mutual aid, anarchist groups destroy themselves through mutual recrimination.

Another hangover of authoritarian thinking in anarchist groups is the tendency to treat personality clashes and factional fights as catastrophic. Intramural conflict is as common as colds in winter in all groups, authoritarian and anarchist, in this culture. Among authoritarians such clashes frequently lead to splintering or to the annihilation or expulsion of one faction. But most authoritarians treat serious conflict as being intolerable. It is – if one wants to achieve the machinelike unity and discipline that is the authoritarian ideal. But conflict should not be intolerable for anarchists. In fact, people are attracted to anarchism because they feel they should be able to fight in peace.

Anarchists also frequently retain the authoritarian idea that there must be formal approval for a project. Anyone with an idea in mind feels a need to get a consensus before acting. Frequently, since majority rule is not accepted as a principle, nothing will be done unless there is unanimous approval. I have seen one person's objection stymie action on a perfectly sound idea because the rest didn't want to go ahead without total approval.

Right now, it seems to me, there is a flourishing mystique of excessive reverence for groups, of deification of the collective will. Team spirit is expected to replace leadership. In part this is the result of a feeling that the movement of the 60s was conned and ripped off by some of its leaders and spokesmen. In part it comes from a general revulsion from patriarchal authority spurred by the women's liberation movement. In part it seems to be an identification of the evils of capitalism with individualism. This belief in the superiority of the communal mind goes a long way back; in post-Revolutionary Russia there were experiments with conductorless orchestras (but not, so far as I know, with captainless ships). This attitude is understandable and healthy, but it assumes that there are only two ways of getting things done, authority or consensus. Carried to excess, this supposed respect for the group's opinion can mask laziness, apathy, timidity, inhibition, obstructiveness, unwillingness to take responsibility. Everyone sits paralyzed, waiting not for a leader but for a mythical entity to take charge, the group mind. And because there's no such thing as a group mind, the energizing impulse never comes. This worship of the communal spirit is authoritarianism without authority, all followers and no leaders.

It is simply very difficult to take the individual seriously. Over 10,000 years of authoritarian programming work against it. The I.W.W. anthem refers disparagingly to "the feeble strength of one." Individual desires are small, mean, petty, selfish – "mere." Almost all moral systems are based on the belief that to be binding a moral code must be authoritative for everyone. An ethical theory based on the idea that each person's morals are binding only for him or her is dismissed as being based on sentiment, whim, subjectivism. Much traditional U.S. rhetoric, like much anarchist ideology, pays lip service to individualism, but authoritarianism is rampant in this country. Ayn Rand's Objectivism, supposedly the individualist ideology *par excellence*, rigorously throws out heretics and dissenters. In the mysticism that has captured the imaginations of many bright people, ego is a dirty word.

And yet, individuals are really all the anarchist movement has to work with. A big step toward learning to be an anarchist is to look for and follow the light within. Only when anarchists start taking their own individuality seriously will the movement get off the ground.

If a meeting seems boring and purposeless, why blame the group and wait for someone else to do something? Require yourself to produce positive proposals and speak out. Don't wait to be told what to do; think of things for yourself to do and announce that this is what you are going to do. If you need help, ask for it. If you get help, you have a group united by a common project, rather than a collection of people bound only by an amorphous commitment to anarchism and a vague agreement about the terrible state of the world. If no one wants to help, then you, the person who had the idea, should try if possible to carry it out alone. Anarchists have to learn self-discipline and self-sufficiency.

Don't expect the anarchist movement to match the performance of authoritarian political organizations. From the point of view of real freedom, the marvels of capitalism or Communism mean little. The source of real creativity is the unfettered individual mind, and its accomplishments permeate a culture subtly, without the help of marching masses, disciplined parties, overwhelming technology or armed force. Let us be content to accomplish things on a small, local, human scale – a Cro-Magnon scale – believing that such achievements take deeper root and have more value in the long run.

Those who have learned to be thoroughgoing anarchists do their work because they enjoy it. They get pleasure from the excitement, the commitment, the hope for the future. They are full of ideas of their own and not terribly concerned about what others think of them. If they think something is worth doing, they'll do it, without taking an overt or covert vote. Therefore they don't get discouraged if others don't help. Some people simply have an abundance of energy and dedication and some do not. Just expend as much as you have, without looking over your shoulder to see how much others are doing.

Not every anarchist can be a bundle of energy and a model of total commitment. Since they consider themselves more important than any group they are part of, real anarchists may withdraw from projects that don't interest them. The group has no claim on anyone; it exists to satisfy the needs of individual members.

Groups do not do things. Everything begins with an individual impulse. Even something that looks like teamwork breaks down, on close examination, to the resultant of a number of individual contributions. It all starts, not with a group soul, but with a single person. Each anarchist has the right and the responsibility to define the total picture of the movement, what its principles are, what its aims are, where it is going, what its strategy and tactics should be.

No one should sit back and let a few ideologists do all the thinking about the big picture.

We are all victims of an authoritarian mindset that dates back, at least, to the neolithic era. The anarchist movement, little more than a century old, represents a beginning effort by some members of our species to erase that programming and try to think about human problems in a new way. This new thinking, and doing, whatever it may become, will not originate with leaders or groups. It will come from individuals, from the voice and the light within.

Ꮆ

Obscenity Laws and the First Amendment

In the Nineteenth Century a grocery clerk named Anthony Comstock was inspired to lead a holy crusade against eroticism in the arts, which he termed "filth," after being shocked by seeing the painting *September Morn* in a store window. At the end of his life Comstock gloated over how many people he'd sent to jail and how many others he'd driven to suicide. Today we would consider him a little bit nutty on the subject of sex. But his influence, his nuttiness, is still with us. Indeed, the Comstock Act, passed at his behest in 1873, is still the law of the land. It was the law under which *Deep Throat* was recently prosecuted in Memphis. That we should now, 20 years into the space age, have such laws on our federal and state books is an indication that this country is still a little bit nutty on the subject of sex.

This irrationality extends to our most respected levels of government. To uphold obscenity laws the most learned judicial body in the land, the U.S. Supreme Court, has perverted the plain meanings of words, arguing that speech or writing dealing with sex is not really speech or writing, and that the words "no law" in the First Amendment actually mean "some law." How ironic that this assault on language occurs in interpreting an article in the Bill of Rights that has to do with communication.

Those who claim that obscenity laws are Constitutional

have a favorite straw man to knock down, the First Amendment absolutist. Pro-censorship people will point out that many generally-accepted laws limit freedom of expression, such as those pertaining to military censorship, regulation of advertising, libel and copyright. But they ignore the point that in all such cases the law can be justified because it prevents tangible, demonstrable, measurable, obvious harm to individuals or to society. In the case of pornography, or sexually explicit material, there is not one shred of evidence that it injures anyone.

The lack of evidence against sexually explicit material is amply demonstrated by the fact that a federal commission was set up and maintained at great public expense to look into the matter. Have we ever felt the need for a federal commission to determine whether libel or false advertising injures people?

The Commission on Obscenity and Pornography surveyed all the research that had been done previously on the effects of sexually explicit material. Pro-censorship groups have always been saying that pornography harms people. The Commission found no evidence for this claim. The Commission went on to assign further research projects to psychologists and sociologists all over the country. The reports of these studies fill 13 volumes. To this day, the material gathered or produced by the Commission represents all the research on sexually-explicit material that exists. Very little, if any, has been done since.

All of this evidence supports the conclusions that pornography does not cause antisocial sexual behavior, that it does not alter the sexual tendencies of people exposed to it, and that it does not endanger children. The Commission recommended that adults be legally free to obtain sexually explicit material.

This represents, not the final word, certainly, but the final word *to date* on the harmlessness of sexually explicit material.

Those who are embarrassed by the findings will sometimes claim that a number of distinguished academicians have found fault with the *Report of the Commission on Obscenity and Pornography.* They always produce the same half-dozen names, you've heard 'em all. Only those few, most of whom have a pronounced conservative bias, have ever attacked the *Report*. And nobody has attempted to repeat the Commission's research and come to contrary conclusions.

During the Commission's lifetime a vacancy opened up, and President Nixon appointed Charles Keating, a professional wowser, to fill it. Keating immediately launched a public attack on his fellow Commissioners for conducting extensive studies of the effects of pornography on those exposed to it. Keating did not want this research to be done, and he tried to prevent the results from being published. This, in itself, was an admission of defeat by pro-censorship forces. Apparently they knew, or suspected, that scientific research would destroy their long-standing claim that pornography is harmful.

It is no accident that Keating was a Nixon appointee and that Nixon himself, whose high moral tone we all remember so well, did everything he could, when the Commission's report was published, to repudiate and bury it. Social issues, in this decade, are increasingly the battleground between liberals and conservatives. Since the end of World War II liberal and conservative views on foreign policy and economics have become virtually interchangeable, especially if one ignores the rhetoric and looks at what both sides do when they're in power. Nowadays, conservatives are distinguishing themselves from liberals by their stands on such issues as abortion, the Equal Rights Amendment, capital punishment, marijuana, homosexual rights and pornography.

The anti-pornography drive, rejuvenated by Supreme Court decisions made after Nixon's appointments changed the complexion of the Court, is part of an overall conservative push against liberalism on the social front. (Nixon always praised his selections for the court as being "strict constructionists," but they are hardly that when it comes to the First Amendment.) Ironically, conservatism has always offered itself to the public as rugged individualism. That may have been accurate when government regulation of big business was the issue. Now, however, there is no rugged individualism for the woman who wants control of her own reproductive process. There is no rugged individualism for the person who wants to smoke pot. And there is no rugged individualism for the person who wants to make up his or her own mind about what books and magazines to buy and what movies to see. In those areas our liberty-loving conservatives desire to see the state as all-powerful as it is under the Communist regimes they profess to abhor. (It is no accident that pornography is *verboten* in totalitarian countries; puritanism and police states always go together.)

Back in the Nineteenth Century, liberalism was the doctrine of those who believed in individual freedom. It lost this association during the New Deal era, when liberals started relying on government to accomplish their aims. Now, as the battleground shifts from the economic to the social arena, liberals find themselves once again taking the side of the individual.

Some of the people who support censorship of obscenity ought to know better. There are many among the leaders of the anti-pornography movement who are capable of understanding a scientific argument and who therefore should be aware that pornography is harmless. Because it is not in their interest to know this, they pretend, perhaps to themselves as well as the rest of the world, not to know it.

There are others who, lacking intelligence or education,

do not understand what constitutes scientific evidence and so believe the claims that pornography causes sex crimes and breaks up homes. Or they know nothing about Constitutional law and believe that there's nothing wrong with banning books, magazines or movies that offend them. Every year some newspaper somewhere in the country sends a reporter out to show a copy of the Bill of Rights to people on the street. Many people don't recognize the document and are unaware that it is already part of the law of the land. Among those there are always some who condemn it as being anarchistic. These are the sort of people who give their time, energy and money to anti-pornography crusades.

It is sometimes charged that opposition to censorship is merely a fashion among intellectuals and literati who want to be considered "smart people." It happens to be true that smart people tend to oppose obscenity laws. It is also true that smart people tend to know that there are at least nine planets, that the Earth revolves around the sun, that the theory of evolution is a highly probable explanation for the development of life on this planet, that environmental pollution is something to worry about and that racism and sexism is based on scientifically unsound premises. This general agreement among smart people is not the result of conspiracy or snobbery but springs from their ability to follow reasoned arguments and grasp factual evidence. That's what being smart means. Only in a country that still has a strong anti-intellectual tradition (one remembers the attacks on Adlai Stevenson for being an "egghead" and George Wallace's diatribes against "pointy-headed intellectuals") could the word "smart" be used to attack a position.

Obscenity laws have no practical justification. They evolved out of religious blasphemy laws. Until the Nineteenth Century all prosecutions for obscenity were conducted under blasphemy laws, on the assumption that sexual explicitness in writings or pictures were offensive to the deity. Today, the real motive behind anti-obscenity campaigns is not the discredited belief that erotic materials are injurious to people in some way. The real motive for censorship is a religious one. Pornography depicts people doing things that violate traditional religious rules of sexual morality. Of course, if the anti-porn crusaders came out and admitted that it is their *religious* beliefs that are offended by pornography their position would be untenable in a society which honors the principle of separation of church and state. Therefore they cling to the screen of pornography's supposed harmfulness to hide their real reason for wanting to ban it.

By any reasonable standard obscenity laws are unconstitutional. They are an unwarranted restriction on freedom of expression and a violation of the principle of separation of church and state. They are an embarrassment for a country as technologically and scientifically advanced as this. Their continued enforcement is a waste of scarce public resources. The more enlightened a judge, a prosecutor or a police official, the lower priority he or she will ascribe to obscenity laws.

It is my hope that intelligence will eventually rise to a level where obscenity laws will be declared unconstitutional or repealed totally.

Ꞡ

The Empire of the Rising Scum

Originally published in Loompanics Catalogue 1990

> A thousand reforms have left the world as corrupt as ever, for each successful reform has founded a new institution, and this institution has bred its new and congenial abuses.
>
> – George Santayana

When I tell people that I am an anarchist (if I want to be treated somewhat politely I say I am a "libertarian") often the first challenge thrown at me is, "How would people get along without organization? If it was every man or woman for themselves, the human race would die off."

I could point out that this is quite possibly the fate we're headed for with the help of our many and mighty organizations. But instead I usually say that, though it may surprise them, I too believe in the necessity of organization. Indeed, if our ancestors of millions of years ago hadn't learned how to care for one another and hunt in packs, they'd all have ended up being eaten by leopards.

The key element in tragedy is that heroes and heroines are destroyed by that which appears to be their greatest strength. Of all human inventions the organization, a machine constructed of people performing interdependent functions, is the most powerful. Because it is so powerful, the organization is more dangerous than any other human invention, including nuclear fission (itself the product of an organized scientific project).

Even while we busily attend meetings, contribute money and perform our assigned tasks, we suspect that we may be helping to create a force that is inimical to many values we hold dear. This suspicion of anything organized is manifested in the often-heard remark. "I'm not against religion, just organized religion." Indeed, the term "organized religion" is never used except by people who are against it.

There is folk wisdom in this. An organized religion tends to require that its members live in certain specified ways and accept certain specified beliefs. What's more, those requirements are presented as a package deal. To reject even one major tenet of the religion or to violate one major rule of behavior is enough to get one kicked out – or worse. Organized religion provides a model of the way all organizations, from the state down to the village garden club, cost a price in terms of a member's freedom of thought and action.

Elaine Pagels, in *The Gnostic Gospels*, suggests that when two sects are competing the one with the more authoritarian structure, stricter discipline and more rigid belief system will tend to win out. The early Gnostics were egalitarian in structure and acknowledged that any member – even females! – might have a valid theological insight. The Gnostics were rapidly driven out of business by the hierarchical orthodox Christians. It doesn't seem possible for an organization to be egalitarian, democratic and allow its participants great latitude in belief and behavior and still outdo competitors more tightly controlled. Just as predatory animals follow a similar general design and behave in similar ways, so organizations, especially those in competition with one another, must follow certain design principles if they are to succeed and prevail.

Military organization, like religious organization, can be seen as a paradigm of organization in general. Indeed, one of the most successful and influential religious organizations in history, the Society of Jesus, was consciously modeled along military lines by its founder, Ignatius Loyola. The very nature of military operations – organized violence – requires a highly authoritarian structure. As Napoleon put it, "One bad general is better than two good generals."

That the more authoritarian organizations survive and prevail goes generally unnoticed because people focus on the objectives of organizations, which are many and varied, rather than on their structures, which tend to be similar. Whenever people see a problem, an opportunity or a threat, their first reaction – even before saying, "Pass a law'" – is, "Let's start an organization."

But the more an organization succeeds and prospers, the more it is likely to be diverted from its original ideals, principles and purposes. While Francis of Assissi was still alive, the religious order he founded, dedicated to poverty, had already started to acquire real estate.

Every combination of two or more human beings has both a useful aspect and a political aspect. These tend to conflict with each other. As the political aspect becomes more and more influential, the organization ceases to be useful to its members and starts using them.

Why does this happen? Because the better an organization is at fulfilling its purpose, the more it attracts people who see the organization as an opportunity to advance themselves.

The ability to get ahead in an organization is simply another talent, like the ability to play chess, paint pictures, do coronary bypass operations or pick pockets. There are some people who are extraordinarily good at manipulating organizations to serve their own ends. The Russians, who have suffered under such people for centuries, have a name for them – apparatchiks. It was an observer of apparatchiks who coined the maxim, "The scum rises to the top."

The apparatchik's aim in life is to out-ass-kiss, out-maneuver, out-threaten, out-lie and ultimately out-fight his or her way to the top of the pyramid – any pyramid. Appropriately, Russia produced a superb specimen of homo apparatchikus – Josef Stalin. Many American novels have described the wheeling and dealing of apparatchiks in various occupations; perhaps the classic fictional character of this kind is Sammy Glick, the movie tycoon in Budd Schulberg's novel, *What Makes Sammy Run?* Niccolo Machiavelli wrote a handbook for apparatchiks that is unsurpassed to this day – *The Prince*. But the most successful of this breed need neither exemplars or hand-books; they seem to know instinctively what to do.

It often happens that when a person possesses a particular ability to an extraordinary degree, nature makes up for it by leaving him or her incompetent in every other department. Thus we see owners of baseball teams who lack any understanding of the sport, heads of banks who couldn't balance a checkbook, industrialists whose main industry is riding around in fancy limos, and generals who know more about playing golf with congressmen than they do about fighting wars.

Unfortunately, the existence of this talent means that every successful organization will sooner or later be taken over by apparatchiks. As such people achieve influence within the organization, whenever there is a conflict between their own interest and the interest of the organization, their interests will win out. Thus, over time, the influence of apparatchiks will deflect the organization further and further from its original intent.

For this reason, the most admirable time in the history of any institution is its early days – Ford and his Tin Lizzie, Edison at Menlo Park, Jesus wandering through Palestine, Castro in the Sierra Maestra, Hefner at his kitchen table. These are the days when organizations are most visionary and goal-oriented and are least encumbered by internal politics.

It is instructive, for instance, to trace the computer industry's decline in vision, idealism, creativity, romance and sheer fun as it becomes more and more important and prosperous. In a few short years the hackers, those talented, inventive people who created this industry, have been shuffled into the background with the explanation that "they don't know how to run a business," and the apparatchiks have moved in like buzzards after a buffalo hunt. The truth is that apparatchiks don't know how to run a business either, but it is their gift to look as if they do. When it comes to inter-corporate fighting, an engineer who knows how to design a superlative computer has no more chance against an apparatchik than he would in the ring with a sumo wrestler.

Whatever the original aim of the organization – to publish books, to heal the sick, to share information about computers – once it has been taken over by apparatchiks, it will acquire a new aim: to get bigger. It doesn't matter whether a bigger organization will fulfill its purpose as well, serve its customers or constituents as well, or be as good a place for people to work. It will get bigger simply because those at the top want it to get bigger. Apparatchiks do to organizations what cancer viruses do to cells; they promote purposeless growth.

To quote Santayana again: "Fanaticism consists in redoubling your effort when you have forgotten your aim."

The apparatchiks not only want their own organization to get bigger; they also want it to swallow up or defeat and destroy all other organizations. Thus we see, in Communist countries, the party runs everything from the state police to the local chess club; whereas in capitalist countries one corporation will manufacture cars, rent out security guards, publish newspapers, bake bread, launch space satellites and pave over rain forests. The tendency of capitalist corporations, whose greatest achievements are due to free competition, to try to eliminate competition and form monopolies is typical of what happens to institutions that get taken over by apparatchiks.

The apparatchik seeks with the same blind inevitability to expand in yet another direction – beyond the agreed-upon limits of authority. Anyone who seeks power wants absolute power. Every Roman emperor, every Medieval and Renaissance monarch who succeeded in getting an armlock on the job immediately sought to expand his power beyond the limits set by law and custom. Every U.S. President who has been accorded the title "great" by historians has attempted to exceed his Constitutional authority, from Jefferson purchasing Louisiana to Lincoln setting aside habeas corpus to Roosevelt trying to pack the Supreme Court.

The ultimate means for determining the top apparatchik is war. This whole phenomenon of the diversion of organizations from their purposes and ideals does not seem very serious when the scum rise to the top in the bridge club or the offices of a small magazine publisher. But today it is happening on a global scale. At the moment the threat of war between the world's two most powerful apparatchiks, the President of the U.S. and the Premier of the Soviet Union, is receding. But we'll be turning another corner soon, when people like the Ayatollah get the Bomb. The world's leaders will then have to decide whether to swallow up smaller nations run by voracious apparatchiks or let the whole world go up in smoke. Whatever decision they make, it will probably be a bad one.

I don't wish to convey a "nothing works and everything is futile" attitude. I think there may be ways to tame the organizational beast, though I have hardly room in this essay to do more than suggest that such means exist.

Could we do away with organizations? A few fringe philosophers are attracted to a vision of what might be called the heat death of society – the idea that only dummies participate in organized activity and that the smart folks live on the margins, shoplifting and eating out of garbage cans.

The obvious drawback to this notion is that it requires a multitude, living in the organized way they do now, to keep the garbage cans filled and the store shelves stocked. Thus we're still stuck with organization as we know it.

One simple way to keep organizations from becoming cancerous might be to rotate all jobs on a regular, frequent and mandatory basis, including the leadership positions. While it may seem wasteful for people to spend part of their time working at jobs they are not particularly good at, and even detrimental to the organization's goals, the healthiest societies do seem to be those that encourage people to do a variety of things – as in pioneer America. A permanent division of labor inevitably creates occupational and class inequality and conflict. As Robert A. Heinlein said through Lazarus Long, '"Specialization is for insects."

Speaking of insects, entomologists have found that life is pretty good for those insects that live as self-sufficient individuals; they have plenty of food, lots of leisure and are good at protecting themselves from predators. Whereas among the so-called social insects, the individual's well-being is largely sacrificed to the needs of the group.

Individuals, too, who cultivate a variety of skills seem brighter, more energetic and more adaptable than those who know how to do one thing only. Not all of us can be polymaths, like Leonardo, Thomas Jefferson or Steve Allen, but we can all learn how to do a few more things than we know how to do now, and the adding of skill to skill can be a lifelong and most rewarding process. And, of course, the more self-sufficient we are, the less we will be dependent upon organizations.

Ultimately we may still ask, why can't humans design a perfect society? But there is no reason why anything in the universe should work perfectly. Only Dianeticians and Christians start from the assumption that humans should be perfect and that an explanation is needed for why they are not. The rest of us know that life is the trial and error product of billions of years of fumbling by what biologist Richard Dawkins calls "The Blind Watchmaker." It's a wonder it works as well as it does.

Ǥ

The Non-violent Bear It Away

From the New Libertarian, August 1978

I'm sorry, but the more I think about it – and I find myself thinking about it often – the more I become convinced that a general policy of non-violence is the one essential of a truly free society.

I say I'm sorry about this because I realize that non-violence isn't fashionable any more. Most anarchists seem to admire the assassins, bomb-throwers and militia leaders of an earlier time (even though anarchism *should* be trying to live down its bomb-throwing reputation.) Many libertarians want to abolish the state, but many also want to keep a little-bitty police force and a little-bitty army to protect private property.

Fashions in thinking about violence and revolution seem to have gone through three phases in recent years. First, roughly from 1960 to 1968, non-violence was in vogue. But peaceful demonstrations didn't bring about the immediate capitulation of militarists, capitalists and racists. Instead, the demonstrators were greeted with police riots and National Guard bullets. The trend-setters in the "Movement" decreed that non-violence doesn't work.

So we entered a second phase in which people began talking about taking up the gun. *The New York Review of Books* printed its famous Molotov-cocktail diagram cover. Clearly, guerrilla warfare was working in Vietnam. Maybe it would work here, too. Even anarchists, to whom, one would think, the goals of the National Liberation Front would be repugnant, frequently found nice things to say about guerrilla warfare.

The third phase, which developed during the long night of the Nixon era and is still with us, is one of despair. Nothing works. There are no trend-setters anymore (unless Jerry Brown, God help us, is a trend setter) and there is no "Movement" to speak of. Instead there are government-engineered rallies for solar energy. Most of the radicals of yesteryear are going into conventional politics – or into business. In Europe and the Middle East the atrocities of radically-oriented terrorist groups become steadily more atrocious – and more pointless. For the most part they don't expect to accomplish anything, only to mess things up. Violence becomes less a means and more an end in itself.

These positions all assume that resorting, or not resorting, to force is merely a question of strategy. Violence is just one of the options we may select in trying to bring about social change. It is equally applicable no matter what kind of society one is working toward. Conceivably, one could, if conditions warranted, make use of violence to set up a democratic, a socialist, a fascist, a communist or an anarchist society.

I would argue that this may be true for all of the above except the last. Because by definition an anarchist society is one without government, and government *is* violence.

"Whoa there!" calls a voice from the audience. "Son of Sam was a *government*?" Well, that's not as ridiculous as it sounds. In other times, in other climes, a man with an irresistible urge to kill women might become an honored part of the state apparatus. Aztec and Mayan priests killed young women regularly, and the Medieval witch hunters went after women young and old. There is no pathological tendency government can't find a use for in carrying out its self-appointed tasks. No government, certainly not that of the U.S., is without its nut cases doing their duty in various corners of the executive, legislative, judicial, law enforcement, intelligence and military machines.

David Berkowitz pleaded guilty to six murders. Think how many young women a legislator helps to off when he votes against the use of public funds to pay for abortions for indigent women.

In a free society there wouldn't be public funds to pay for anything. But in a free society no woman would have difficulty in getting an abortion. In the context of this political/economic system, to make it difficult for any group of women to get abortions is murder.

The same voice cries, "All you are saying is that governments *resemble* violent criminals. You haven't proved that they're identical!"

Well, what are the differences? Governments claim a monopoly on the means of violence in the areas they control, whereas violent criminals do not prevent others from using violence. Governments are supposedly constituted to benefit people, whereas violent criminals don't benefit anybody but themselves. Governments are always somehow legitimated – divinely appointed, hallowed by tradition or popularly sanctioned – whereas violent criminals are by definition not legitimate.

All these differences boil down to differences in scale. The violent loner may not look much like a government, but multiply him by a hundred acting in concert and the resemblance becomes uncanny. The larger a criminal enterprise grows the more it seeks to monopolize the means of violence, claim to benefit people generally and claim legitimacy. A triangle is still a triangle, whether its altitude is a few inches or a mile.

The essence of government is the use of power of inflicting physical harm to coerce people. The reason the anarchist objects to government is precisely this use of physical force to coerce people. If anarchists are to be consistent, they should object to any physical coercion – including the use of physical force to make an anarchist revolution or to protect an anarchist society.

What about self-defense? Only those who adopt pacifism as a moral position object to a person using violence when there is no other way to protect oneself from being hurt. And I am not advocating pacifism as a moral position. Indeed, I avoid moral positions as zealously as I avoid potholes on the road.

But once a society institutionalizes defensive violence, setting up a police force or an army, it *is* a state and those who command the police force or the army *are* a government, regardless of what the state and its rulers call themselves. The institutions of violence take on a life of their own, develop needs of their own, grow larger and more aggressive and invasive. Once a society is committed to using force to resist internal or external violence, it finds as time goes on that it needs larger and larger doses of force to do the job. And self-defense becomes more and more an excuse for empire building. Hardly a nation in recent years has gone to war without claiming it was acting to defend itself against aggressors.

Anarchists or libertarians who propose to work for the abolition of government should consider carefully just what it is they want to abolish. Is it government as the preserver of the economic and social inequities that mar our society? Is it government as enemy of individual liberty? Or is it the very core and essence of government – the coercive use of physical force?

People who aim to abolish the very essence of government and all that resembles it can't do so by fighting government with government. The tool shapes the user. Those who live by the sword shall perish by the politician.

Letter to the editor on freedom of speech

Glencoe News, July 6, 1989

When the Ayatollah declared open season on Salman Rushdie for blaspheming Islam, many Americans looked down their noses at the tyrant and his followers and thought, "How irrational!" But doubtless many of the same people were outraged with the U.S. Supreme Court decision declaring flag burning to be a protected form of expression under the First Amendment. The truth is, when it comes to the symbols we hold sacred, there is a little tyrant in all of us.

Probably we wouldn't kill someone whose expression, communications or symbolic act offended our deepest convictions, but many of us would be happy to see that person in jail. Many of us simply can't accept the idea that the freedom of expression guaranteed by the First Amendment means freedom for precisely those utterances, artworks and acts of protest that make us furious.

The Bill of Rights was written two hundred years ago, but it sometimes seems to be a 21st Century document. Many of us, like the Ayatollah, are just not rational enough to accept it.

Now I read that President Bush is seeking a way to circumvent the court's decision exempting destruction of the flag from punishment. But we honor the flag because it stands for freedom, especially the freedoms guaranteed by the Bill of Rights. To chip away at those freedoms is itself an act of desecration.

Robert Shea

G

Come Back Lyndon!

(With Robert Anton Wilson).

(This piece ran in the July 1971 issue of The Organ, an underground newspaper in California. The editor).

God, how we miss L.B.J.!

The confession comes with weeping violins, thunder off-screen and shadows gathering in the corners. There is the gnashing of teeth and the commotions at the other end of the alimentary tract causing a noticeable tightening of the ass-hole, while the liver dies a little, and the damage to key glands and trunk-line nerves will not be discovered by conventional medicine. Still, the confession, at last, must come. We were there, we marched with the others and chanted, "Hey, hey, L.B.J., how many kids didja kill today?"; yes, we signed the petitions and wrote to the Congressmen, we even gave some credence in Garrison and Mark Lane and *MacBird;* we longed for the day and dreamed of the day when that Texas Turd was sent home to gather flies on the banks of the Pedernales and was replaced at the Helm by somebody, anybody, who didn't have the soul of a cattle rustler and a face like a study in the mesmerization of the anal sphincter. Back in Texas was where we wanted him. We most definitely wanted him back in Texas.

Well, we didn't get somebody. We didn't even get anybody. By the malice of a left-handed and sardonic God, we got "Richard Milhouse Nixon."

We repent all of our sins and heresies; we recant in public. We want L.B.J. back. The next time our troops withdraw from Vietnam into another Asian country, we want old Lyndon there to explain it, with those crafty lines of ham Summer Stock piety crinkling around his eyes – not "Nixon" with that no-echo sound in his voice that makes it seem as if his throat is lined with styrofoam, and that Insect Trust remoteness from all human emotion. Confronted with the alien, the perhaps mechanical, the possibly Outer Space quality of seeming motiveless malignity in "Nixon," we are beginning to appreciate how American, how human, how *downhome* Lyndon Baines Johnson really was.

And the L.B.J. jokes – remember them? They were so folksy and real and earthy – remember? Remember, "Terrible accident at the L.B.J. ranch today – somebody left the gate open and the cattle all went home?" Remember the legends about his enormous schlong, and Paul Krassner's great line, "When he calls a joint meeting, everybody cringes?" Remember, "The White House reporters can now tell when L.B.J. is lying. When he scratches his ear, he's telling the truth. When he rubs his nose, he's telling the truth. But when he open his mouth – he's lying!" Who tells jokes about "Nixon"? Perhaps the computers at the Rand think-tank do, exchanging ghastly electronic jests as they calculate scenarios for the next Asiatic incursion. But do you know any *people* who relate to "Nixon" enough to joke about him? Behind the name "Richard Nixon" is there anything substantial enough to jest about?

Remember the quick adrenalin flashes and the screams of rage in the old anti-Johnson demonstrations, the most exhilarating hate-trip many of us have ever been on? Do you know anyone who hates "Nixon" that way? Turn anywhere, look at the hardest-working and most dedicated peace crusader you know, and is there any personal feeling toward "Richard Nixon"? Never. At the most, there is distaste and an attenuated metaphysical dread, a hunch that behind the seeming void of the public persona might be a secret so dreadful that the human mind would crumble on confronting it. Worse: that there is no horror behind the void, nothing but another void, which conceals a still deeper void, in a mad series of 0-dimensional Chinese boxes regressing infinitely always to another void, another mask, and still another void masking another void, forever?

History is a game for any number of players, but that's the key – you need real players to enjoy it. The one thing that, sooner or later, any hyperactive participant (as we sometimes think we are) has to learn is that a good game requires a spirited opposition. We of the Left need a Right. Realizing that, you come to see that your enemy is not really your enemy in any total sense – he is as necessary to you as your friend. At that point you come to value the fact that your enemy is a human being; who can work up a good political enthusiasm against a moving van, the tobacco mosaic virus or the weather in Chicago? But we have reached this point of understanding only to have the universe swat us upside the head once more: Sitting across the table from us is "Richard M. Nixon" and we have the stale, disappointed feeling of being up against a chess-playing robot. If he wins, does it matter – if we win, does it matter?

People have humanized hurricanes and other disasters, they have even anthropomorphized the plague bacteria and projected malice into its invasions, but it is simply impossible to humanize or anthropomorphize "Richard Nixon." The best public relations brains in the country have worked on the job for years, and all they produce when the TV cameras turn on is the same dead-level computer readouts of some very unconvincing used car salesman's pitch of fading memory. How different it was when L.B.J. said, "With a heavy heart, I once again resume bombing," and the delivery was so Riverboat Gambler that you could feel an almost tactile relationship with the conniving but *human* sonofabitch who rehearsed the words over and over until they almost captured the ring of sincerity.

L.B.J. was a bad father, a father you could hate, an old Huck Finn Pap of a reprobate who lied his head off and stole everything not nailed down but probably cackled with obscene glee over every swindle and laughed like hell when he told his cronies about it. You might want to ride him out of town on a rail, but you knew he'd make out all right in the next town and swindle the folks there, too, and you had a sneaking admiration for that incorrigibility. But nobody can think of "Nixon" as a father, good or bad, or any kind of brother, or even a very remote cousin. Being conquered by the Martians would be existentially believable compared to being governed by "Nixon" – at least the Martian, if inhuman, must be protoplasm. Who is that sure about Nixon? If he abruptly answered a press conference with "That – does – not – compute," who would really be surprised or feel aught else but that a buried suspicion has been confirmed?

Even "Nixon's" admirers don't admire "him" and this clearly communicated early to "his" circle who thoughtfully built up Spiro as a human and believable spokesman whom people could love and hate.

Consider what could have been "Nixon's" finest moment, the day he announced that he was against abortion because of his belief in "the sanctity of human life." Imagine how Lyndon-Baby would have handled that line, every crease on his face emphasizing the depths of emotion and spiritual revelation, the quiver in his voice on the key words "sanctity" and "life," the whole effect mounting to a crescendo of righteousness on a level with Fields himself saying, "What? Five aces in the deck? What scoundrel could have done that?" Do you remember any of "Nixon's" performances? Nobody does; Nobody remembers any of "his" speeches. They just remember that "he" was on TV again and said something and nobody can quite recollect whether "he" was selling his latest invasion or Ajax, the Foaming Cleanser.

Or, look at the other side of the picture. Recall the great oration that terminated L.B.J.'s three decades of opposition to racial equality, that Falstaffian performance in which he pledged all his loyalty to civil rights and concluded raptly, "And we *shall* overcome." It was pure Rod Steiger, right out of the scene in *The Harder They Fall* where Steiger, the gangster, tells his gunsels to "show some respect" for the man they just killed. You felt a deep human identification for L.B.J. and Steiger in those scenes and wished that they could succeed in making someone believe them, wished almost that you could believe them for a moment. Can you imagine "Nixon" handling that bit? Can you hear him saying, "We shall overcome," and getting any response any more sympathetic or antipathetic than a yawn?

Obviously, given that people aren't completely stupid or tasteless, it is hard at times to understand how come the American electorate made the trade – the monstrous human being for the robot monster. The best explanation we've found is the Conspiracy Theory. In our novel *Illuminatus!* (to be published by Dell later this year) we dramatize the notion that just about every catastrophe in history can be explained by the machinations of the Ancient Illuminated Seers of Bavaria, a conspiratorial organization which runs international finance, all major political parties everywhere in the world, all communications media, the Catholic Church, and the Chicago Transit Authority. While doing the research for *Illuminatus!* we came across the fact that on April 1, 1968, Johnson was opening his morning copy of *The New York Times* while spooning a heavily-sugared wedge of grapefruit into that lugubrious face (which, as he himself quite frankly stated after viewing Peter Hurd's portrait, was "the ugliest thing I ever saw"), when a pink slip fell out. The message read, "It's April First and you're It," and it was signed "The Fellas." Under this there appeared a peculiar symbol, printed in red, an eye inside a glowing triangle. A somewhat similar eye can be seen – if "Nixon's" stewardship of the economy left you any bread – on the U.S. dollar bill, back side on the left.

Shortly after receiving this message, Johnson opted out of the 1968 Presidential race. We learned these facts in a teenager's magazine called *Teenset* for March 1969 in an article on the Ancient Illuminated Seers of Bavaria by a writer named Sandra Glass. The writer disappeared before the article was published, *Teenset* changed its name to *Aum*, and *Aum* itself subsequently ceased publication.

Assuming – as do most Illuminati experts such as ourselves, Howard Bickler and Robert Welch of the John Birch Society – that Johnson's masters are the ones who continue to rule the country through "Nixon," can anyone visualize them disposing of "Nixon" by sending him a pink slip? They would simply pull the plug.

We blamed the war on the Democrats. When the Ghostly Old Party gave us "Nixon" as its nominee, the proceedings were as genteel as a wake in Grosse Pointe, Michigan. When the Democrats met in Chicago, the boil burst in full color on television and all over the parks and streets. Richard J. Daley, rumored in some documents we've found to be the fifth Illuminatus Primus, destroyed Humphrey's chances of winning by making the nominating process look as democratic as parliament run by Oliver Cromwell. Can this have been an accident? Then why did Daley shout "*Ewige blumenkraft!*" (an Illuminati slogan used by Beethoven and Goethe) at Abraham Ribicoff at a most heated moment, on the evening of August 26, 1968? The boil burst, but it was not allowed to drain. "Nixon" plastered it over, that it might suppurate more in the darkness.

So you Illuminated Seers, if you be human and not a race of interplanetary invaders who are all "Nixons," you, too, must be fed up with the banality of this particular brand of evil. You've outdone yourselves this time. Let us have a man back in the White House. A shrewd, stupid, crafty, clumsy, eating, breathing, spitting, belching, balls-scratching, nose picking, guilt ridden, boasting, overcompensating, naive, corrupt, evil and innocent human being – another L.B.J. or the original L.B.J. himself, brought back for a re-run. Do not, O Illuminati, leave us out here in the twilight with no more for host than a sincere Coca Cola machine.

On Science Fiction: Its purpose and the effects of critics

The idea that science fiction doesn't really try to predict the future, or other imaginary marvels, to comment on the present is an interesting one, and one I think that explains a lot.

I've heard William Gibson make this assertion about his own stories and about the works of other well-thought-of SF writers, such as Ray Bradbury. It also seems to me that when so-called mainstream writers turn to SF they do it to satirize or warn against current trends. Certainly this is what Orwell was doing in *1984*. And recently I read an article in the *New York Times Book Review* that pointed out that H.G. Wells wrote *The War of the Worlds* to show the British what it would be like to be on the receiving end of a visit from a ruthless, technologically superior imperial power.

But any statement that tries to explain "the purpose" of a literary genre has to be qualified by the recognition that there may be as many purposes as there are practitioners. Indeed, as many purposes as there are readers, because a writer may invent an imaginary world to teach me a lesson, and I may choose to ignore the lesson and read the story for sheer entertainment. All my life I've enjoyed *War of the Worlds* in all its versions without once thinking of it as a criticism of imperialism.

Perhaps I missed the point of *War of the Worlds* because I tend to root for the Martians.

I like SF, not because it comments on or satirizes present conditions, but because it allows me to vicariously experience strange and wonderful things that *cannot* be found in the world around me. And it tells me that such things are scientifically possible. Damon Knight is closer to my motive for reading – and writing – SF when he talks about the "sense of wonder."

The kind of fantasy I like best, similarly, stands on its own feet as storytelling. I don't buy the idea that Tolkien in *The Lord of the Rings* was writing an allegory about British democracy versus Continental totalitarianism, or about the destruction of the beautiful medieval English environment by the industrial revolution. I think Tolkien was trying to tell us stories about a marvelous new world that had manifested itself in his imagination. And that is pretty much what he tells us he was trying to do in his essay, "On Faerie Stories," where he describes stories as "subcreations," self-contained universes that exist for their own sake, not necessarily as commentary on the big creation we all inhabit.

[As for criticism's effect on the genre,] criticism can be helpful to writers if it points the way to what they want to do, but it can be harmful if it deflects writers from doing what they are naturally attracted to or talented for. For example, I think certain critics are responsible for the low esteem in which science fiction is held in U.S. intellectual circles, such that writers like Margaret Atwood won't even admit that they're writing SF.

For example, in a review of *The Child in Time* by Ian McEwan, about the sudden and inexplicable disappearance of the main character's daughter, we read, "The thought that the central event was constructed of the stuff of science fiction seriously undermined my involvement in Stephen's tragedy, and with those aspects of the book that resonate with psychological reality: the beautifully realized relationships, the tracing of the many-layered love between father and child, husband and wife." For this reviewer, one Rebecca Goldstein, herself a novelist, the thought that McEwan *might have included* a science fiction element spoiled the novel. She didn't even have to be sure. Is that prejudiced, or what?

This critical notion that science fiction clashes with psychological reality is one Algis Budrys remarks on in the December [1988] *Fantasy and Science Fiction.* He mentions the term "serious" novelist, often used by critics, and says, "That's another one of those terms full of assumptions, including the pernicious ones that descriptive fiction is the superior literature and that the average practitioner of descriptive literature is one of a more elevated talent and sensibility than the average practitioner of other forms of writing." This idea is pernicious, I would think, because it influences both writers and readers.

This is only one example of the ways critics can have a harmful effect on literature.

Ǥ

Robert Heinlein's Rules for Writers

Heinlein's Third Rule, "You must refrain from rewriting except to editorial order," means not doing any major revision of a piece before submitting it.

This gives me a chance to quote extensively from Heinlein's speech, "Channel Markers," given at the U.S. Naval Academy in Annapolis on April 5, 1973, in which he offered advice to would-be writers. (It was published in the January 1974 issue of *Analog.*)

You may wonder why Heinlein would make a speech on how to become a freelance writer to a bunch of Naval cadets, but it makes perfect sense in the light of his own life. An Annapolis graduate himself, he was discharged from the Navy for health reasons and turned to writing as a way to make a living. He could well have imagined that the same thing might happen to some of the cadets in his audience.

He gave his five rules for success in writing as follows:

First: You must write.

Second: You must finish what you write.

Third: You must refrain from rewriting except to editorial order.

Fourth: You must place it on the market.

Fifth: You must *keep* it on the market until sold.

He went on to talk about how few people follow all five of these rules. About not rewriting he said, "Of those who do not finish a manuscript, nine-tenths of them won't leave well enough alone. They start fiddling with it, rewriting, polishing, changing . . . until they have squeezed the life out and lost interest."

Later he returned to the subject of rewriting: "Take a cabinetmaker specializing in handmade furniture. He must make furniture and he must complete each piece he makes. He never tears up a chair he has finished because he has thought of a better design. No, he offers that chair for sale and uses the new design to build another – this is the 'no re-writing' rule."

I guess he knew that of the five rules the third would be the most controversial, because he went back to it yet a third time in the lecture. This time it becomes clear that he isn't recommending that the aspiring writer let the first draft stand exactly as written. The professional writer, according to Heinlein, should go over his work, to improve the language and to cut wherever possible. What he's arguing against are structural changes, such as rewriting a scene from a different point of view, adding or removing an important character, new plot developments, the kind of big changes that necessitate redrafting part of all of the story from scratch:

"A beginner finds it hard to believe that no-rewriting rule. A myth has grown up that a manuscript to be suitable for publication must be rewritten at least once.

"Utterly false.

"Would you refry an egg? Tear down a freshly built wall? Destroy a new chair? Ridiculous!

"This silly practice of rewriting is based on the hidden assumption that you are smarter today than you were yesterday.

But you are *not*. The efficient way to write, as with any other work, is to *do it right the first time!*

"I don't mean that a manuscript should not be corrected and cut. Few writers are perfect in typing, spelling, punctuation and grammar. Most of us have to go back and correct such things, and – above all – strike out surplusage and fancy talk. The manuscript then needs to be retyped – for neatness, retyping is not rewriting. Rewriting means a new approach, a basic change in form.

"Don't do it!

"A writer's sole capital is his time. You cannot afford to start writing until you know what you mean to say and how you mean to say it. If you fail in this, it is not paper you are wasting but your sharply limited and irreplaceable lifetime.

"An instructor in English who requires a student to rewrite is reinforcing the worst possible habit in the use of language, the inability to say it right the first time."

Heinlein then talks about the need for naval officers to be able to write efficiently, and he describes a course he took at Annapolis called "Order Writing," which required students to write orders for various situations, after which the instructor and the rest of the class would try to misconstrue the order. No chance to write a second draft. If the order could plausibly be misunderstood, the writer got zero. If it could not be misunderstood, the writer got a perfect mark for the day.

"It was a wonderful course!"

Frank Robinson, who interviewed Heinlein for *Playboy* (an interview that was never published) told me that Heinlein wrote his novels straight through, one draft, then went over them with a felt-tipped pen, cutting out about half. And that was it.

Talking to aspiring writers, I often quote Heinlein's five

rules, and the one most people object to is the third rule. This is because, more than any other, it flies in the face of what is generally believed.

To take a typical example of the conventional wisdom about writing, I ran across the following in a *New York Times* review of a program designed to teach creative writing, written by former publisher Sol Stein:

"Good writing, as Mr. Stein tells us time and time again, is rewriting: adding, subtracting, polishing and otherwise changing the product until it is just right . . .

"The program leads you through successive rewritings, creating a heroine, a villain, a young son and two key scenes of a novel, and continually exhorts you not to be satisfied with your first try . . ."

Precisely because this is so widely perceived as the unquestioned and unquestionable truth, I like to quote Heinlein's views. One of Heinlein's great virtues as a science fiction writer was the way he encouraged people to question the unquestionable. I think the conventional wisdom encourages too much reliance on rewriting. I think many aspiring writers (such as myself at an earlier stage in my career) spend time rewriting which could more profitably be used writing new material. I think a writer can improve – and get published more often – by writing more and revising less than by writing less and rewriting more.

Not every writer, of course, but certainly some writers. And the "good writing is rewriting" doctrine is usually presented as if it applies to everybody. People need to at least consider the possibility that it isn't right for them.

Heinlein, like Asimov and Bradbury, who also say they are pretty much one-draft writers, come out of a generation that learned to write for pulp magazines paying very low rates. The only way to make decent money was to write a lot. For writers of that generation it was a common practice to write one draft, go over it with a pencil once or twice, then type a clean copy and send it in. I think that for Heinlein, Asimov and Bradbury, that which was a necessity also happened to be a congenial way of working.

Like any advice to writers, Heinlein's Third Rule cannot be followed blindly. The only absolutely infallible rule of writing I know is: *What works for one writer will not necessarily work for another.*

For myself, I find that one-draft writing doesn't work well. If, while writing my first draft, I think, this is it, this is what I'm going to be sending in, I tend to choke up while writing it. I need to do a draft in which I feel free to write whatever comes into my head without worrying whether it is good or bad. For me, the main value of Heinlein's Third Rule is to remind me to have reasonable confidence in my first draft and not to do *too much* rewriting.

Though Heinlein talks about revision rendering a piece lifeless, I don't think that's always true, either. I think there are many writers who can go on revising over and over again, and each revision will be an improvement. I don't think rewriting is *bad* (though it may be for some writers). The question is, how good a use of one's time is it? The answer will vary from one person to another, but for each person there will come a moment when it becomes more profitable to move on to something new than spend any more time reworking the old.

Peter Elbow's approach to composition seems like a sound and sensible one to me. I especially like the idea that students should be educated away from excessive concern with a perfect final draft and encouraged instead to view writing as a process. I am surprised though, that he doesn't attach more importance to the preliminary work – finding an idea, developing it, thinking it through, researching, making notes, organizing the notes, outlining. It seems to be that doing all that stuff right is at least half the battle.

But Heinlein doesn't talk much about preliminary work, either.

Acting Without Lusting for Results

If it is better not to care about results, then why not make futile gestures on behalf of one's ideals? As I have written earlier, I'm intrigued by people who do this, such as Yukio Mishima, and I am not intrigued by the widespread notion, which strikes me as terribly vulgar and corrupting, that winning is the only thing.

Here are some thoughts I've had lately about pursuing practical ends but not getting hung up on succeeding:

An action is a whole, and the end is part of the whole, part of the action. The end should have a probability of being achieved. Otherwise, the action is futile and self-destructive. So, one should not undertake any action that seems "good," regardless of whether the action is likely to end in failure. I would even go so far as to say that a well-done action is one so designed as to have every chance of accomplishing its purpose. But having embarked on an action that has a good chance of succeeding, we always know that the outcome depends on Goddess or luck or the gods or God, and we are willing to have it so and willing to accept whatever outcome, because we've done our best. In this state of acceptance we liberate ourselves from anxiety and are free to do our best.

In the above formulation I'm very uncomfortable with all those moralistic "shoulds," but I'm letting them stand because I need to get on with these comments.

But –

What we consider to be a worthwhile end depends on our value system. An apparently self-destructive action, like attacking a missile silo, doing no damage and going to prison for ten years may be in the eyes of the doer a successful action because it called national attention to her cause. This, not wrecking the missile, may have been the end of the action. And what about Mishima's raid on the army base and subsequent suicide? Was spectacular seppuku the very result he was aiming at?

A Sufi sage in *The Saracen* says, "The fool does nothing and leaves the future to God. The ordinary man acts and prays that God will give a good result. The wise man acts and leaves the future to God."

How can we eliminate the lust for results and at the same time base our actions on doing what is useful and avoiding what is harmful? Doing what is useful may be the basis of our value system. But another value might be to achieve a more central consciousness – i.e. awareness of one's intrinsic illumination. Any activity pursued for increased awareness yields value regardless of what it accomplishes. So it's not a case of either/or. The Japanese admire noble failures more than they do successful people. Of the rival Minamoto brothers of the twelfth century, the Japanese admire Yoshitsune, who lost the power struggle and died, more than Yoritomo, who won and became the first Shogun. They admire Yoshitsune, not because he lost, but because he was of finer character than his successful brother. So it is possible not to reject the practical end, but at the same time to pursue, over and above it, the – let us call it – psychological end.

Another way to aim at a practical end without lusting for results is to aim at accomplishing something, period, without worrying about whether you'll be rewarded for that accomplishment. After all, one can try to write a book and get hit by a truck before finishing. Success then lies in having been working toward the goal.

You can secretly lust for the result, but should always focus on the process.

I like what Linus Pauling says about this in the issue of Trajectories Bob Wilson included in Golden Apa No. 56. Asked what contribution the average person could make to peace work, he said, “Well, I say, do what you can. Don’t worry about how effective your contribution will be. Just go ahead and do it . . . Do something. Don’t think that you’re not going to be of any value. You might be of great value. But altogether, if everybody is doing this, it’ll be effective.”

These are all ways that a person can work towards a worthwhile goal without being caught up in the lust for results.

Ǥ

Robert Shea's 'Letters to the Editor' policy

In what was apparently the final issue of "No Governor," issue 11, Robert Shea explained that he no longer had room to run every letter to the editor he received and that he would have to implement a new policy for handling them. I was delighted by the policy and thought I would reprint it here:

I will publish letters that are surly and hostile in tone advocating positions that I consider a crock of shit, as long as they are not excessively long.

I will publish letters that are surly and hostile in tone and excessively long, as long as they do not advocate positions I consider a crock of shit.

I will publish excessively long letters that advocate positions I consider a crock of shit, as long as they are not surly and hostile in tone.

But I will not publish letters I consider a crock of shit, are excessively long and are surly and hostile in tone.

I get to decide what is excessively long, what is a surly and hostile tone and what is a crock of shit.

Ǥ

Comments about *Illuminatus!*

Robert Shea's comments to other members of The Golden APA often referred to Illuminatus!, *and I thought it might be useful to try to put the comments about the famous trilogy in one place.*

[In a comment to Robert Anton Wilson]:
I was stunned by your comment [to] Kevin, wherein you say you brooded over why you couldn't finish a long book and then, collaborating with me, finished one. You see, I've been going around telling people that I never completed a book project before writing *Illuminatus!* and it was my collaboration with *you,* and your example of joyful productivity that taught me how to write and finish novels. I never realized that *Illuminatus!* was a breakthrough book for both of us. I guess I sort of assumed that you had never before written a book simply because you hadn't gotten around to it, whereas I, who had started a number of novels and never finished any, had a "problem."

• • •

TODAY IS JUNE 22, 1988, FEAST OF THE MARTYRDOM OF ST. JOHN DILLINGER. HAIL ERIS. ALL HAIL DISCORDIA. 23 SKIDOO.

• • •

Bob Wilson on the myth of John Dillinger's penis – Wilson may answer this, too, but I can't resist – ah – inserting my own recollections. We first heard the myth about the Smithsonian keeping Dillinger's penis stashed away when a *Playboy* reader queried the "Advisor" about it. One of our researchers called the Smithsonian and said, "What I'm about to ask you may sound ridiculous, but we've received a serious question from a reader about it." Before she could continue, the man on the other end said, "No, we do not have John Dillinger's penis here." He went on to say that people called to ask about it several times a year.

As for it being 23 inches long – when Dillinger was cruelly assassinated and murdered a photograph of him lying on a tilted morgue table was published in the Chicago Daily News. He was covered with a sheet and seemed to have an enormous erection. Actually, the sheet was thrown over him and a lever that controlled the tilting of the table, but in the photograph the lever looked like part of Dillinger. Some Chicago papers published the photo retouched, with the sheet flattened out.

• • •

There is and always has been an awful lot of hokum around everything to do with the uncanny, esoteric, the occult, the paranormal, the supernatural, the mystical. Throughout this century and in past centuries as well. That is why I appreciate, as a needed corrective, even the knee-jerk skepticism of such groups as the Committee for the Scientific Investigation of Claims of the Paranormal.

But it also happens to be true that people can get useful philosophical and moral ideas from dubious sources. I've quoted Robert Anton Wilson's observation that Buddhism would still be valuable even if the Buddhist texts turned out to be forgeries. A lot of people have the same feeling about Castaneda; it doesn't matter whether Don Juan ever really existed.

I hope it won't seem too immodest to say that there are people who claim to have gotten a lot, philosophically, out of *Illuminatus!* and *Shike*, even though both novels are clearly labeled fiction. It seems to me that ideas have a life of their own, and that it may be important, in evaluating an idea, *not* to consider the source, but rather to consider its possible usefulness to one's own belief system.

But ideas are ideas and facts are facts (yes, I know this is a terribly stodgy Aristotelian/Newtonian/Cartesian way of looking at things, but there it is: I seem to be stuck with it).

• • •

Do you still read/like Korzybski? Wilson says Korzybski's ideas, though absorbed by him many years ago, are still influential in his thinking. Mine, too.

• • •

Indeed Jim Frenkel does have good taste; he was one of the five editors at Dell who worked on *Illuminatus!* He's the one who described it as, "The anarchist acid-rock answer to *Lord of the Rings*."

> *[The origin of this description is disputed; in the other interview, Wilgus attributes it to Dell editor David Harris. – The editor.]*

• • •

I've run into a fair number of people who believe world events are manipulated by the Illuminati or some similar conspiracy. This always poses a moral dilemma for me, because I want to be honest and tell them the novel was intended to spoof such notions, but I don't want to take away their reason for buying the book and recommending it to their friends.

• • •

The Masons have always been pretty open about being behind the U.S. government. Look at the eye and the pyramid on the dollar bill. They're so brazen they even put their headquarters on 23rd Street.

• • •

Re: Fans wanting to be disembodied intelligences: It strikes me as interesting in this connection that there are a number of SF stories on the theme of brains in boxes or brains removed from people and installed in machines, or minds or brains transplanted from one body to another, sometimes to an alien body. And higher intelligences are sometimes portrayed as beings of pure energy. We used this idea in *Illuminatus!* – but note that it was the Illuminati who wanted to get rid of their bodies, not our heroes and heroines.

• • •

I'm a student of Zen, and Zen teaches that mind and body are one.

I don't feel knowledgeable enough to comment on Judaism's attitude towards the body, but Catholics are taught that the body is "the temple of the Holy Spirit," and that they are obligated to take good care of it. The obligation to maintain good health comes under the Fifth Commandment, "Thou shalt not kill." This is interpreted to mean that it is forbidden to injure oneself. My sense is that many Catholics don't give much thought to this obligation, or to the rest of the Fifth Commandment.

• • •

Another thing I want to make perfectly clear, to quote a famous Illuminatus, that, as I have said again and again and again, to quote another one, that I am not only not an expert on conspiracy theory, I don't even believe in the damned things. I cannot speak for Bob Wilson on this point, but I know one of my intentions in writing *Illuminatus!* was to poke fun at the conspiracy paranoia besotting both Right and Left in the U.S. in the late 60s and early 70s.

• • •

Bob Wilson and I once had a bit of a run-in with Roger Ebert at a press party at the Biograph Theater promoting a book called *Dillinger, Dead or Alive*, which asserted that Dillinger had not been killed at the Biograph in 1934 but is, in fact, still living. Since this idea had also occurred to the authors of a Certain Trilogy, we showed up to express our support of the proposition that Dillinger lives. Ebert got the notion that we were making fun of his friend's book. A contretemps ensued. Hail Eris! [*Dillinger: Dead or Alive?* By Jay Robert Nash and Ron Offen was published in 1970].

• • •

Your essay caused me to think some more about how I feel about people masturbating to sex scenes I have written, and I've decided my attitude is more complicated than just being flattered that I had written something sexy enough to turn somebody on. I definitely would not be embarrassed and would be rather pleased, but it's occurred to me that I did have different intentions in writing the two scenes you refer to. In writing *Illuminatus!* Bob Wilson and I agreed that we would incorporate some out-and-out pornographic writing into the novel, and pornography is meant to turn people on sexually. So that was what I was trying to do when I wrote the cocksucking scene between George and Mavis on the beach, which is what drove my actor friend to bring himself off.

When I was writing *Shike* I was trying to bring to life on paper an imaginary world and its people. I was thinking more about clearly expressing what was in my imagination than about how it might affect the reader. Jebu and Taniko's first erotic encounter was something happening between them, and it was my job to describe it as well as I could and not to manipulate the reader's sexual feelings. The George-Mavis scene was written somewhat in the crude style I recall from the typewritten pornographic stories that were passed around in my high school classes. Even after passing through Bob Wilson's typewriter, it retains that flavor. The Jebu-Taniko scene was written in what I hoped was a subtle, delicate style that seemed appropriate for the Japanese characters. Which is to say that while I wouldn't *mind* somebody being moved to masturbate – or to look for some nice person to have sex with – after reading the Jebu-Taniko scene, it would seem to me that the reaction wasn't all that relevant to my intention. After all, I wouldn't want to write anything that would make people want to stop reading.

• • •

Last September, Yvonne and I saw the Lyric Opera's production of *The Magic Flute.* I'm becoming more and more of a lover of Mozart's music, and this has certainly done much to hasten the process. Of the libretto of *Die Zauberflöte*, no less an illuminated being than Goethe declared its "high meaning will not elude the initiated." Besides the music, I was entertained by the sets, which were, of course, full of pyramids. One pyramid had the word "WEISHEIT" over its entrance, which I at first misread as "WEISHAUPT." At the end, an orange sun arose and appeared centered in a gigantic triangle. The evening would have been complete if the sun had opened a bright red eye and winked at me. Highly recommended, in whatever form you might have access to it. *Die Zauberfloete* was first presented in Vienna on Friday, Sept. 30, 1791, fifteen years after the founding of the Bavarian Illuminati and six years after its suppression by edict of the King of Bavaria.

• • •

It is relatively easy when you are writing a wild book like *Illuminatus!* to come up with funny stuff. But most historical novels tend not to lend themselves to a lot of humor although there are exceptions, and when my head is in the historical novel mode it does not produce much humor – except in minor ways, like a couple of Perrin's songs in *All Things.*

• • •

Yes, there really is a Fernando Poo. It is named after the explorer Fernando Poo, who landed there in 1492. Whence comes the well-known rhyme, "In fourteen hundred ninety-two, Fernando Poo discovered Fernando Poo." Some people spell his name Po, but they are just spoilsports.

Ǥ

Footnotes to An Unwritten Text: Brief bits

Editor's note: Many of the issues of Shea's zine "No Governor" have a feature called "Footnotes to An Unwritten Text," a section of brief comments about a variety of topics. Many of these are comments made to other members of The Golden APA, an amateur press association that both Shea and Robert Anton Wilson belonged to. Here are some highlights from the feature.

Want to do something agin the government but too old to refuse to register and unable to resist paying taxes? Refusing to vote is a form of nonviolent resistance to government. That it disturbs governments is underlined by the fact that it's a crime in Australia, punishable by a $5 fine. In totalitarian countries, where over 90 percent of the population is routinely dragooned into voting, not voting is even more of an act of resistance. The use of voting by dictators to legitimize their rule may have been started by Napoleon I, who in 1804 had himself elected as hereditary emperor of France by 98 percent of those eligible.

• • •

When I first started using a computer for my writing, my first feeling was dread that I'd have to waste a lot of time experimenting with this expensive machine before I got the hang of it, and meanwhile my writing wouldn't get done. After working with a computer for well over a year and a half, and having found it very useful for my writing, I now wish I could spend *more* time experimenting with it. My attitude at first was, how do I make this thing useful, right away? My attitude now is, let me learn what else I can do with the computer, and it will probably turn out to be useful later. In fact I'm thinking of making exploring the computer a reward or recreational break. Such is the fascination of computers.

• • •

After seeing *Revenge of the Nerds,* which I heartily enjoyed, I started thinking about the last scene, at a pep rally in which the nerds invite everybody who has ever felt like a nerd to come down from the stands and join them. And from what I could see, everybody does. Made me wonder, is there anybody who does not, in real life, think of him or herself as a nerd? I'll bet even the handsome football players who date the beautiful sorority women – and the beautiful sorority women – think of themselves as nerds in relation to other people still more beautiful, who in turn have even more exquisite beings before whom they feel like nerds. When you get right down to it, nerdity is part of the universal human condition.

• • •

That death is the worst thing that can happen to a person is not an objective fact. It is a truth only for those who believe it. And nobody lives as if they fully believe it, because nearly all of us risk death every day. We do it because one can't lead a normal life without some risk, so most of us value what we consider to be a normal life over an indefinitely prolonged life.

Between the person who says, "I would rather run the risk of death than give up traveling on airplanes," and the rebel against tyranny who says, "I would rather risk death than give up my freedom," the difference seems to me only one of degree.

• • •

When I use the term ego in connection with Asian mysticism, I don't mean self-awareness. That I take to be a given of experience. I mean rather the social identity that is imposed on us by our families and our cultures, and that we come to think of in an illusory way as being "really" us.

• • •

Each level of life that we examine seems to have its own level of purpose, which is not particularly relevant to other levels. On the level of molecular biology organisms are collections of molecules whose workings are governed by the laws of probability, and everything including the workings of human intelligence can be explained as the inevitable result of the functioning of these molecules. But that need not cause us to change our psychological, philosophical or religious views in any way. Tell me I'm nothing but a collection of molecules looking to replicate themselves and I'll still enjoy Beethoven's Ninth as much. Our minds can impose our own meanings on our lives and the world. In between the level of molecule and the level of mind are many other levels. The way living things act as organisms is a bridge between the molecular and the mental. A tiger pursuing its prey has imposed a kind of non-molecular meaning on its universe. The universe in general may have no purpose, but nothing can take *our* purposes away from us.

• • •

Every day is a *good* day.

• • •

When I lift the hood of my car, all I see is a jumble, and I'm happy to pay somebody to fix it for me. When hi-fi addicts start talking about tweeters and woofers, I yawn. Basically, I'm a literary person. So now comes along computers, and I'm hooked. My idea of a good time is sitting in front of that green screen for hours punching keys until I'm bleary-eyed. I haven't quite figured out why this should be so, but I recently read a profile of one of the new young computer tycoons and found that he was a literature major in college. And he mentioned that many of the other people involved in the development of the personal computer were people with similar backgrounds. In an interview in the February *Playboy* Steven Jobs, chairman and cofounder of Apple, says, "If we can inject that liberal-arts spirit into the very serious realm of business, I think it will be a worthwhile contribution." Apparently working with computers is decidedly attractive to people with an aesthetic or philosophical bent. I'm still not sure what this is all about, but I like to think it presages, at long last, a reunion of what C.P. Snow called the two cultures – the arts and the sciences.

• • •

Efficiency is never that important when you are playing. I think this is the Great Basic Truth. It may be, then, that by not trying to be efficient, when we are working, we can turn work into play.

• • •

The notorious CIA manual for anti-Sandinista guerillas in Nicaragua is a perfect example of the way hostile states come more and more to resemble one another. The manipulative and terrorist tactics advised by the manual are a replica of tactics used effectively in Viet Nam by the National Liberation Front. Politicians opposed to the Reagan administration may condemn U.S.-sponsored terrorism as antithetical to the American way, but the fact is that there is no American way in these matters. There is only the way that works, and once a people chooses to dominate others by coercive force the technology of terror is the same, whatever the ideology chooses to call itself.

• • •

A major purpose of my political – or anti-political, if you will – efforts is to guarantee that I and everyone else can enjoy baseball, music, movies, novels, comic books – yes, even pornography – freely and fully. Politics and economics exist to make all that fun stuff possible. This is what totalitarians ignore in their efforts to herd the arts into line.

• • •

Ideology is a trap. Having no principles, or principles that are easily compromised, is also a trap. The trick is to use your ideology without becoming a slave to it.

• • •

Every so often, after a bomb goes off or a public figure is assassinated, a group claiming "credit" explains that it has adopted armed violence because peaceful ways of changing society have not worked. How short-sighted this view is! Over the centuries it is armed violence that "has not worked," leaving people's lives unchanged or worse than they were before. Humanity has taken its major steps forward in spite of armed violence. To change our lot for the better requires actions far more creative than lighting a fuse or pulling a trigger.

And as for people who use violence (including the violence of legal censorship) to try to suppress movies, magazines or books that they consider evil, they don't seem to realize that such actions are an admission of defeat. To use force to keep people away from such materials is to admit that your side has nothing equally persuasive or attractive to offer. In the war of ideas a rifle or a bomb is the weapon of one whose ideas have run out.

• • •

I agree with your view that Shakespeare wrote for the masses, but he wrote for the classes as well. The example you quote from *Hamlet* is indeed silliness that doubtless made common people in the pit laugh, but it's cleverly conducted silliness that furthers the characterization of Hamlet as an extraordinarily witty man pretending to be mad. Smart, educated folks would relish it, too.

• • •

Much as I love Tolkien, I'm uncomfortable with the attitudes toward women implicit in his work (the main female Hobbit character I remember is a virago) and also the attitude toward non-European cultures. That is, it seems very clear to me that the Orcs and the Haradrim are modeled after a xenophobic view of African, Middle Eastern and Asian cultures, whereas the cultures of the good guys are clearly derived from northern Europe.

• • •

Why would one want to see a movie in a big theater full of people? Well, many observers have noted that in recent years there has been a deterioration in the behavior of theater-going audiences, but given ideal conditions, a large, darkened theater with a big screen allows one to be overwhelmed by the movie, to feel drawn into it. And being part of an appreciative audience greatly intensifies the emotional experience. Ever seen a movie in an almost-empty theater? I have, and it isn't the same at all.

• • •

The Stoic philosophers say that we can't always control what happens to us, but we can control our attitude toward it. However, if we don't practice controlling our attitude in other situations, we're not likely to have the skill ready to hand when we find ourselves in deep trouble.

To compose one's mind and feelings in a crisis might be considered prayer by a religious person and just composing one's mind by a non-religious person. Either way it strikes me as a good thing to do. The religious person might say it is better than asking the deity to rescue one. Again, to compose one's mind in a crisis is much easier if one makes a point of composing one's mind any time a challenge, even a small one, arises.

I have a notion that the *higher* philosophical and religious impulses are those that reconcile us in a healthy way to the situation we're in; whereas the *lower* ones are those in which we ask whatever we have faith in to give us goodies or get us out of a bad spot. "Give me strength," which appears in so many cartoons, is actually a pretty good prayer, or affirmation.

By healthy reconciliation I mean a realistic acceptance of a situation that encourages one to make the most of it.

• • •

In 1832 Chief Black Hawk led his Sauk tribe's resistance against federal seizure of their lands. His view of land ownership is close to that of many modern anarchists:

"My reason teaches me that land cannot be sold. The Great Spirit gave it to his children to live upon, and cultivate, as far as it is necessary, for their subsistence; and as long as they occupy and cultivate it they have the right to the soil, but if they voluntarily leave it, then other people have the right to settle on it. Nothing can be sold but such things as can be carried away."

• • •

A point you made that fits my own experience is that writing is most interesting when one is thinking about specific wordings for things – almost always one specific sentence, turn of phrase, or (more rarely) extremely good way of conceptualizing an idea. My writing tends to bog down when I struggle with abstract plot, structure or characterization problems; it goes well when I think about a particular line of dialog or bit of description or specific action. A detail. The real creativity in writing, for me, is in the bits of material, the details. As Vladimir Nabokov (quoted in *The New York Times Book Review* by Patricia Hampl) wrote, "Caress the detail, the divine detail." And Hampl adds, "This is the atom that generates all the stars."

• • •

Yukio Mishima is one of my heroes because he is a wonderful novelist. *The Temple of the Golden Pavilion* is one of the best novels I ever read. And because he was a romantic who so loved his vision of Japanese culture he was willing to die for it.

• • •

Re: hereditary guilt, Elaine Pagels in *Adam, Eve and the Serpent* claims that the notion that the whole human race inherited guilt because of the sin of Adam and Eve goes back only as far as Augustine – Fourth Century C.E. Prior to Augustine Christian theologians accepted suffering and death as natural aspects of the human condition, rather than divinely inflicted punishments. If Pagels is right, Augustine was as pernicious an influence on Christianity as Paul. A fascinating and surprising book, backed up by what appears to be the soundest scholarship.

• • •

Best general suggestion I can make on getting into classical music is to listen to your local classical station, which will probably be an FM station and may be a university station. Listen to a lot of stuff and make a note of the pieces that give you most pleasure. When you encounter something that gives you a particular thrill, buy a cassette or CD and play it a lot at home. Ignore all critical bullshit about what you *should* like or not like; most music critics are the worst snobs in the world and just out to fuck up people's heads. Just be a musical hedonist; follow the pleasure principle. Your taste will change as you familiarize yourself with the stuff, but you must be true to your feelings. I used to think Mozart was for the birds; now I can't get enough Mozart. So it goes. That is my advice. I have spoke.

• • •

When *Illuminatus!* was playing in Seattle, Bob Wilson and Yvonne and Yvonne's Aunt Laddie and I made several trips to the top of the Space Needle. I was absolutely dumbstruck by the sight of Mount Rainier. Getting a better view of Seattle's surroundings really sold me on the city. We (Yvonne and I) still think we might move there some day. Although New Mexico is a bit ahead at the moment.

• • •

I think the concept of "bearing witness," which Christians are sometimes taught to do, may be relevant to suppressing one's feelings for fear of rejection. To bear witness, as I understand it, is simply to make one's position known, not necessarily to get into a big argument. Sometimes simply to state our disagreement openly with the prevailing attitude can make us feel a lot better about ourselves. Indeed, I think that's a good reason for doing it.

• • •

I think the fact that the samurai took up Zen proves your point that there is less Buddhism and more Taoism in Zen than is generally realized. Buddhism places certain human actions beyond the pale, unworthy of an enlightened being. Taoism, as I understand it, doesn't rule out any phenomena; it says that the dark side as well as the light side of life must be accepted. Buddhism has a rule against killing. Taoism says that when you try to follow rules you have lost the way. I also think that by studying Zen the Japanese warriors did not corrupt Buddhism but ennobled their profession. It seems that many activities are useful for learning Zen, from flower arranging and poetry to archery and swordsmanship.

• • •

Examples exist in real history that people would find too implausible to accept in fiction. One of the best is one I actually wrote about: The thwarting of two Mongol invasions of Japan seven years apart by, each time, fortuitous typhoons. If I'd made this up and had it happen in a fictitious country it would have been condemned, as a deus ex machina solution.

• • •

I share your opinion of Holocaust revisionists. Some libertarians have gotten involved in defending Holocaust revisionism as a freedom of expression issue. While I believe people should have the right to publish *anything*, no matter how pernicious, I have priorities about which cases I want to crusade for, and Holocaust revisionists are near the bottom of the list, above the out-and-out Nazis, but under the child pornographers.

• • •

Yvonne and I saw a man reduce his son and daughter (estimated somewhere between 8 and 10) to tears, in a video shop, with a steady stream of cruel, sarcastic remarks, mostly about their taste in movies. "Rubbish" was the kindest word he used. Many abusive parents hit their children; this guy was able to hurt them without lifting a finger. It was obvious that the guy was very intelligent (confirmation of a comment Andrea recently made in the Golden APA about the possibility of intelligence and evil going together), and very articulate and very sure of himself, and that a verbal remonstrance would be just a case of getting into a pissing match with a skunk. We discussed killing him and/or kidnapping the kids but ended up just going home and feeling bad.

• • •

I concur with the ambivalent views you express on Timothy Leary. I like and admire him, but each time he announces a new scheme I know he's going to promise a lot more than he can deliver. A used-car salesman of the spirit.

• • •

Maybe two out of three of Leary's ideas are valuable. The third can be quite off-the-wall, as with his remark that Mother Teresa is performing a disservice to the world in trying to make people's dying more comfortable. This is like the old Trotskyite argument that it is wrong to give money to unwed mothers because by easing their lot you postpone the revolution by that much.

• • •

I think the job of a writer about the paranormal – and a job most of them shirk – is to ascertain whether the events described actually happened. Many writers tend to assume that episodes of psi, UFOs, strange animals, out-of-body experiences, Bermuda Triangle stuff, reincarnation and whatnot are established fact, and to offer their explanation of how these phenomena might have occurred.

But then I also hold the unpopular view that the job of historians is to find out what actually happened, rather than assume they know what happened and philosophize about it.

• • •

I never go to the hospital without a book. In fact, I carry

a particular book in my car – not just for the hospital – but in case I have to wait in my car for any reason – at a railroad crossing or a drive-in bank, for instance – or have to go somewhere in my car and then sit, as when I take someone to the hospital. (So far my trips to the hospital have all been on behalf of others.) Currently the book I'm using for this purpose is *The Mote in God's Eye* by Larry Niven and Jerry Pournelle. It's been in the car for nearly a year, and I'm about half through it.

• • •

I consider myself a materialist only provisionally, in that I am ready to accept the existence of spiritual or supernatural phenomena if sufficiently compelling evidence comes along. Materialism feels good to me because it is what I escaped to after thirty or so years as a believing Roman Catholic. Because it seems so reasonable to me, and it feels good to feel reasonable. Because it fits in with my anarchism and individualism, in that I do not worry about a higher intelligence telling me what to do or keeping score on me, and I can ignore people who set themselves up as spokespersons for such a higher intelligence. I regret what I see as the shortness of life, but I see nonexistence as a state that is by definition totally painless, and I feel that death is something we have to come to terms with, and that belief in an afterlife is a comforting fantasy that doesn't really help. I think I am comfortable with materialism because I am strongly influenced by the Stoic and Buddhist philosophies. They have taught me to live in this world and in the present, and that as rational beings we can control how we feel about things.

• • •

[In a comment to Robert Anton Wilson]:
Chicago seemed more like home to us, too, with you visiting. I get more interesting, new ideas in a few hours of talking with you than I get in six months of my day-to-day life.

• • •

As I see it, the value of the human race's spreading into new territories would be the opportunities it would create for an enormous variety of cultures to develop. Cultures developing apart from each other and then meeting and cross-fertilizing seems to be the way we've made such progress as we have so far. On the other hand, if the Earth remains our sole habitat, our culture is likely to become more and more homogenous as time goes on, and if historical experience is any indicator this means more static.

Well, that's the optimistic side of it. The pessimistic side is that if we stick to one planet our chances of becoming extinct, by blowing ourselves up or destroying our environment, or through some natural disaster, are much greater.

• • •

Actually the sexual revolution of the 60s and 70s would never have gotten off the ground if it were primarily of, by, and for men. It was women's sexual decisions that made the difference. I have some doubt as to whether the revolution was touched off by the pill, as many people think, but certainly a big change that made a sexual revolution possible – as I perceived it – was a change in women's attitudes. The main change I noticed in men was that they were willing to stop expecting virginity or chastity in the women they loved, what was called the double standard. I think when the sexual revolution petered out (so to speak) it was because women's attitudes changed again . . . I think the pop magazine philosopher of the sexual revolution was not Hefner but Helen Gurley Brown.

• • •

As I understand it, the Hindu teaching that the world is *maya* doesn't mean that the world itself is an illusion. It means that we are under the spell of *maya* if we take our ideas and perceptions about the world as the reality. This is similar to what the General Semanticists say. Buddhist hold essentially the same thing, adding that the notion of a separate, individual self is *maya,* too. Most of the Buddhists I have met, or whose works I have read, are not materialists, but I find that Buddhism can be interpreted in a materialistic way.

• • •

There are various versions of the Voltaire story. The one I heard, from Bob Wilson, was that the Marquis de Sade invited Voltaire to one of his disgusting orgies, and Voltaire attended and acquitted himself admirably. After a decent (?) interval had elapsed, the Marquis sent Voltaire an invitation to another orgy. Voltaire turned him down with, "Once is philosophy. Twice is perversion."

• • •

On the different meanings of "self," I also posit that, transcending all other selves, there is a Universal Self that is identical with the universe. When in intuitive contact with the Universal Self "I" can be said to be anywhere and everywhere in the universe and in contact with all of it. From what I know about modern physics, I'm not sure it makes ultimate sense to speak of psychological states as being inside or outside of the epidermis or to think of my consciousness as being separate from anyone else's consciousness. To try to answer your question in a few words, then, I think there is a Universal Self which transcends the limitations of what I call the deeper self.

• • •

I believe death is the end of consciousness, that consciousness requires a physical brain to support it. To some people this is an awful thing, but to me it isn't, since where there is no consciousness there can be no suffering, no negative feeling of any kind. No positive feelings either, of course, but their absence cannot be missed.

• • •

The reason I repeat "Every day is a *good* day" at the end of all my apazines is that I hope it will have the effect that it did on you: One day sink in and become meaningful.

Robert Shea met his wife, Patricia Monaghan, at a conference of the Association for Consciousness Exploration in Cleveland. This photo shows, from left, Timothy Leary, Robert Shea, Patricia Monaghan, Jeff Rosenbaum and Gillie Smythe. Rosenbaum, an ACE founder, introduced Shea and Monaghan.

Ꞡ

Physics and Grief

By PATRICIA MONAGHAN

Robert Shea's last wife, and his widow after he died, was Patricia Monaghan (1946-2012), a college professor and a writer who penned more than 20 books, including "The Encyclopedia of Celtic Myth and Folklore," "The Red-Haired Girl from the Bog: The Landscape of Celtic Myth and Spirit" and "Encyclopedia of Goddesses and Heroines." She also wrote four books of poetry, was a founding member of the Association for the Study of Women and Mythology and was a professor at DePaul University. Shea and Monaghan met at the Starwood Festival, an event that at the time was presented by a Cleveland-based group, The Association for Consciousness Exploration, founded by Jeff Rosenbaum and Joseph Rothenberg. Other speakers at that time included Robert Anton Wilson and Timothy Leary.

"Physics and Grief" is Monaghan's Pushcart Prize winning memoir about dealing with her grief in the aftermath of Shea's death. It is reprinted with the kind permission of Michael McDermott, who was married to Monaghan when she died.

I have sometimes written about Shea at my blog at RAWIllumination.net, and when I would write to Monaghan for information about Shea, she was always kind and helpful. Monaghan was only 66 when she died, so this beautiful piece also can be read as a requiem for her, too.

> In nature nothing remains constant. Everything is in a perpetual state of transformation, motion, and change. However, we discover that nothing simply surges up out of nothing without having antecedents that existed before. Likewise, nothing ever disappears without a trace, in the sense that it gives rise to absolutely nothing existing in later times.
>
> –David Bohm

"Actually," Dan said, "I've been reading a lot of physics." He looked down at his empty paper plate and shrugged one shoulder, then the other. "I don't suppose that makes any sense."

Dan had not spoken to me in almost a year. We'd seen each other occasionally; we had too many common friends for that not to happen. But when it did, Dan made certain to stay on the other side of the room, to find himself in need of a drink when I came near, to turn suddenly away when I tried to catch his eye.

That was the year when I was a new widow, and Dan was about to become one, his partner, Steve, descending into a hell of lesions and pneumonia and fungal invasions of the brain. Even in the blur of my loss, I felt no anger toward Dan – though anger is so predictable a part of grief – for avoiding me. I knew the cause: I already was what he most feared to become.

Six months after I was widowed, Dan joined me in that state. Steve gave up his obdurate struggle to remain alive, asking to be kept home when the next crisis hit. It was only a week. Friends told me that Steve's death was gentle and that Dan bore up as well as could be expected. Dan dropped from sight for a time, disappearing into memories and pain.

Now it was summer, and we were sitting under blue canvas at an outdoor festival. Dan had approached me with an apology for his actions. I had embraced him with understanding. We were sitting companionably together, catching up on each other's lives, when I asked him what most helped him deal with his grief.

Physics.

Dan met my eyes, and his brows came together, then raised. "Relativity. Quantum mechanics. Bell's Theorem. You know?" I think he expected me to be surprised. But I was not. It had been the same for me.

To explain how physics came to be important on my journey of grief, I have first to describe the problem with my keys. There were five of them, bound together with a wide steel ring: a big silver skeleton key, for the embossed brass Victorian lock on the front door; a round-headed key that opens the more modern deadbolt; a little golden key to the garage; an institutional "do not duplicate" key to my office; and a black-headed key to the Ford station wagon.

I remember the day – the hour – that the keys disappeared. It was late spring, less than three months after Bob died. Walking out the door to go shopping, I had reached into my jacket pocket, where I always kept my keys. They weren't there.

At the instant, it seemed inconsequential. I'd mislaid keys before; hasn't everyone? I was inside the house, so I had used the keys to enter. They were, therefore, somewhere in the house with me. I merely had to look carefully and I would find them.

I was unperturbed. I did what I did whenever I had mislaid something. I looked in all the logical places: in my coat's other pocket; on the shelf near the front door; next to the telephone; in the kitchen near the sink. Nothing.

I was still not overly concerned. I must have been distracted when I entered, I reasoned with myself; I must have put the keys in some unlikely spot. So I began methodically searching the house. Entry hall. Living room. Pulling out furniture, looking under pillows. Nothing. Dining room. Kitchen. Opening cabinets, reaching to the back of shelves. Nothing.

Okay, then, I must have carried them upstairs. Guest room. Bathroom. Moving around each room slowly, looking especially in places where keys were unlikely to be. Behind pictures. In rarely-opened drawers. Study. Nothing. Linen closet. Nothing.

In my bedroom, I suddenly grew frustrated. I needed my keys! The only key to my car was on that ring; I could not go to work without it. What would I do without my keys?

I started to cry.

I had been crying for months, ever since Bob had finally died, fighting cancer to the last. The six months before his death were exhausting. For three months I was his sole caregiver; then, during his final hospitalization, I visited him two, three, even four times each day. Economics forced me to continue working, so I had neither physical strength nor emotional resources left when he died.

In the days before Bob's death, I had been with him constantly, telling him stories of the future we should have had, praising his work and his son to him, reminiscing for him about happy times when he could no longer speak. I did not sleep for perhaps forty-eight hours as I held vigil by his bedside, leaving only for necessary moments, for he had been shatteringly fearful of being alone at the moment of death. And so I was with him when that moment came, holding his hand as his breathing slowed, singing old songs to him, stroking his face through its paralysis.

It was the hardest thing I have ever done, witnessing as he "departed from this strange world a little ahead of me," as Einstein said when his oldest friend, Michele Besso, died. When I left that hospital room, bearing with me the amaryllis that had bloomed only the day before, I felt that I was leaving all happiness behind, that my world had changed unutterably, and only for the worse.

I lived the months afterward in a trance of grief. There was a memorial service that I planned, I remember that. I remember a brick meeting hall with red tulips, a jazz pianist, readings from Bob's novels, visitors from many states. For the rest, I barely recall anything. I apparently kept working, and doing laundry, and feeding the dogs, and planting the garden. My body kept moving through the Midwestern spring. But my soul was in the desert, in winter.

That day in May, the loss of my keys reduced me to tears, though of course I was weeping for my greater loss, which every other loss would now reflect. Possibly I wept for hours; I did such things at that time. Finally the storm passed. I got up and set determinedly about to find the keys. To survive, I had to work. I needed to drive to my office. I could not manage without my keys. I would find them. I had to.

And so I repeated my search. I must have missed the keys the first time, I told myself. I started again at the front door and scoured the downstairs. Living room: no. Kitchen: no.

And so it went. After an hour or so, I found myself again in the bedroom, still keyless.

I began to weep again. This time, my desolation seemed endless. I could not stop crying. I lay on the bed, sobbing and flailing my arms. I soaked several handkerchiefs. I buried my head in pillows and drenched them with tears.

Then I became enraged. I got up from the bed and began to scream at Bob, furious at him for dying and leaving me so helplessly besieged by grief. I screamed that he was cruel and heartless, that I'd been there in his hour of need, and where was he when I needed him? I raged and wept, wept and raged.

I had not, before Bob's death, spent much time thinking about the question of whether or not there is an afterlife. I had been brought up with a conventional picture of heaven and hell. And I had studied enough other religions to realize that many wiser than I believed in some kind of survival after death. I had read believable-enough accounts of those who claimed to have been contacted by the dead. But the possibility of an afterlife was not something I dwelt upon. I did not wish to make moral decisions by weighing the possibilities of future reward or punishment for myself. Nor did the survival of my own small person seem especially important in comparison with the universe's vast majesty. So, for myself, what happened or did not happen after death was not a very important question.

Bob, by contrast, had been quite clear about his beliefs. A natural mystic, he had practiced Zen for twenty years. But he was also an unrelentingly hard-headed empiricist who believed the universe to be a mechanistic place in which consciousness was only a byproduct of the body's functions. Thus, when the body died, consciousness ceased as well. Bob believed, as Fred Alan Wolf put it in describing the Newtonian worldview, that mind – or soul, or spirit, whatever you call it – was just "a convenient by-product of the physiology of . . . the mechanisms of the brain, down to the remarkable electrical and mechanical movements of the nerve firings and blood flows."

He never changed his belief once he entered the hospital that final time, even though I, desperate for some reassurance that our love could continue after he faded from this life, talked to him about reincarnation and other possible survivals. But Bob would be no foxhole convert; he marched gamely toward that abyss which he saw as the likely end of his being. Death was painful to him; he had much to live for; but he would not grasp at hope of continued life just to ease his pain. Unless he had time to ponder, unless he could become completely convinced, he would believe as he always had. Happy lies held no appeal for him.

One thing I loved about Bob was this: he had more integrity than any person I'd ever met. That integrity remained to the end. He met his death with his long-held beliefs intact. He was frightened, but he was very, very brave.

Because I had no personal convictions on the subject, I held true to Bob's beliefs after he was gone. It was a way of remaining close to him. I, too, would refuse to grasp at imaginary straws just to ease my pain. If Bob believed that all traces of his consciousness would evaporate at his death, that only his physical works would remain, then I would loyally uphold that belief.

And so I lived in the desert. Life has never seemed so dry and meaningless to me as it did then. I would watch lovers kiss in a coffee shop and a whirlpool of pain would open beneath me, as I thought of one of them holding the other as they parted forever. I would stare at parents playing with their children near the lake and imagine sudden illnesses and accidents, wondering how life could create such joy only to obliterate it. I wept constantly: when I heard beautiful music, when I saw painful news, when I saw new flowers, when I went to bed, when I woke up.

But I adamantly refused to settle for those happy visions

that religion held out, of dreamy heavens full of harps, of other lives to come, of eventual reunion in some cosmic void. I even rejected nonreligious spiritualism. When friends said they had dreamed of Bob, or felt him near, I received the information in silent disbelief. It was their need of solace, I told myself, that caused these apparitions. They had just imagined them. I, loyal to Bob's beliefs, would not settle for such self-deluding comfort. I would tough it out, looking reality right in its cruel face.

But the day I lost my keys, I could not be brave like Bob, not any longer. Seeing those loving eyes go dim had been the single most painful moment of my life. The idea that the universe could so wantonly create beauty, could bestow upon our lives the kind of love that seems like ultimate meaning, only to destroy it in a breath, had finally become too much for me.

I wanted so desperately to believe that Bob, and Bob's love for me, still existed somewhere in the universe, that in my furious pain I flung down a challenge. Standing in the middle of the bedroom, I demanded that he come back. Find my keys, I insisted. Find my damned keys! If there's anyone there, if there's any love left in this universe for me, find my keys!

After the fury had passed, I felt mortified. I had been screaming at a dead man. Standing in my room alone, screaming at a dead man. Worse, it was all so trivial. If I were going to throw down the gauntlet to the universe about whether there is life after death, couldn't I have chosen something more important as proof? World peace? Personal economic security? A beatific vision?

But I'd spoken. I'd insisted that Bob prove his continuing existence by finding my keys.

Even writing about that day, I feel embarrassment cover

me. It was such an excess of emotion about such a small matter, about such a minor inconvenience. Why had I broken down over such a silly thing? Why had I challenged the universe over something as unimportant as a key-ring?

But break down I had, and challenge the universe I had. And I could not bear the answer to be silence, negation, the absence of Bob forever, anywhere. Now I truly had to find the keys. So I resolutely began, yet again, to search. I started once more in the front hallway. But this time, I took a new tack. I might as well do spring-cleaning, I decided. I'd clean the entire house, front door to attic, and in doing so I would certainly find the keys.

There was more than a bit of desperation about all this. If I did not find the keys, all was indeed lost. If I did not find the keys, there was no vestige of Bob in the world. If I did not find the keys, I was alone in the cruelest universe imaginable.

Three days later, I was back in the bedroom. Except for that one room, the house was now clean, ammonia-and-paste-wax clean. I had taken down curtains and washed them, cleaned out closets, pulled up rugs. I had upended sofas and searched their bowels. I had repotted plants. I had pulled books from shelves and dusted both.

The house sparkled, indeed.

But I had not found the keys.

The bedroom was the final outpost of possibility. From the first corner around to the last, then spiraling in to the center, I cleaned and searched. I opened drawers and rearranged them, shaking out their contents on the floor. I moved pictures and dusted their frames. I worked slowly, with mounting despair, for the keys had still not appeared. I moved the bed and polished the floor under it. I shook out the bedclothes and aired out the mattress.

Finally, I was finished.

There were no keys.

I collapsed. This time my grief truly knew no bounds. I had asked for an answer from the universe, and I had – I believed – received one. Bob had been right. Consciousness was a byproduct of our body's functioning, and now that the ashes of Bob's body sat on the bookshelf in a white box, there was nothing, anywhere, left of the curiosity and passion and brilliance and love that had been him.

The depression that began that day incapacitated me. I was unable to work for nearly a week. Finally, however, I called the car dealership and got new car keys. I found the spare house keys. I began to reconstruct the openings to my life. I knew now that I was indeed alone, that I could not call upon Bob for help, that he was no longer present anywhere, in any form. It was a bleak and cruel universe, but at least I knew the truth of it.

What I experienced during that next year was more than simple grief and certainly more than emotional depression, although I suffered from both as well. It was stark existential despair. Life had no meaning, much less any savor. I tried to find what comfort I could in friendship, in earthly beauty, in art, in learning. But at my center was an abyss of meaninglessness. I could as easily have gambled all my resources away as built a garden; as easily have crashed my car as driven it safely across the Midwest; as easily have drunk slow poison as cocoa for breakfast. That I did one thing rather than another seemed only an arbitrary choice.

At last, however, I began to awaken from my coma of sorrow. I began to argue with Bob in my mind. As I gardened, I noticed again the resilient connection of matter and energy, how nature never destroys but only transforms. As I walked in the woods with my dog, I saw spring flowers emerging from the withered leaves of autumn. What hubris, I began to think, to imagine that human consciousness is the only thing this universe cares to obliterate. Surely we are not that important.

But these were fleeting thoughts, unconvincing, evanescent, ideas which did not in any case reach to the root of my grief. It was easy to accept that Bob's body would eventually nourish other beings, through the cycle of decomposition and recomposition. But it was Bob's self that I'd loved – not only his body, though certainly that. And although I knew and accepted, with piercing pain, what had happened to his body, that told me nothing about where the unique energy went that had invigorated it.

Every once in a while, I would think of the lost keys and sigh. I had, after all, asked for a sign, and I had been given one.

That was when I began reading books on physics. I had been reading a lot of spiritual literature, looking for answers to the appalling questions life presented. But I only grew more isolated, angry at the serenity that seemed forever beyond my grasp, despairing at my continuing inability to find any sense in death's senselessness. It was not that the answers which spiritual literature offered seemed implausible or incorrect; it was simply that I could not believe them, could not make the leap into not-doubting. The more rigidly codified the religious insight, the more it seemed to exclude – even to mock – my anguished confusion.

I can't remember exactly which book, which author, brought me to physics. Most likely one that pushed the boundaries of science to include spirituality. Fritjof Capra, perhaps, or Gary Zukov. One of those wild minds who saw bridges where others saw barricades. But it wasn't the spirituality that gripped my attention. It was the science.

Where religion had failed me, being so certain of itself, physics offered paradoxes and complexities so bizarre that my hatred and fear of the universe began to be replaced with what can only be called awe. I'd known Newtonian physics before, from my days as a science reporter, but I had never ventured into quantum mechanics. There I found the most astonishing ideas, ones which smashed the clockwork universe just as Bob's death had torn apart mine. Ideas that read like Bob's beloved Zen koans, statements that strained the limits of my linear thinking. "Our universe seems to be composed of facts and their opposites at the same time," I read in Louis de Broglie's work, and "everything happens as though it did not exist at all."

Such statements seemed eminently sensible, reasonable, even straightforward. Yes, I responded passionately. Yes, the universe was that strange, that indescribable. Death is not an equal and opposite reaction to life; consciousness is not some strange form of inertia. I needed a new physics to describe the wild movements of my grieving soul. And a new physics I found.

Like my friend Dan, I found quantum theory immeasurably consoling. With an uncertainty-loves-company kind of logic, I lost myself in Heisenberg and the reassurances of the Uncertainty Principle. If we cannot conceivably know everything about the physical universe, then the abyss of doubt whereon I stood was as good a standpoint as any from which to view life. If we cannot know something as simple as two aspects of a subatomic particle's motion simultaneously, how can we know for certain that there is no life after death – or that there is? If our measurements may alter the reality that we measure, could not consciousness be a form of measurement, subtly altering the universe?

My deepest consolation, however, was not in speculating

about whether a consciousness suffused, as mine was, with grief altered the world in a different way than one flooded with happiness. Rather, I drew solace from the dumbfounding absoluteness of Heisenberg's theory. We could not know everything, not ever, because in the moment of such knowing we may change what we know. I could not know – I could never know – if or where Bob existed, for each time I sought for him – each time I measured this universe in terms of Bob's existence or nonexistence – I was perhaps changing the conditions of the very universe through which I sought. It was as though Heisenberg, by enshrining uncertainty at the center of perception and knowledge, made anything and everything both possible and impossible at once.

Suddenly the world seemed to make sense again, although in a deeply paradoxical way. Where religion's certainties had left me bitterly bereft of comfort, quantum uncertainty allowed for unimaginable possibilities. Whatever measurement I took of the universe, I understood now, could be only partial. There would always be something that eluded my grasp. This was an enormous comfort.

It was not only uncertainty that captured me. Because this new physics was all about time and space, Einstein spoke to me like a voice from a burning bush. I, who lived in a time and space from which my love had disappeared, found respite in considering the ways that time and space were linked. "Any two points in space and time are both separate and not separate," David Bohm said. What salvation that seemed! As incomprehensible as this new spacetime was, it was more lively with possibilities than linear and planar realities. My separateness from Bob was real, but in some way, we were also still together.

In some way – this was most important to me. For this was not a metaphoric togetherness, a trick of language. This was science, after all. And not just science but the queen of sciences, physics. Physics which did not ask me to believe, did not ask me to have faith. Physics which observed and experimented. Physics which offered a description of the world, admittedly bizarre but as accurate as blundering language could make it.

I did not have to believe. I only had to wonder.

The fact that, as Max Born pointed out, the quantum world is utterly unvisualizable presented no problem to me. Visions of the subatomic world were metaphors, whose richness and limitations I amply understood. But unlike religion, which seemed hypnotized by its own articulations of the ineffable, physics acknowledged that any picture we hold of the subatomic world is by definition inaccurate, limited, inexact. No one has ever seen a quark, much less a Higgs boson. But they act; we see their traces. Such quantum strangeness spoke to my condition. I had witnessed something deeply incomprehensible when Bob died. Studying what Bohm called the "unanalyzable ways of the universe" mirrored that experience.

My grief did not disappear, for grief is a chronic disease which exists in the body. My body would still regularly writhe with sudden memories: when I automatically reached for Bob's favorite juice at the Jewel, when I passed the lake where we had taken our last walk, when someone uttered a phrase he had relished. The tape-loop of his last hours ran constantly in my mind, so that I would see the doctor, my friends Natalie and Barbara arriving, Bob's son Michael leaving, the amaryllis, Bob's paralyzed face, the doctor, Natalie, the amaryllis, the doctor . . .

Because of the power of these death-watch memories, relativity especially absorbed me. The paradoxes of time preoccupied me for days on end. Einstein had seen the connection between the study of time and awareness of death's approach, arguing that death really means nothing because "the distinction between past, present and future is only a stubbornly persistent illusion." I envisioned those points in the universe where radio waves of Bob's voice, from a long-ago interview, were still new and bright. I invented scenarios in which I stretched time out like taffy, making Bob's last days as eternal as they had subjectively seemed. I relished that consoling insight that Einstein's equations were time-reversible, that perhaps time does not move in one direction but can flow backward as well as forward. I imagined moving backward through time, intersecting with a healthy Bob and recreating our life, always hopping back on the time machine before the diagnosis, living those happy times over and over and over. I knew these were fantasies, but I also knew that I no longer knew what time really was. There, once again, were limitless possibilities.

If my grief did not disappear, that crazed existential doubt did. Life no longer was so utterly senseless. It made sense again, but in a more marvelous way than I'd ever imagined. I found myself staring at graphs of the Schrödinger wave collapse, imagining a cat alive, dead, alive, dead, all at the same time – imagining Bob's continued existence as such a wave. I pondered the complementarity between particles and waves, especially the way an observer seems implicated in the emergence into reality of each. Particles dancing and leaping in a virtual world, flickering in and out of measurable existence. Or perhaps they were not even particles at all, but what Henry Sapp called "sets of relationships that reach outward to other things." To David Bohm, too, particles exist not so much as nuggets of virtual and actual matter, but as "on-going movements that are mutually dependent because ultimately they merge and interpenetrate."

Matter disappeared, at this scale, into flashing energy, particles into momentarily observable comets of being. Bob had been composed of these miraculous particles, these miraculous relationships reaching outward toward me, these mutually dependent and interpenetrating movements. And perhaps he still was, in some way, in some unmeasurable place. Our lives together had been lived in a space and a time, within a universe through which the mighty and unfathomable river of spacetime flows. Were we still connected, as Bell's Theorem hints, in some intricate and inexpressible way? Was I somehow still affected by the changes that he experienced – in whatever state those blinking-into-existence particles that had been Bob were now? And did my changes affect him still as well?

Far from compelling me toward certainty about where and how Bob still existed, quantum theory removed from me any urge toward stapling down reality within one interpretation. In the quantum world, Nick Herbert has pointed out, there are at least eight possible pictures of reality, any of which is more consoling than the Newtonian vision of the universe. Maybe there is an "ordinary reality," as de Broglie and Einstein believed; in that case the hard stuff that made up Bob is somewhere still in existence, and even now I am breathing atoms that had been part of him during his life. But the Copenhagen hypothesis of Bohr and Heisenberg questions whether there is any such "reality" at all. In their view, Bob and I had lived something like a dream together, and that dream had as much reality without him as it had with him. An alternative reading of the Copenhagen hypothesis is that we create our own realities, that reality exists only as we observe it doing so; in that case, I could create the reality of his continued existence by believing strongly enough.

These were only some of the possibilities. There was David Bohm's theory of the implicate order, which argues that there is an undivided wholeness that could wrap both Bob and me, in our varying current states, in what he called "indivisible quantum processes that link different systems in an unanalyzable way." There was the fantastic many-world hypothesis, which permitted me to envision that Bob and I still lived happily in another spacetime, after he had survived cancer; in that reality, we are writing an essay together, perhaps this very one.

Or possibly, the quantum world is based upon no logic that we would recognize. In that case, life's either/or does not exist, and Bob's apparent lack of existence is no more true than his apparent existence had been. Or perhaps I created him, or he me; perhaps neither of us existed before we met, we came into being complete with memories when we created each other, and thus he continues in me, his creation. Perhaps, as Fred Alan Wolf has argued, the mind does not "exist in the physical universe at all. It may be beyond the boundaries of space, time and matter. It may use the physical body in the same sense that an automobile driver uses a car."

Or maybe all of this is simultaneously true. Maybe this world is so full of mystery that we cannot ever grasp its actual probabilities and probable actualities.

I pondered these extraordinary possibilities as I moved through my ordinary life. Slowly, the pain of my loss began, not to diminish, but to find its place in my life. If I did not feel joy, at least my pain had become a familiar companion. I continued reading physics, but with less crazed compulsion. I even began to accept the cruel existence of thermodynamics, with its arrow of time that threatened my happy time-travel imaginings, once I realized how connected to the richness of chaos it was.

Every once and again, I thought of the lost keys. In fall, as I was raking the front yard, I imagined that perhaps I had gone to the car for something, that spring day, and had dropped my key-ring into the crowded bed of hosta by the door. But no. In winter, when I decided to move the piano, I thought that perhaps I had missed the hidden keys during my frenzied cleaning by not moving that massive upright. But no. That next spring, after preparing for a dinner party, I sat in Bob's recliner and noticed a side pocket I had missed. There? But no: the keys were not there either. The seasons passed, and the keys remained lost.

Each time this happened, I thought to myself that finding the keys no longer mattered. That I had moved beyond the challenge I had flung out to Bob, to the universe, on that wild sad day. That unless the keys found their way back to me in some utterly strange way, I could not regard it as an answer to my desperate plea. I said to myself that finding the keys would be – just finding the keys. That if I found them in some ordinary way, it would prove nothing, one way or the other: I lost the keys, I found them, there was no connection.

And then I found the keys.

Friends were coming to dinner, and I was sitting in my study feeling sad, as I often did, and thinking of Bob, which I always did. I wistfully imagined him being with us, thought how much he would have enjoyed it. I felt my loss again, but poignantly this time, as a sad melody rather than as painful cacophony.

Then, for no special reason, I looked at the door of my study. It was open after having been closed all day. I kept it closed to keep my dog out and to keep visitors from wandering into my private space. That door had been opened and closed scores of times in the preceding year. When I entered, nothing unusual had caught my eye.

My study door is decorated. There is a Celtic knocker in the shape of a squirrel, a St. Bridget cross made of Irish rushes, and a poster. The poster, mounted on heavy blue cardboard, is a memento from the publication of my first book. Issued by my publisher for promotional parties, it shows the book's cover, my name, and the huge black words "it's here!"

The door is one of those old wooden doors with six deep panels. The poster is tacked tightly to the middle of the door, covering the two center panels and resting on the lower. The edges of the poster are flush against the door, especially at top and bottom, with the exception of two areas on each side, halfway down the cardboard, where small gaps exist. From one of these gaps, I noticed a key coyly poking out. I walked to the door and pulled sharply. Immediately, out tumbled the entire missing set.

I held the keys loosely in my hand and stared at them. I looked up at the poster, with its emphatic proclamation. And then I smiled and said aloud, "You always did have a great sense of humor, Bob Shea."

It would make a good story to say that everything suddenly fell into place, that all my questions dissolved, that I was somehow transported to a place of certainty and confidence in life's meaning. That I no longer felt that the universe was a place of uncertainty and chaos. That I recognized and accepted the proof of Bob's continuing existence.

But that would not be true. What I felt was bafflement and curiosity, together with a startled amusement. This could not be the answer to my crazed prayer. No. There had to be some other, more common sense answer. The keys were behind the poster: effect. Someone must have put them there: cause. I had been alone when the keys disappeared. Ergo, I had put the keys behind the poster. I did not remember doing so; it must have happened accidentally. Somehow, it was clear, I must have dropped the keys behind that poster, that day a year previously when I'd lost them.

I set out to prove my thesis. I tried to drop the keys behind the poster. I stood at the door, held the keys up in my right hand, and dropped them on the door. They caught at first on the cardboard's edge, then bounced off the door mounding and slid down to the floor.

I tried throwing the keys at the poster from a few feet away. The same thing happened: they slid down and did not hold. I tried walking past the door with the keys dangling from my hand, to see if they would catch in the poster and hold. They did not catch and hold.

There was only one way to get the keys into the position I had found them. I had to pull the poster forward, push the keys along a little groove in the door, and shove the poster back in place. Anything else would result in the keys either not lodging behind the poster at all, or dropping out as soon as the door was moved.

I spent a half-hour trying to make the keys stay behind that poster. Natalie, when I told her the mystery of the found keys, did the same. We stood in the green-carpeted upstairs hallway, two grown women flinging keys at a door, over and over. Thinking of more and more peculiar ways that the keys might have wound up resting on that hidden shelf. Unwilling at first to accept that only careful, conscious effort could bring the keys to rest as they had been, but unable to find any other way to make the keys stay in that place.

A year previously, the answer that I had wanted was a simple one: that Bob still existed and, hearing my call for help, would return my keys to me. But once this particular and peculiar miracle had occurred, I resisted accepting it as an answer to that crazy challenge. I attempted to catalog all possibilities. I had gone into a fugue state, placed the keys behind the poster, and forgotten all about them. A visitor had found the keys and whimsically placed them behind the poster. A worker – the plumber, say – had found the keys and hid them rather than giving them to me.

These scenarios are possible, though fairly unlikely. Were this a court of law, I would argue that there was no motive for anyone else to hide the keys, and no evidence that I have either before or since gone into a state of mindless fugue. That my beloved Bob had somehow answered my request seems as likely as any of these interpretations. Also: Bob had a unique sense of humor, and he tended to procrastinate. So it would be in character for him to have taken a year to get around to giving me the keys back, and then it would be in a suitably clever fashion.

I have, many times since the keys reappeared, asked myself how I would have responded had I found the keys, in exactly the same place, during my original frenzy of grief. I would, I think, have accepted it as a dramatic proof of Bob's continued existence. Look, I would have said to myself, he returned to me in my hour of need. He loved me still; I could still call upon him and rely upon him; there was life after death. In retrospect, I am glad that I did not find the keys then. Although my pain might have been greatly lessened at the start, I would have been left with only an odd anecdote which, over time, would have grown less and less vital, would have held less and less consolation.

Instead, the loss of the keys had propelled me into discovering a way to live with the unresolvability of our most basic questions. During my period of grief, I became familiar – even comfortable – with relativity and uncertainty. Indeed, those theories polished the world so that it shone with a strange and compelling luster. The world could never again be ordinary once I had plummeted through the rabbit-hole of quantum mechanics. If there was uncertainty at the basis of the universe, there was also a ravishing mystery.

After the keys reappeared, as I considered the various possibilities for how they got where they did, I did not feel compelled to prove any one or another. I did not call every visitor and worker who had entered the house in the previous year; I did not have myself examined for unsuspected fugue states. Neither did I convince myself that I had proof of life after death. I was, and I am, willing to live with all the possibilities. I will never know exactly how those keys got on my door, but it does not matter. The loss of the keys did not pose a question to me; it set me on a journey. Finding the keys was not an answer to my question; it was just another station on the way.

I once asked a techno-junkie friend where my email is stored. I think I pictured a huge computer somewhere, where I had the electronic equivalent of a little mailbox. I think I pictured that mailbox sometimes full with mail, sometimes empty. But where on earth was the mailbox?

My friend guffawed. "There's no big computer," she said, "it's all in the fiber-optic network."

This answer was utterly mysterious to me. In the fiber-optic network? Where is that? How can messages be in a network, rather than in a place? My mind boggled.

But quantum theory teaches us that this is not, ultimately, a universe of hard mechanistic reality where mail has to rest in mailboxes. It is a universe of connections and relations, of particle-waves in spacetime where order explicates itself in form and enfolds itself in pattern. The universe is not a great machine, Jeans said, but a great thought. A great thought that expresses itself in matter and energy, ceaselessly changing places.

Whatever part of that great thought once appeared as Bob Shea still exists, I now believe, somewhere in the network of this universe. He has only “departed from this strange world a little ahead of me.” Perhaps, as Einstein said, “That means nothing. People like us, who believe in physics, know that the distinction between past, present and future is only a stubbornly persistent illusion.” If I cannot access the codes to find Bob in the universal network, it does not mean that he has ceased to be. But “being” in that other world must surely be something beyond our imagining in this one, something as different as messages surging through networks are from little metal envelope-filled boxes.

I am comforted by having my keys again. We live in story, and the story of the keys now has a pleasing symmetry. But I do not know what that story means. Or, rather: I know that it can mean many things, some contradictory, but perhaps all true at the same time nonetheless. And I am most deeply comforted by knowing that I cannot ever truly know, that the universe is so far beyond our understanding that miracles, even peculiar and rather silly ones like this one, are very likely to keep occurring.

Ǥ

Appendix 1: Horseman, Pass By

By Robert Anton Wilson

This piece is reprinted from Green Egg, Vol. 27, No. 107, Winter 1994-5, with the permission of the Robert Anton Wilson Estate.

In a procedure that had grown habitual in the last year, I made my coffee as soon as I woke up (grinding my own gourmet beans: a ritual in honor of Epicurus) and then carried it to the phone alcove. I dialed Bob Shea's hospital number and recited a bawdy limerick to make him laugh. But his voice sounded weaker than ever, and I had that terrible feeling again, the feeling that I just didn't know how to do enough to really help.

We talked about NYPD Blue, a new TV show we both liked.

"I'm feeling better," he finally said in a near-whisper. "A lot better, but I'm tired now." In retrospect, I don't know if he wanted to sell some optimism to his own suffering body – to rebuild its immunological defenses with the potent neurochemistry of hope – or if he only said it to spare me further worry and pain, to relieve my anxiety.

The next time I called the Bob Shea Information Line on Voicemail, the message told me he had gone into coma and no more phone calls should be made to the hospital. Even then,

I didn't believe, didn't want to believe, the truth. When the voicemail message finally changed, after about three more days, and said simply that Bob Shea had died, I went into shock. I should have expected the news, but I didn't. I had tried to instill hope into Shea and, by contagion, had instilled so much into myself that I had come to expect a miracle.

I sat at the table like a cartoon cat who just got hit with a hammer but doesn't know it yet and doesn't know he should fall over. I slowly put down the phone, still unable to believe the truth, still in shock. Shea had seemingly beaten the Big Casino (no new tumors in six months); how could he go and die of the side effects? I looked out the window. The sun had barely appeared – I rise early, with only cinnamon and tangerine streaks coloring the east – but already the breakfast crowd, as I call them, had arrived in my patio. House finches, blackbirds and sparrows hopped and flapped about, pecking at my bird feeder. A mourning dove made its usual grieving sound in a tree, as if it didn't believe things would ever become less depressing, and a car drove past, invisible behind the patio wall. I still could not make the concepts "Bob Shea" and "death" fit together in my head.

I thought of a grave in Sligo, the wild west of Ireland:

> Cast a cold eye
> On life, on death.
> Horseman, pass by.

Another car rumbled in my street, and the mourning dove complained about life's injustice again. I became abnormally conscious of Nature outside my glass patio door. Then another damned noisy car went by, racing: some guy late for work maybe.

Bob Shea and I had never seen birds and flowers and trees in the first years when we knew each other, but we had heard a hell of a lot of noisy cars. Our friendship grew in Chicago, amid the rattle and scuttle of industry, the blood-and-shit smell of the stockyards: I remember it as Dali's (or Daly's) asphalt purgatory. The friendship became closer when Bob and I inhaled the haze of tear-gas and Mace during the 1968 Democratic Convention, the one they held behind barbed wire because Mayor Richard P. Daly (emphatically not Dali, although the idea sounds surrealist) decided to prevent Americans from meddling in their own government.

The protesters chanted, "ONE, TWO, THREE, FOUR, We don't want your fucking war! Five, six, seven, EIGHT: Organize to smash the State!" Another canister of tear gas exploded nearby and, eyes streaming, Shea and I ran down Michigan, cut into a side street, and evaded the clubbing administered to those who couldn't run as fast as we did. If you want to know what happened to those less fleet of foot than us, you don't need to call some archive to dig out the 1968 footage; just look at the Rodney King tape again. Cops have simple ideas of fun, which do not change much over the generations.

I counted back, sipping my coffee, and decided Shea and I had known each other for just a few months less than thirty years. A human can grow up in thirty years, from diaper to the first tricycle, to the first orgasm and even to a Ph.D. A human can learn to work at a regular job or learn how to beg on the streets, or court and marry and become a parent, or join the army and get a leg blown off. Most humans in history, before 1900, did not live longer than 30 years. A friendship that long becomes more than friendship. Shea meant as much as any member of my family.

Way back in '65, when Shea and I both started working for

The *Playboy* Forum/Foundation, we drifted into the habit of lunching together. Soon, we developed the tradition of going to a nearby bar every second Friday (read: payday), and drinking a half-dozen Bloody Marys after work while discussing books, movies and every major issue in civil and criminal law, logic, philosophy, politics, religion, and fringe-science – insofar as one can distinguish between those two topics or any of the others, which explains why each of us found the other's ideas so stimulating, and why, in our years, the *Playboy* Forum discussed more far-out notions than it has before or since.

I remember our WHO OWNS ERIK WHITETHORN? series, in which we publicized a woman, Mrs. Whitethorn, who had sued the government for trying to draft her son, Erik, 18. She claimed she owned Erik until he reached 21, and that the government could not take him from her. Shea and I gave that case all the coverage we could, since we wanted people to really think about whether an 18-year-old belongs to himself, to his mother, or to the President (Richard Nixon, in that case.)

Alas, Erik, like many young people, didn't want to become a tool of his mother's idealism, and finally ended the debate by willingly enlisting in the Army. (Madalyn Murray's son also rebelled against becoming a battering ram in her assault on Organized Religion.) We had to drop the debate after Erik donned his uniform and went off to napalm little brown people. I like to hope that some *Playboy* readers of those years still occasionally wonder whether humans belong to themselves, to their parents, or to the State.

Mostly, in the *Playboy* Forum, we followed the ACLU's positions, which Shea and I passionately share (as does Hefner, or he wouldn't have started the Forum and the Foundation) but often, as in the Whitethorn case, we pushed a bit further and sneaked in some anarcho-pacifist propaganda – never in *Playboy's* voice, of course, but as the voice of a reader. Some of those "readers" later became more renowned as characters in three novels we wrote . . .

Among my sins, I turned Shea on to Weed. I turned a lot of people on to Weed in those days. I had a Missionary Zeal about it, but now that I think back, so did a lot of others at *Playboy* in those days. Maybe I should say that I helped turn Bob on to the Herb.

On one gloriously idiotic occasion we got our hands on some super pot from Thailand and had the dumbest conversation of our lives.

"What did you say?" Shea would ask. I'd grapple with that, but amid millions of new sensations and a rush of Cosmic Insights, I'd lose it before I could find an answer. "What did you say?" I would ask slowly, trying to deal with the problem reasonably.

"I asked… uh… what did you just ask?"

And so on, for what seemed like Hindu yugas or maybe even kalpas. That night inspired the "Islands of Micro-Amnesia" in *Illuminatus!*. Maybe a similar night inspired the Lotus Eaters in the *Odyssey*?

One payday Friday, when Bob and I sat in our favorite bar consuming our usual Bloody Marys and gobbling our usual peanuts, a priest at a near-by table struck up a conversation. Soon he had joined us and I quickly became convinced that I understood why the conversation persistently veered toward the Platonic ideal of true love between (male) philosophers. I then pulled one of my nastier pranks. I said I had to get home early, and left Bob to navigate for himself. A half-hour after I arrived home and got out of my shoes, the phone rang. Shea had called and asked me, with awe – as if somebody had killed a goat in the sacristy – "Do you think that priest was a homosexual?"

I admitted the suspicion had crossed my mind.

"My God," Shea said. "You really think it's possible?"

He became much less naive in only a few months after that, since a lot of our Forum/Foundation work involved consultations with the Kinsey Institute. I regard this incident as atypical, and hope it doesn't make Shea seem obtuse, even for a time almost thirty years ago (when the Church brazenly denied all priestly shenanigans and bullied the media into not even printing the cases that got to court). But this adventure had something strangely typical of Bob Shea also, in showing a kind of innocence that, in some respects, he never lost.

Shea probably, at that time – still young, remember – would not have believed that Roy Cohn, who made a career of driving Gay men out of government, himself led an active Gay life. Shea took a long time to learn how much deception exists in this world, because he himself always acted honestly. He accordingly thought clergymen who preach celibacy will practice celibacy, and even that politicians who call themselves liberals will act and think liberally.

Anyway, that cruising priest caused enough Deep Thought, for Shea and then for me, that he finally became transformed and immortalized as Padre Pederastia in *Illuminatus!*.

Around the time we met the priest, Shea told me that he had remained Catholic until the age of 28 (if I remember correctly after all these years. Maybe he said 27 or 29?) Aside from his shock at the thought of gay clerics, he did not seem like somebody newly escaped from Papist thought-control and I never did understand how he had stayed in that church so long.

(Having quit Rome at 14, like James Joyce, I had assumed all intelligent people go out at around that age . . .) Shea never did explain why he stayed in so long, but he once told me, in bitter detail, why he finally bailed out.

His first wife, it appears, went totally mad shortly after the wedding. After a lot of agony and psychiatric consultation, Bob finally accepted the verdict that he had married an incurable schizophrenic. He found it more than he could handle, and sought an annulment, which led to a meeting with a monsignor.

To Shea's horror, neither psychiatric evidence nor any other evidence nor church law itself had anything to do with the monsignor's conversation. The monsignor only wanted to know how much cash money Bob could pay for an annulment. Shea offered as much as he could afford, as a young man beginning at the bottom of the magazine industry, in a cheesy imitation of *Playboy*. The monsignor told him to go home and think hard about how to raise more money. End of interview.

Shea got a civil divorce and never went into a Catholic church again. Still, when I first knew him (only five or six years after he quit the Church) he considered abortion a criminal act – and didn't know that gay priests existed. He learned a lot, in those wild last years of the '60s, and he learned it fast. His Kennedy liberalism got gassed to death by Daly's storm troopers and he became another fucking wild anarchist, like me.

I remember one night when we got stoned together (Bob and his wife, Yvonne, and Arlen and me) and looked at Frankenstein Meets the Wolf Man on TV. They still had cigarette commercials in those days and one of them, that night, showed a guy and a gal walking in a woodland and passing a lovely waterfall etc. As they lit up their ciggies, the slogan said, "You can take Salem out of the country, but you can't take the country out of Salem." I guess they wanted us to get the association "Smoking Salems = breathing good fresh country air." As soon as the commercial ended, Lon Chaney Jr. came back on screen and started suffering acutely (remember his expressive eyes?) as he turned into a wolf. "You can take the man out of the jungle," I said with stoned solemnity, "but you can't take the jungle out of the man." Like most of my marijuana whimsies, that went down my Memory Hole and I forgot it immediately.

Imagine my astonishment when the complex Darwin/Wolf Man, Salems and all, showed up in *Illuminatus!*. Shea hadn't forgotten.

In 1971, after we finished *Illuminatus!*, I quit *Playboy* in the midst of some midlife hormone readjustment. I didn't understand it that way at the time; I just decided that I could not live out the second half of my life as an editor (read wage slave) who only wrote occasionally; I had to become a full-time-free-lance writer, or bust.

Instead, I became a full-time writer and busted. It took 5 years to get the Shea-Wilson opus into print and meanwhile Arlen and I and our children damned near starved: but that's another story. While we wandered about, looking for the least horrible place to live in poverty, Shea and I started writing to each other almost every week. Later, as we both became more "commercial" and hence busier, the letters dropped to two a month or fewer, sometimes; but for 23 years we wrote about every important idea in the world and filled enough paper for several volumes. I hope some of that will get published someday.

When *Playboy* fired him, Shea endured terrible anxiety about keeping his house, and dashed off a few novel outlines while looking for another job. He sold his first novel before finding a job and never stopped writing again. I still treasure his comment on why the Bunny Warren cast him out. "I worked hard and was loyal to the company for ten years." he wrote. "I guess that deserves some punishment."

Whenever I had a lecture gig in or near Chicago, Shea

invited me to stay at his house. Yvonne always went to bed early and Shea and I talked and talked and talked for hours, just the way we did in the early days of our friendship. I always felt that Yvonne didn't like Shea's literary friends, but I never took it personally.

And then, suddenly, Yvonne left him for a much younger man, and I don't know (or really want to know) about the details. I worried for a while that Bob would die of depression, and I shared in empathy the vast wasteland he must have felt around him, 60 years old, alone in a big house, and dumped by a wife who ran off with a young stud who might call him "Gramps." Maybe I project too much here. At 62 myself, I perhaps see in Bob's desolation the deepest anxieties of all aging males.

Oh, well, Yvonne just split the scene. She didn't Bobbitize the poor bastard on her way out.

Then, at a Pagan festival where we both had lecture gigs, Shea met Patricia Monaghan. I saw what happened: a kind of magic, real love at first sight. Pat gave Shea's last two years a transfinite boost of TLC and almost youthful joy. The day before he lapsed into coma, he arranged to marry her. I think of the wedding ceremony as the last thing he could do for Pat, and the last thing she could do for him.

For years and years, in many places – in Ireland, in Germany, in Cornwall, in Switzerland, on the central coast of California – I often found myself wishing Shea could visit me and see the panoramic views that I found so wonderful. I still feel that at times, and find it hard to understand that he will never visit me now. Never.

Shakespeare made the most powerful iambic pentameter line in English out of that one word, repeated five times: "Never, never, never, never, never." I first realized how much pain that line contains when my daughter died. Now I realize it again.

The birds have all flown away and the patio stands empty. Empty? Could an old-time acid-head like me believe that? I looked again and realized anew that every plant and vine pulsed with passionate life in it, millions of cells joyously copulating. I started to remember a line from Dylan Thomas but couldn't quite get it: "The force that through the green shoot drives the flower, drives my something something." I grinned, remembering Shea's wit. Once I had written, in one of our disputes, "I find your position amusingly rigid."

"I'm glad you find me amusingly rigid," he wrote back. "Many women have paid me the same compliment."

Ɠ

Appendix 2: Three Bobs and the Origin of the *Illuminatus!* Trilogy

By Tom Jackson

Editors are in many cases the unsung heroes behind the literary classics that we love. *Dune* by Frank Herbert, for example, considered a classic and never out of print since it came out in 1965, was rejected by more than 20 publishers before Chilton, best known for automotive manuals, took a chance on it. Who was that editor? It was Sterling Lanier.

I'd wondered for years who the editor was at Dell who decided to publish the *Illuminatus!* trilogy – an odd literary work, written by two unknowns.

Well, now I know. You know who two of the "Bobs" are who were involved in *Illuminatus!* – Robert Anton Wilson and Robert Shea – but this article is about editor Robert "Bob" Abel (1931-1981), a former Dell Publishing Co. and Warner Books editor and former sidekick of Paul Krassner at *The Realist*. Abel, also a published author, was only 50 when he died and left behind Carole Abel and two young sons.

So *Illuminatus*! is really a story of three "Bobs." And without Bob Abel, there would have been no *Illuminatus!* Publishing that book launched the literary careers of both Wilson and Shea.

Abel was a friend of Robert Shea for many years, and it was this friendship that helped get *Illuminatus!* off the ground. Shea mentions him in an interview by Neal Wilgus, published in the fanzine Outworlds (issues 28/29) in 1976:

> Wilgus: Since you and Wilson were both editors at *Playboy* at the time ILLUMINATUS! was written, I'm wondering why Playboy Press didn't publish it. Or was that too close to home?
>
> Shea: At the time we got the idea for ILLUMINATUS!, Playboy Press wasn't publishing original novels, and a very good friend of mine, Bob Abel, was an editor at Dell. I was looking for an opportunity to write paperback fiction, so I wrote Bob a letter briefly sketching about half a dozen ideas for books, of which a book about the Bavarian Illuminati was one. He thought that one had the most possibilities, so Wilson and I did three sample chapters and an outline and sent it in. On the strength of that we got a contract and began writing the book.

Abel had left Dell when it was time to edit *Illuminatus!* for publication, so Abel apparently did not work on the book. Two other Dell editors, Fred Feldman and David Harris, edited the manuscript and turned it into a trilogy of paperback originals, shaping it for publication and also making cuts that Wilson and Shea complained about.

But who was this "Bob Abel" who got the book published? After I found the Shea interview, I wanted to learn more. *The New York Times* published a brief obituary (three paragraphs) after Abel died. His widow, Carole, still lives in New York City and let me interview her, and his friend, Krassner, also answered my questions.

Carole Abel raised his two sons while making a living as a literary agent. She talked to me and faxed me copies of two of Abel's old resumes, as there is very little biographical information about him online.

Abel was an important player in New York City's publishing and literary scene, an author, an important book editor and a trusted co-editor for Krassner at *The Realist.*

Some of what he accomplished is largely unknown. According to Abel, it was her husband who really wrote *The Happy Hooker*, a bestselling call girl memoir by Xaviera Hollander.

"He wrote the book for her. And then they did a couple of other books. She was kind of a character," Carole Abel said.

Abel had a bachelor's degree in English from the University of Connecticut, and a master's in journalism from Boston University. He moved to New York City and married Carole in 1959.

Bob Abel was an expert in American popular culture. He wrote *The Beer Book* and *The Book of Beer* (it's too bad he didn't get to see the rise of the craft beer movement) and edited two books of cartoons, *The American Cartoon Album* and (with David Manning White) *The Funnies: An American Idiom.*

"I got to know most of the New Yorker cartoonists," Carole Abel said.

Abel's knowledge of cartoonists was helpful to Paul Krassner when Abel was Krassner's trusted assistant at *The Realist*, Krassner's seminal publication. Abel was an editor at the publication, but Krassner didn't use normal editorial titles. Abel was "The Featherbedder."

Krassner explains, " 'Featherbedder' was his title among other staffers. For example, John Francis Putnam, the art director of MAD magazine, was 'Dirty Old Man.' My assistant,

Jeannie Johnson, was my 'Scapegoat.' She became my 'Scapemate' when she became my first wife. Bob Abel and I became close friends in the process of his filled-with-variety contribution to *The Realist*. He brought in cartoonists who reeked with irreverence. Not to mention journalists and satirists alike, fake news in its time. Bob brought in clippings I missed that were essential for my pieces, and he also wrote a column of offbeat media. Although he worked at home, we had meetings at my East Side office loft, where he gave me thoughtful advice. Appreciation was the name of the game. Oh, yeah, and my title was 'Zen Bastard.' "

Abel and Shea both worked for magazines, so that may be how the two men knew each other and became friends. (As far as Krassner knows, Abel and Robert Anton Wilson did not know each other). Carole Abel recalls her husband working for "girlie" magazines, and Shea also worked for such magazines. Shea was an editor at *Cavalier* magazine and Abel contributed to it.

Abel was perhaps most prominent as a book editor.

He was senior editor for Dell Publishing from May 1968 to July 1972. He bought books not just for Dell Books but for the company's Delta and Delacorte Press divisions. Aside from acquiring *Illuminatus!*, he published books such as *The Happy Hooker*, *Scientology: The Now Religion* (a groundbreaking expose by George Malko that drew the cult's wrath) and *Saint Abortionist: The Legend of Dr. Spencer* by Paul Krassner.

As executive editor at Warner books from 1972 to 1975, Abel put out paperback reprints of books such as *All the President's Men* by Bob Woodward and Carl Bernstein, and *The Palace Guard* by Dan Rather and Gary Paul Gates. As editor-in-chief for Manor Books in 1977 and 1978, he created a line of historical fantasies, "Time/Past Editions," about which I've been able to learn little.

At the time of his death, Abel was involved in various freelance ventures and was editorial director of *Harvey*, a new men's magazine he had helped create.

Who knows what else Bob Abel would have been able to accomplish, or if he would have played a role again in the careers of Wilson or Shea? He died young, from cancer. His death occurred on Dec. 21, 1981, according to a brief obituary in the *New York Times*, and he was only 50. He had been quite sick for about two years.

He left behind two young sons, Douglas and David, and his wife, Carole Abel, who raised the boys and had a successful career as a literary agent, from which she is now mostly retired. She handled books such as *The Spirituality of Imperfection*, which is still in print, and many books in the "Idiot" series. One of the sons, Douglas, is a film editor who at the time of this article was working on a project with Michael Moore.

(Article originally published July 23, 2018, at the RAWIllumination.net blog).

Ğ

Appendix 3: Looking Back at the Golden APA

By Tom Jackson

Before *Maybe Logic Academy*, before the annual Maybe Day celebration, and before many other attempts to carry Robert Anton Wilson's work forward, there was the Golden APA, an amateur press association founded by Arthur Hlavaty back in 1979.

An amateur press association is a group of zine writers who agree to put their zines together in a common mailing; the zines are sent to a person who assembles them all into one bundle and mails them back to the APA members. This might occur every other month. Members typically have "minac" requirements – they have to provide a "minimum activity," perhaps at least one zine every other mailing. Although there is usually no formal obligation, members generally are encouraged to do "mailing comments," about zines in a previous mailing.

Discussions on apazines are often quite personal in nature, with the understanding that the comments will not be circulated to the world at large. That was certainly true of APA-50, the apazine I belonged to for many years, and Mr. Hlavaty is still quite protective of the privacy of his APA's former members.

Apas in some cases can last for decades, although that is

uncommon. (One particularly famous apa, FAPA, the Fantasy Amateur Press Association, was founded in 1937 and is still going.) Like other forms of fanzine fandom, however, apas have taken a hit in the age of the Internet, because it is easier to write for a blog or a website than to produce a zine.

I asked Hlavaty a few questions about the apa he founded:

Q. When did you found the Golden APA? Is it still with us, or has it ceased publication?

A. I started Golden APA in1979. I put out 100 issues, then (mid-90s) turned it over to others while remaining a member. It lasted a few years longer, but the Web killed it, as it did most apas.

Q. So when did the Golden APA come to an end?

A. I think the last Golden APA mailing was 2003.

Q. What was your motivation in founding the Golden APA?

A. I read *Illuminatus!* in 1975, volume by volume as it came out, and it blew my mind; *Stranger in a Strange Land* is the only other book that influenced me anywhere near as much. I wanted to talk with others about sex, dope, sedition, conspiracy, self-programming, guerrilla ontology, etc. For that and other reasons, I started doing a zine, first called The Diagonal Relationship, in 1977. I then learned about apas, and took to them immediately. Tossing out quick comments on what I read was fun back then and still is, though I now mostly do it via livejournal.

Q. When was Robert Anton Wilson an active member of The Golden APA? Did he interact with the other members, i.e., did he do mailing comments or otherwise demonstrate that he read the zines of the other members?

A. Wilson was an active participant from the early 80s through somewhere in the 90s. He did mailing comments as well as essays. Note for scholars: A number of Golden APA zine titles appear in the list of groups at the end of *The Homing Pigeons*; mine was the Bloodshot Pyramid. Also a quote about Wilson that appears on the covers of several of his books ("Stupid") comes from the apa.

Q. As we are providing information to scholars, can you give me other examples of zine titles that turn up as the names of bands in *The Homing Pigeons*?

A. Other zines mentioned are Seeds of Discord, the Benton Harbor Rat-Weasel, and Wascal Wabbit.

Q. I met Robert Shea at a Golden APA room party in 1989 in Boston. (You were nominated for "Best Fan Writer," and when you came into the room, the others applauded.) Was Shea a member of the Golden APA, too, and if so, did he apparently read the other zines?

A. Shea likewise appeared in the apa from the early days through the mid-90s (when he died), doing mailing comments.

Q. Did the Golden APA operate according to the usual apa rules, i.e. were there minac requirements and dues?

A. It was pretty much a standard apa. Shea & Wilson were ex officio members; others were expected to participate in at least every other mailing, and pay for their postage & printing. There was no membership fee or dues as such.

Q. Did the Golden APA draw many members from the ranks of fanzine fandom, or did it draw in many "mundanes" attracted by an interest in *Illuminatus!* ?

A. I tried to recruit people whose minds seemed in tune

with the trilogy wherever I found them, but those without a zine/apa background tended to lack staying power.

Q. Has there been any discussion of digitizing issues of the Golden APA? Are any copies of the mailing publicly available, i.e, in a fanzine collection at a library, for example?

A. I know of no public digital or print archive of the apa and have no interest in starting one. It was an apa, and thus ephemeral and private (though not secret).

Q. Is there a particular Wilson book you'd recommend to someone who wanted to try him? And what is your personal favorite RAW work?

A. I'd suggest starting with Illuminatus! because that's how I did it. Not sure what nonfiction I'd recommend. Maybe Prometheus Rising. I would not recommend starting with The New Inquisition, because that shows much of Wilson's flaws of argumentativeness and pig irony, though there's good stuff if you can get past that. Schrödinger's Cat is my favorite, though if he'd completed the Historical series, that might have passed it.

Ǥ

Appendix 4: A Brief Reader's Guide to Robert Shea's fiction

By Tom Jackson

Here is a brief guide to Robert Shea's fiction. As I will explain, it is possible to acquire ebooks of most of his work without spending any money at all, or to get paper copies without having to spend very much money.

Aside from a few short science fiction stories Shea published in science fiction magazines in the 1950s (not very good, but available at Project Gutenberg if you are curious), Shea's work falls into two phases.

The *Illuminatus! Trilogy* – e.g. *The Eye in the Pyramid, The Golden Apple* and *Leviathan* – was originally published in 1975 by Dell as three separate mass market paperbacks, cowritten by Robert Anton Wilson. Although it was a genuine collaboration – Shea came up with the original idea for the work and got the pair a contract with Dell – it is undeniable that stylistically, the work is more Wilson than Shea.

Since the original publication, the work has remained in print as a one-volume omnibus, available in paper and as an ebook and also available as an audiobook from Audible.

Shea's other fiction, begun after he was laid off from his longtime job as a *Playboy* magazine editor, consists of historical novels published from 1981 to 1991.

The last novel, *Shaman*, is set in what was then the American West, during the Black Hawk War of 1832.

All of the other novels, however, have settings in the Middle Ages, mostly in Europe and the Far East. They include *Shike*, set in Japan and China and originally published as two separate books, *Time of the Dragons* and *Last of the Zinja*. *Shike* was followed by *All Things Are Lights*, which takes place in France during the time of St. Louis and which includes descriptions of the Albigensian Crusade and the Seventh Crusade (1248–1254).

The Saracen, set a little bit later than *All Things Are Lights*, takes place in medieval Italy and also was published in two volumes, *Land of the Infidel* and *The Holy War.*

It should be noted that while Shea's historical novels are stylistically very different from *Illuminatus!*, written in straightforward prose with fast-moving plots, they also are linked to *Illuminatus!* All of them, except for *Shaman*, feature secret societies not unlike the Illuminati, and it is hinted that these secret societies in Europe and Asia have ties with each other.

There are other affinities with *Illuminatus!* The hero of *All Things Are Lights,* Roland de Vency, is essentially a "model agnostic," to use a term used by Robert Anton Wilson; he believes that all religions essentially are equally good (and bad) and is dragged into two crusades very much against his will.

There are bits in *All Things Are Lights* that subtly tie it to *Illuminatus!* For example, here is a scene in which Roland's lover walks into an old pagan temple:

> "She walked into the circle of columns and dropped to her knees on the marble floor. She looked for and found a carving that she and Roland had talked about the night they came

> here. It had fallen from the temple roof and showed a naked young man facing three naked women and holding out an apple to one of them. Roland had said the one receiving the apple was the Goddess of Love. She reached out and with her fingertips touched the smooth shoulder of the young man."

The carving of course depicts the Judgment of Paris, the cause of the Trojan War, when Paris, a prince of Troy, was asked to award a golden apple to the most beautiful of three goddesses, Aphrodite, Hera and Athena. Aphrodite offered the bribe, Helen, that appealed the most to Paris, but the losers did not take it well. The golden apple was from Eris, the goddess of discord and also the goddess of Discordianism.

Robert Shea's literary executor, his son Michael Shea, has released all of Shea's solo novels under the Creative Commons license, and they are available free from various Internet sites, including Bobshea.net, Project Gutenberg and the Internet Archive.

Used copies of the original paper editions also remain available. BookFinder.com is a good Internet site for searching multiple vendors to find a reasonable price for a used book.

Shea also published a fanzine, *No Governor*, which mostly focused on anarchism and which sometimes had contributions from Robert Anton Wilson. All of these zines are available as PDF documents at Bobshea.net.

Ǥ

Acknowledgements

Thanks to Michael Shea, Robert Shea's literary executor, for giving me permission to put this collection together. Thank you to Warren Asa Wilgus for permission to reprint the two excellent interviews with Robert Shea conducted by the late Neal Wilgus. Thanks also to the people who helped me locate articles: Chris Hibbert of the Libertarian Futurist Society; Adam Gorightly, author and keeper of the Discordian Archives; Martin Wagner, who maintains a fan site devoted to Robert Anton Wilson but who helped me locate Shea pieces; Jesse Walker, author and an editor at *Reason* magazine. Steve Jackson gave me permission to reprint the opening piece about *Illuminatus!* Daisy Eris Campbell gave me permission to quote parts of an interview given to members of the audience in her father Ken Campbell's stage adaptation of *Illuminatus!* Christina Pearson, trustee of the Robert Anton Wilson Trust and Wilson's daughter, gave me permission to use pieces that Wilson and Shea co-wrote. Thanks also to Rasa at Hilaritas Press for helping me with questions about publishing and rights, and for his publishing work in the production of this book, including the design, his work on the cover and his many other efforts to improve the quality of the book. Victor Koman helped me with information about Samuel Konkin and Konkin's *New Libertarian* publication, where Shea published some of his pieces. Thank you and apologies to anyone else who helped me who I forgot to mention.

HILARITAS PRESS

Publishing the Books of Robert Anton Wilson
and Other Adventurous Thinkers

www.hilaritaspress.com

www.ingramcontent.com/pod-product-compliance
Lightning Source LLC
Chambersburg PA
CBHW072012190726
48293CB00001B/257